The Year
of the Fox

The Year of the Fox

a burning man memoir 2016

steve arntson

REGENT PRESS
Berkeley, California
2019

ISBN 13: 978-1-58790-475-2
ISBN 10: 1-58790-475-6
Library of Congress Control Number: 201994735

Cover drawing by Karen Davis:
www.moonlightandhares.co.uk

To contact the author:
cozzy2424@gmail.com

Manufactured in the U.S.A.
REGENT PRESS
Berkeley, California
www.regentpress.net

~INTRO & ACKNOWLEDGEMENTS~

It had to be done - For a book that was neatly printed there must be some actual penmanship ~ you, the reader, must find your way through the maze of cursive here at the outset - put up with an erratic hand - it is a nod to the scribbling done that produced THE YEAR OF THE FOX - everything flows from the pen, from the notebooks - as for the book itself, I wanted something that was only approximately chronological, not strictly so - think of it as a brand-new deck of cards, just slightly shuffled - some of what happened before arriving at Burning Man is interspersed with pieces written about Burning Man - like sudden flashes forward ~ Likewise, once there, I referenced earlier experiences - the order of happenings in the desert is also not strict - there is truth and fiction in these pages - not all the conversations took place - a word about the fox - it was while returning from the summit of Old Razorback one night - it is a peak near to Burning Man that I climbed into early morning ~ there were two eyes in the flashlight's beam - continuing the descent they turned out to be the eyes of a beautiful fox and the creature was mesmerized by the bright flashlight - it was such an unusual experience to watch as the fox slowly circled me and then disappeared into the sage - it was a sign of something, but just exactly what, who could say? ~ In 2015 there had been a plan to climb this peak with one of the artists I'd met that year and I imagined that somehow the fox had been expecting more than just myself that night ~ this book is hopefully both a fresh take on the event and a successful protest against the convenience of typing as well as a counter to mainstream coverage of this art festival ~ at times, roaming Black Rock City I felt a little like I was channeling Alain Robbe-Grillet so totally was I absorbed by detail - and it was good noticing little things - time during the desert week was skewered - it was like going through a week of what it was like when you were eight years old and each day was two weeks long - at this point I want to thank my friends for being there and encouraging - in particular Mel C. Thompson for listening to many of these poems and giving helpful feedback - I am indebted as well to Harry Scott Boggs who brought me out there in the first place in 1996 - this was when Burning Man was still relatively small at some 8,000 attendees - I should mention Kirk Lumpkin who always brings the message of ecology and sustainability - he is a fine writer and musician who performed many times at Burning Man - I want to thank my friends in the Bay Area poetry community - the question of audience is an important one - writers keep me writing - special gratitude for Richard Loranger, Jan Steckel, James Cagney, Jr., the amazing Judy Clarcy, Mary-Marcia Casoly and the Waverley Writers in Palo Alto, Tom Stolmar who, along with myself searched in vain for the Temple of Rudea in the middle of the night - 1998 - my thanks to Anna Wolfe for getting me notice and enjoy ballet and for having a profound understanding of what it means to Be Here Now - Oh, and as for those long days, child-hood-length, well that is reason enough for loading the car with supplies and heading for the playa - it was a joy to be a part of the camp called "Minstrel Cramp" - the music was great and Greg kept the red piano tuned every day - oddly enough, though I have been to this event many times and wrote on each occasion, I never wrote about the actual burning of Burning Man himself until this book - well, that's about it - I couldn't include all of the pieces, much as I would have liked to - hope you enjoy YEAR OF THE FOX and that you are moved to explore Black Rock sometime your-self if you haven't already - Mark Weiman at Regent Press has graciously assisted during this project - thanks, Mark and much love to Loie Johnson, sine qua non!

~TABLE~

for Loie
bringer of light

1. ESTHER'S BURNING MAN

It was Esther's fires begun before she ever arrived
    her 2016 just a theory of digits
      her Black Rock City unbuilt

And this preview   a plan to see her there
And what I wear in the dark is hopeful evocation

She will see such lights as these minimal adornments
It will be some evening of the week
      when she ventures out   the desert cool
        her bicycle aglow for safety

Or perhaps she will board an artcar
        hitching her way
It might be a ship
    a double-decker palace
      the shark machine   redly-outlined

She will cruise all the bonfires
Their ancient glare a primordial comfort

There will be lasers, too
Mysterious tipis   softly luminous
The diffuse ambiance of the Pink Heart
          discoveries by accident

The Flaming Lotus waits
    to fulfill its propane promises

1

that seem years-at-a-time
        with every "whoosh" and flare

She will hear the hot talk of the Fire Conclave
        rising on stilts and spinning their batons
                        with Promethian authority

And she will stroll the Esplanade
        its discreet kerosene lanterns
                        like a modesty emplaced.

These are Esther's fires   before her coming
        the even-numbered year 2016
                allowed to beckon unevenly
                        from almost Iranian distance

She has said she will journey
        her very own silk road to complete.
Samarkand, Nevada   just over there
The nearest East chilled to midnight's degrees

And in those early a.m.'s winds
        her lights will "flicker and glow" like Yeats
                and blink their own fantasias
                Fellini enlisted
                        to enhance her dreaming
                                of more inscrutable warmth

What she brings to the desert
                is fire already made
And what she imagines
                will burn as surely
                as the outsized central effigy

On Saturday   the end
Or Sunday   the *second* end
                the temple hugely engulfed
                                sacred

She is in advance of future fires set
                        and blazing!

2

2. COMMUNIQUÉ

Friday

If I'm still alive
       I'm still in the desert

Friday!

And you are my friends in the Friends Meeting House

You should know
       that while your words are spoken
              a dinosaur
                     allosaurus to be exact
A dinosaur has materialized
       at Colorado and Middlefield Road

It stomped the Round Table Pizza there
                     and the Seven-Eleven too
And it's heading your way right now!

But keep reading   don't leave
Though you hear it pounding
       getting closer
              the meeting hall shaking
                     with each allosaurus step!

Though you hear it bellow
Like the Id monster of *Forbidden Planet*
              don't worry   you're good!

Just wanted you to know it's really a bird
No, *really!*   Science has said so!
An *early* bird, as it were
Mary-Marcia will know what to say to it to keep you safe!

And now   if I am still alive
          I'll walk way out on the playa
                    and think
                    actually think
                              for the very first time

3. REST STOP STRAYS

They are startled
          "what's he doing?"
          "Does he have any food?"

They start and stop their way away
They seek a safe distance
          "He's *calling* us!   what does he want?"
          "Why is he stepping up and down
                                        from the picnic table bench?"

They had never seen a human do that at the rest stop before
It's a first   he repeats   stepping up and then down again
          they'd *never* seen such behavior!

But the man had never seen *cats* at a rest stop

"They yours?" asked a second man
"Nope!   strays   me, too" came the reply
"That's quite a workout you're doing!"
"Yep"
"Most folks rest at a rest stop   but not you!   nossir!"

The cats heard it all
          and wouldn't come when called
          They just observed   like aliens
                              cute aliens, though

          They went back to wondering
                    why the humans did what they did

4

"Something to do with the number eight"
        one of the cats   the one with more white
"He does it eight times then stops"

"Yeah!" said the duskier alien
"It's very mental   as in 'going mental'"

"I've heard the expression" said the other
"You know, I wish they'd all go to sleep
        so we can scavenge in peace   damn!
        here comes another bunch   they're *gigantic!*
            look at how they stagger around!"

The gray cat pondered
"Hey, I think I figured it out
        why this guy is stepping up and down like that
            it's beginning to make sense
            sure!   he doesn't want to look like *them!*"

"Okay," said white streak   "he's smarter
But if he really wanted us to let him pet us
        he'd have opened a can of salmon in our presence
I mean, he's smart
            but not smart enough to win our affection"

The gray one then said,
        "You know I'm not sure I want to interact in *any* case"

The man at the table did another eight repetitions
        staying restless at the rest stop
            and the man who'd spoken with him
                walked away
And the enormous travellers gazed at everything
                        with wonder

4. WEED, CALIFORNIA

You won't see the damage
     the night is black as the ashes
     the night is censor   selecting
The destruction is an edit performed
     and the unimaginative are assuaged

Burning Man has an evil twin at large
     incinerating wrongly
     the fuel uncaring
The torch has been applied

Weed   under cover of darkness
     hides away the object of a morbid curiosity
What the fire's left will not stand up to blind scrutiny
The carbonized timbers shy of dawn
     demure   wishing to stay concealed
          past sunrise

It is not a town anymore
It must be a virtual construction
If this is a dream   I know you will wake me
          oh, kindest realist!

5. ISLAMOPHOBIA RISING

It's a crescent
It's orange Islam
     just starting its journey to the zenith.

Just the iconic moon in the Digger pines
Just suggestion
     late night   and getting later

There's something about *hejira*

Is that the word?   for flight?
        as in   got the heck out of Mecca?
This crescent rises
And the higher it goes the more Islam there is

  It's a curious conquest
Windy as rumors portending
                maybe a phobia
                maybe more

Near to the horizon the orange kept it human
But now   having arced through the Digger branches
                and left the lower layers
It is whitening with self-important purity

Soon *no* one will please this moon
No one will be good enough
        and "How was your day?" will be moot inquiry
                for all of them must be so perfectly wrong

6.   THE RANGERS, THE TRUTH

Something's up with the park rangers of Crater Lake
They're behaving strangely
They're saying what they *really* think
                        instead of talking ranger talk
            and they're making stuff up, too

It isn't exactly intentional   it just *is*
And   *surprised* by what they find themselves saying
      they appear to be enjoying it
      liking the novelty
      it feels *so* right!

"Look at that one, Bob!
What's she see in him?"

They're loud
        so that the tourists cannot help but hear
"You wanna' know *what?*   when the next boat ride is?
Hah!   you missed it
        and there aren't any others!"

When asked about the hike on Garfield Peak
        a couple was told
        "You'll never make it, don't bother
                why don't you just vegetate   *much* better!"

When the Troop 19 brats complained
        and whined about the nature talk
                the ranger-lecturer said

"What?!   ya' wanna' stay stupid??
Now pay attention!
        or I'll see to it you get on the bad side of your parents!
        forever!"

And   in answering a dorky question
        about how many thousands of years ago
        some explosion occurred
                a ranger was mercilessly blunt,

"It doesn't *matter!*
It will have no effect on your life whatsoever
        and is worthless information besides!"

Other tourists were asked why they'd come

"Why don't you just turn around and drive to Disneyland?!
        where you belong!"

Then the rangers all got together
        and decided to *really* have some fun
Outside the expensive lodge they began shouting
They used bullhorns   megaphones   a siren

"All right, now listen up!
We've had word from the United States Geological Survey!
New magma has refilled that chamber down there

The volcano's gonna' blow
        and it's going to be worse than the last time
Leave the park   *repeat,* leave the park   immediately!
Get gone!   hurry up!   I don't see you running!
Panic is okay!   you only have minutes!   go!   GO!!
You may not survive!
            hurry!
            faster!   *now GO!!"*

And they did   screaming
There were frantic scenes
        and desperation
        the rv's lurching
            horns played like a vast Doomsday organ!

After the manic exit
And after the rangers
        (the only ones left)
            had ceased rolling in the pumice
            in hysterics   uproarious!
They quit their jobs and went to Burning Man

A place   they all agreed
        where they could all be even better
                        at being themselves!

7.   SHADOW ROCKS

With sunglasses   or without
The shadow rocks will trip
        the trail not warning enough

And the shadows may be purple
Be deep blue umbra   in the color-coded descent
                        all you are is clumsy

Just as in real life

Though a camera's used
        all it sees is metaphor
            twisting the sense out of all those pines
                that perfectly inform what's grown up or not

Easy!   you stumble
The blue-and-purple shadows were playing
            playing with your footfalls
The rocks' way of saying, "Remember me!   remember!"
                    learn another way of walking
                down the crater's walls"

Though it's daylight
        it's the contrast allows those shadows to so deceive
        there is no real safety
                no matter *how* much safety is craved

The stone in the way   dusted
Or the larger boulder   half-buried
        also dusted
                tan as the trail you walk

Makes one blind
Makes one mindful of all sorts of blindness
When Crater Lake stops being photo-op
        and becomes ·   an illustrated philosophy
            some kind of coming close
                to the mark of sage scenery
View Master's retro
        where the stereo teaches more than one sense

Your concentration's not enough
        "one foot in front of the other"
                unreliable skill

It is to be in the black that counts
In the shadow rocks
Then *only* is a remedy   found
        stopped   the way everyone wanted that
        all along
        and still
                because going somewhere and returning

was always distraction

We are cancelling directions
Staying in the shadows
      where invisible obstacles do not deter
      cause injury   downfall

Peace has a color
Blue-purple   stopping is good
You are helped
      and complete the climb of Garfield Peak this way
            the unexpected companion
            the *peculiar* claiming one's attention

As if the extinct smilidon had appeared
      and followed you home
      its saber tooth   moot ferocity
                        its hunger appeased

This is shadow talk made
      while the west wind blew a hot summer's day away
This is the dream of your body
                  in all the places of the planet
                  staying true to itself

8.   WHERE YOU PROPOSED

It was after the Marienbad of the Crater Lake Lodge
With Robbe-Grillet whispering his own sweet nothings
      about corridors and colonnades

It was after waking to a blue day's coda
                        that a return was possible
And the history-making timbers creaked their longings
The debonnaire hostess *complimented* you and me
      on something neither one of us knew about
      or thought about before

so that it was flattery barely understood

It was after perfect coffee with elegant strangers
After   after all
       you took my hand
       with Mozart in my earphones   at first
              then Tchaikovsky
              and you guided me to matrimony

There   at the edge
Under trees that had crowded into an evergreen shade
       the same that Handel composed for
At the end of a very short lane to a vantage concealed
An obvious tryst
              a bench   that   when you see it
                                   you know to propose

It seemed to *speak* this proposal
              and the shelter *was* needed
              because it was just you and I
And maybe   walking there
              I knew you'd have a question

The mountain that fell all to pieces suggested as much
A feeling the crater could teach
              have something left to instruct
              a state of beauty
                     like the lake's equilibrium

It might have stayed "Deep Blue Lake"
              the first name found for it
              that made it into print anyway
And quiet as those waters
              was your voice inflecting
              lifting the last part of the question
                                   as questions require

No one besides ourselves embowered
Our stroll was all   before and after your question
              which I answered *well,* I think
              such a moment so very unusual
                     I might have faltered   talked to myself

12

It was alright, though
I spoke to *you*
        and over and over assented
        as if there had been *many* questions
        and perhaps there were in what you asked
                like Tchaikovsky's Russian dolls contained
And I said "yes!" to all of them

Our agreement disturbing even the sunshine
        what it's all about
                usurping all else
Like a ripple in Time discovered
        after certain glorious   transcendental collisions
                                        in Space

Robbe-Grillet will include your proposal
Say things in French   sustained   mesmeric
The way things are between us
        though to tell the truth
        what's between us has vanished
                like the distance that was closed
                a billion light years away
                when gravity   and such a *good* gravity
                                        won out.

As what had seemed dense apart
        did the only sensible thing   and joined

9.   SOLAR COOKING   DONE WITH THE SUN

"Is it ready?   huh? huh?   when? when?"
"What's the hold up?"
"We're hungry!"
"How's it work?"
"What's it called?"
"What's for lunch?   I'm a vegan"

The bright flaps of the thing were maybe aluminum
        bending the sun so the oven can heat
            it *was* getting hot in there!
            it was hot but it was empty

"When do we eat?"
what do we eat?"
"Who's cooking?"
"Who's in charge?"

Whatever lunch means   the cook isn't telling
It's a demo   it's live   but he needs permission
        he cannot serve the unseen chow
        his proxy's in touch with the organizers
                there's a need for "Okay!"

There are two models
        the aluminum "flower"
        and the barrel thing with inserts
Both being taken very, very seriously solar
solar!   say it like you just learned the word!

Passersby are mystified
"What *is* it?!"
"What's it do?"
"When do we eat?"
"Have any steak back there?"
"Lobster, maybe?"

The man listening to all this?   patient   cryptic
He has the nervous energy of a master chef
                        but the cupboard is bare

"Waiting on a go-ahead
        we need to be certified
            we're not quite authorized
                the operation's pending
                    please be patient   like *I* am
                        the *kitchen's* ready
                            yum!
                                you're going to *love* it!"

"No menu?"
"How *long* does it take?"
"'*I didn't know I was starving till I tasted you...*'"
"Wait a minute!   that's a song *"by the way..."*'"
"Yes!   *'by the way'* is part of the song!   you're good!"
"Let's eat!"
"Eat *what?*   can't you see there's nothing to eat?"

There followed an appeal for calm   and then

"Please, *please*, my friends
      we've sent someone
            It needs to be official
                  it needs to be sanctioned
                        we can't just, well, uh
                              we haven't gotten word"

There was a group sigh

"However, the *oven's* ready
      do you understand the principle?
            let me show you   it's really simple
                  it's just reflection
                        you have to line things up
                              here's how you check it"

Already the mood was changing
Though everyone's invited   everyone is hungry
The morsels there are cannot be found
      and the sunshiny metal hurts the eyes
            the luncheon's fairly blinded

Tea is served   hopefully
They enter the shade of anticipation only
      a pent-up place of wondering when   as in a dream
            when   will the solar oven feed
They wait dead-tired
Malnurished   with rumors of zucchini   tomatoes, corn

Good luck!
Survival an experiment *so* controlled

15

it has succumbed to preliminaries
the relevant chit-chat coming slowly apart
in the famine

10.   THE VIEW FROM UNION PEAK

Let's watch an explosion!   a big one!

The time machine was obviously in perfect condition
Perfect working order
We'd gone back, all right
        to some seven thousand seven hundred years ago
        seven thousand six hundred and ninety-four
                                        to be exact
Yes, Mount Mazama's blowing up!   or was *about* to

We'd be watching from the top of Union Peak
West of catastrophe   west of oblivion
We knew what would happen
        had made a plan and made the climb
        while the preliminary show was underway

And oh, those prevailing westerlies!
Everything the volcano had
        was going to go to the elsewhere
                of northeast and east
                        no ash would be burying us!
The products of the blast   so very lethal
The stratosphere to fill with infernal grit

It was nice knowing in advance
Someone had a harmonica
The weather was pleasant   the ground was moving
We were safe and so were the Indians
        we'd talked some into coming along
                though the name "Union Peak" didn't register
                they called it something else

We shared K-rations left over
        from our recent reenactment of Okinawa
        in which I role-played the Japanese commander
        Isijima

We had earplugs rated an awesome 40
To ensure that   when we went back home
                              we could still hear Mozart
Curiosity   intense curiosity   that's what brought us
It had not been enough to just read about it   that lake
Crater Lake   even the boat ride was wrong
        well, except for the glasses of lake water drunk
                                        pure blue

We just *had* to be there when the lake got its crater
The mountain was getting noisy
What satisfaction!   all that shaking!
At 4:02 in the afternoon of August 16th
        the final paroxism came
                everything fell in and fell down
                        right on schedule

The same as Toba but a modest Toba
The pyroclastics are special   *look* at that!
Just rip-roaring down!
Total obliteration!

I said, "It's very good, Eve"
        quoting that movie again
        Being There
        Peter Sellers   for, just like Chauncy, the gardener
                we like to watch!

Once the rolling is over with
And the textured clouds have thinned that held the ash
        we'll be able to see the waterless lake
        the bottom beforehand
        Wizard Island just a volcano's *theory* of encore
                        the cinder cone to come
                        spewing in the aftermath

It's time to take the duct tape off
The geologist we hired can talk now
About dacite and pumice
        he was talking too much   before   on the trail
        don't you hate that?

But now it's okay
It's time   let him lecture and explain
        tell the scientific names for things
        while the land turns gray
                and the cauliflower tower billows
Thank you, westerlies, for ringside!
For BCE spectacle!

Just make sure no ash gets in the time machine
We'll be needing it!

11. CHERRY SELLER

She's leaving tomorrow
Her brother, too
They've been supplying cherries to Chemult

Dark cherries   cherries for the Chalet
        where they promise to wake you
                when you want to leave
                        the motel   the town   this life
The Chalet with the Raiders on and steak cooking

She lives in Fresno
Been away two months
        too long
She's harried
She's *had* it
        the motel lonely and its air unconditioned
                                her own condition iffy
                                ripe for departure

Ready   *been* ready   for the San Juaquin
That valley again
        she's overdue to ride
                down to more air
                and lower level acres
                Tule Lake   what's left of it
                        verdant   useful
                        the early ducks at home

The cherries were great except for the pits
They inhibit such there were no handfuls at a time
        cherries plural   at once   not possible
        no gorging

I think she's tired of cherries
        just when / was getting interested
Will she start fresh in Fresno?
Feel an ironic homesickness for the Oregon Outback?

She was sad   exhausted
And knew as much of Chemult
        as one could know on a shoestring
The history of motels   told in her posture

May she and her brother prosper
And the Valley turn down the heat a little for their sake

12. THE KIDNAPPED WAITRESS

That was her story
        and she was most definitely sticking to it

She'd been kidnapped and taken
The guy just did it
She had been gone   though not altogether
It had been *awhile* she was gone

She couldn't   or rather wouldn't
         be allowed to see her kids after that
                  or she *was*   I can't remember

But she got the order right
And while I played with my food
         she talked
                  it was most of the autobiography

Chemult history on a Saturday   air-conditioned
The place was minimal *chalet*
         just kind of pretending
         called that   a nod to some European concept
There was a feeling of welcome
                  one was welcomed *back*

She had a necklace of spangles
She looked a little out-of-control
         but nothing Jesus couldn't handle

I felt abrasive and restless but didn't let on
Wouldn't admit that I had no energy
         that I'd entered a food coma after the steak

We worked very well together, however
         waitress and customer
                  willing   to answer each other's questions
                  as many as the air-conditioner could take

The cook roamed about
         saying what he was out of

The waitress who'd once been kidnapped
         could have come to Black Rock City
                  and be Godforsaken as ourselves
We'd be a team *there,* too
Eat well   go on the radio with recipes

"I'm very serious in spite of the jokes I told you"
"You still want a to-go box?"
"Not anymore!   the food was too good to save!"

Is the girl who was kidnapped likely to allow
                                    a second capture?

Will it be windy in the desert?
The next phase intrudes the first
        and being ahead of oneself is very confusing
        makes me want my mommy

In a very short time
        the valley that scared my Anna
                will scare myself all over again
It was as if I kidnapped *her*   that year   2013
The closest she ever got to the art cars

But the red sun in the sky
The forest fire smoke that caused it
        Anna had cried
                "I don't think I can..."
And unlike a kidnapping   she got to go home
The Gate had been as far as she'd dared
                        and it was more than all right

"I told you 'Anytime you wish to return it's okay
                I will love you still'   don't cry"

I think she would have liked Chemult
The menu   the waitress, too
They would have had so much to talk about
        and I could have played with my food undisturbed

It's going to be cold
        the Oregon Outback
                even in summer

The "Whiskey Girls"
That will be their names
        for a song that would be played on Wednesday
                            in Center Camp
                    by the Saloon Ensemble

Since dates and times are shuffling
Since there is no then and later

When "you're hangin' with the Whiskey Girls"
    you're a virtual drunkard   but in a *Good* Drunk way

13.   TAKE THE CRUISE AND FACE THE CLIFF

So much effort
So much patience   relying on others
So much construction
The western road is rough   gravelly
    and the shuttle bus is slow
            seeming about to tip over

It would be another one of those transit disasters
                          you hear tell of
Occurring *not* in a Bolivian ravine
    but on the flanks of an American caldera

But one should get to the boat anyway possible
Walking after the bus quits
    descending   zigzagging
        to a pier
        with others of your kind
            applying sunscreen
            boarding   accepting the circumstances
                the gruff captain   well
                perhaps he was only reticent

A full boat left the dock
The center seats faced outward
Those were the best
    they were benches parallel
    lengthwise to the sides of the craft
        and there *was* a vacancy I seized
        without offending anybody
It was stealth advantage taken in broad daylight

I feel so far from skateboarding here in the crater

22

But strangely   the volcanic wall summons Anna
        who never discussed geology   *ever*
So why *do* these insanely bright slopes bring her back?

How steep they are!
How unfavorable the footing!
How much has fallen   collapsed
The story *can* be told
        the park ranger's telling it
                the others must look sideways
                or even turn around

But I planned well
        and the movie of the inner walls is playing
        at nine knots an hour

Drifting out of Cleetwood Cove
Aware a cone is underwater
        the one called Merriam
Drifting past Llao Rock
Llao, one of the legend's combattants
        Skell   the other

The two of them had fought   and fought hard
Crater's the result

Then there are the dykes in the crater's *walls*
"Dykes"   the term loaded   a contemporary identity
        with orientation
But here meaning intrusion
Molten stuff that hardened and resisted
        what was left
        when what it sneaked into
                through all those fissures
                    itself vanished
                being weaker   softer

Oh, the kind lady instructs!
And it appears there are geologists aboard!
        but they have to twist to see
                twist this way and that
Only myself and two or three others face the cliffs

The ranger has drawn attention to Hillman Peak
                                    and the Watchman
And she explains they'd once been volcanoes
                                    in their own right
For the entirety of Mazama existed composite

The movie's full of slow motion
There *is* a shore sometimes
        more a sort of bench
        and so brief and narrow
                you know it's the waves
                what they do
                    when the lake stays the same
                                        those centuries

Stays balanced   the inflow   the outflow
Like the most tentative agreement
        that lasts because good will was always in play

The ranger would have us gaze into the water
                    so green where it is shallow
Wants everyone to experience clarity
As if it could be relevant   pertain to Purpose
                    why *not?*
                thinking
                inventing
                discovering right there in the boat
        as sentient beings

Everything is contained   weird and crazy in the crater
The Big Questions conceived of as gigantic explosions
What I am proposing's already transpired
Is there a God?   where are we going?
        never going to know?

Mount Mazama
        it's own capacity for truth
                ended up   got into extinction
                all its relationships as well
The center of the Earth had spoken

24

                    its poor technology   more than enough diction

Now Wizard Island is affixed
        blocky where the aa lava piled
The *why* of when this happened
                is a motor in the letters that can spell it
                    the captain careful not to run aground

There is snow   beautiful because so little is left!
Start with the physical
            thoughts   the mind *itself*   relaxed away from

Structure is the wall
        the crater bowl guiding decisions
Structure is the random rockslides
And the particular dimensions of the Devil's Backbone
Hearing the lovely ranger tell it   more structure
        how dangerous it all is and was
                the inside parts   the Chasski Slide
                the loose rock remnants ready to go
                        and topple into a blue galaxy!

I am breathless   I see it happen!

And you have the waterfalls
The little rivulets with moss
The water coming down improbably
        a well
                a spring
                    waterfalls small
                        a seeping persistance

"How *wonderful* it would be to hide up there
        where the Chasski fell!
                I mean   in the part that's level
                    that was once rim-high
                    the level place brought *down*   intact!

"But ranger, dear
        although there's danger
                and a Danger Ranger you certainly are
                    who advises the caldera's a no-go

Don't you think it would be great
        to put a tent in the little trees
                and have that water for a water supply?
Wouldn't that be wonderful?!"

She answered with a qualified "Yes" she said she'd later explain
But *first* the Phantom Ship   the ship of stone
        You'd think it would sink!
        on the way to it   know   it is more ancient
                                        than the rest

And circling this exquisite miniature island
        there's a sense it has many stories to tell
        the several towers like pedestals in a zen forest

"White Pine," she says

The crater is anomaly
What once was here is no longer assembled   all parts
And the Pumice Castle's impossible to see for the sun
The walls are wearing out   *we*   are wearing out
        no one cares
                the Secchi disk
                        additional knowledge

Final thoughts
        one may drink the lake, it's okay
        collect the lake in a bottle
                the lake "to go"

The water's so blue, it's *destiny*
"Destiny," the same as her stage name   ·   confided
        when Anna told her story
        all of it seeming vast as the caldera
        the mountain having hurriedly exploded
                the crater painstakingly examined
                like a patient   seven millennia later

14. THE OTHER TRAIL DOWN

Cleetwood's *one* way to find the lake
Crater Lake's Cleetwood's how it's done
     descending a good and sensible path
     one that's populated too

But there's another   not known that well
Another trail down into
     and why is this so?
     a little history's the answer   what's bygone
        the earlier days when they knew other ways

Let's hike it   with stealth!
Maybe in the moonlight for it's not allowed
Wait till no one's looking
     then   from the rim   to the deep water go
        and starting from this elsewhere
        the Lodge the beginning

Think "old days"
In your bedroom sleeping
     or in the mornings   hyper-aware
Consider reunion   though we're separate now
     and we'll meet at the place of proposal
        to go the old way
        copying others with pioneer minds

It's wooded over and the path's a mere sketch
It might be learned in a day
Wake up together and find the route
     and secretly explore it
        Zigzagging the wall as earlier visitors had done
        the ladies *especially* careful in their skirts

Then   where the lake waves begin
     take an imaginary canoe to the Phantom for lunch

This is disclosure
This is like Burning Man we travel to
        a cry for help that takes you down

minimally impacting
          unafraid of failure
               for obscurity has no critics around

This is not the squandering of time you might imagine
Of resources   of writing
You love life as I do
Life here
     life in the geology
     In the center of the Center   the heart is constant
                                       the canoe well-made

There must have been a Conductor
The first movement was cataclysm
The Indians wrote the music down
          before the instruments were dreamt of
          before even Time's signature was added

If you know just where
          then wildness ensues
               catches up with you
Do not slip and slide too much
               aware the aliens may be ourselves
                         with Seven-Elevens, too

No one okayed it
     but decades have been lost on the trail
The cars above   regressing
The models more rectangular and black
There's even a few electric   the *first* ones

The act of retracing the New World's baby steps!
We'll have such a good time going undercover!
All the music heard in Black Rock City let loose at once
There is even a "perimeter"   the rim drive
                    some enchanted evening of Vulcan
                    by special arrangement

This unused path rededicate
     path so long unbeaten to these same waters' edge
No one can see   it is our own course taken
          our lifeform's amazement savored

The forest is playing tricks   but the coffee's perfect
        unaffected
            believe and belong
                at once spectator and participant

There's a party pretending Crater Lake has a gate
Has Greeters
        and rangers willing to let us take the old trail
Together will we conjure a time of fewer rules

Wilderness hungers for the wayward
The caldera's lonely now the century has turned
        technicolor gone to bed with lysergic acid
            and birthing hybrid intensity

A few short years ago its last song was sung
It was Stravinsky's *Firebird* finale
C Major making the most of its white keys' industry
                Stravinsky hiking
                    the superstar and all of Ballet Russes

Breaking the chains of Nineteenth Century procedures
Spontaneous steps taken
        both of us envision the landscape as clues
        with hints how this can best be done

The other trail is another time brought forward
The Lodge and all its amenities
        helps us to help others
                as the playing of a xylophone
                    endears the player to whomever is listening
Body talk
        the instrument rejoicing it has a part to play

Climb downwards into the heart of Mazama
A second Cleetwood wanting visitation
        where skulls covered with flowers are
The vision quest will succeed   continuous
The rocks have microphones
The volcano is wired
        says it's been there and done that

Llao and Skell!
The warring factions!
Explosions
        tore it apart and put together something new
        true blue

Say, "*Thank* you, walls!   thank you, sky!
            and the canoe we'll take
            and take away as memory.
                carried bright as pumice yellow!"

Enchantment!
Nothing in Nature left out
Dawn's shadows an ironic commonplace
        constancy's apotheosis
            a unicorn is not more strange

Beyond the sky
        will be the national parks of other worlds
And there will certainly be craters brimming on Earth 2
        in orbit about a small red sun
        with just enough heat to bring forth a *Stravinsky* 2
            and other alternate beings

There's a sunken camp out there
            wanting volunteers
            to serve the citizens of a sunken Black Rock
We're almost there   unpredictably there
The way children are
            almost Heisenberg brats
                in two places at once

We have no schedule   no bus has carried us
No boat will depart with lectures
Here   we walk occluded   top secret
        allowed just enough substance to startle the mortals
        gone cuckoo-giddy in the twilight

The City may be imagined
        as the aftermath of Culture capital "C"
            when *little* "c" starts again its roundup

It took all of Mazama to make it happen
            do what it did in disappearing

Well, not entirely, of course
Just as Burning Man builds on what went wrong
        and will try to get right   and soon
            so each footfall is perfect reenactment
                            the whole way through

And as Chauncy Gardener said,
        "It's very good, Eve
        I like to watch!"

I say that balance is desired   necessary
Walk this path   the established trail forgotten
This one   making your way in the slanted woods
        a baby Robert Frost
        his diverging road

Picture this gravity
        gone to sleep in the arms of acquaintance
            allowing hikers wings
                for the planet's gargantuan spaces

This is the second that *was* the first
The other
        the original
            buttermilk to the infant's wants

And there is luxury
Though primitive reigns   it rules with compassion
                its many eyes surveying

So we were winding and threading the trees
        soft-stepping the incline
            still a volatile slope after the millennia
                people talk about it still
Hard radiation adoring all it finds
                    being lovers with the living

15. VIDAE FALLS   EAST DRIVE

As Burning Man waits
So the several
      indeed   the *multiple*
          cascadings that are Vidae   linger
            prior to waterfalling all your intentions
            steeply   as befits the risks
        expertly plunging
    without prerequisite purpose
        a long way dropping
            past angular ledges
              a vertical garden unsuspected
                  except for the hinting mind
              that is always ferreting
          and seeks in the wilderness
       what is strange
in what is already enchanted

The sun has proven hotter
      this side of the gifting volcano
But Vidae splashes ice water even so
And it is good for you and your acrophobia
      the handholds and footholds
         found near to the sound
         like conversation backgrounding

A discussion with *variants*
As if white noise were inconstant chatter

And where Vidae's various landings minutely pool
      the spillway a stop-and-start masterpiece done
There is the stream's pause   like thought
              in a runaway and willful rushing

In Black Rock *too* is that slower moment made use of
The anti-cult.   to balance too swift a patronage
Art   a longing sweetly resisted

that the heart may prolong its adorations

16. SUN NOTCH

He'd said there'd been a glacier
        the man who manned the talk and took questions
And you could call his brood
            those many so resolved
            to let just *one* be a guide

He wasn't loquacious   though he *was* insistent
The way a groove is cut then deepened with repeats

The crowd that followed him   well,
        its collective will was gone
        abrogated by a park employee   a ranger!
He could have lied if he had wanted to
                    for *they* wanted to believe it *all*
                    being hynotized
                            by the whole situation
                                with chipmunks, too!

He said Mount Mazama's glaciers had carved
And when the mountain fell
        the glaciers' troughs were split   cut
            and abbreviated to   drop-offs

His "school" was walking a remnant curvature
Crater Lake's rim where the bowl is lowest
"Sun Notch"
        say it again   the two n's joined   tongue to roof
        one's speech imperceptably paused for effect

There's a "ship" down there   can't miss it
A Phantom Ship quite real in the overexposed day
The ranger's gestures are perfunctory
        though graceful

33

                his uniform pressed to better inform
Out of respect we'll let him talk
Name names   point to points
         the audience earnest as himself
                        and fresh from rub-a-dub

Only the children punctuate   impatient
Prepared to go wild as the butterflies
The rest are a rhapsody of diabetes
        and inert wonder they made it to Sun Notch at all
         the ascent   though very gradual
                still an ordeal

"Can someone say why there aren't any trees?"

"Pumice!" came the answer

It was a little one   proud of the book she'd read

"Well, *well!*   very *good!*"

Pumice, the inhibiter
That's why there's sun   and why Sun Notch
Is it possible the two n's together's the take-away?
        a construct the same as that glacier imagined
        a glacier left invisibly filling
                everything gone but the thinking
                and if *that* would only stop   then   the *Void?*
                        the *crater?*

Yes, the crater filled   with a no-thought lake
And   overall, perhaps   a Nothing
        the concept of "notch"
                large or small
                        is moot undertaking
                                perhaps the sun *alone*   sufficient

17. ON CLOUD CAP, HIDDEN

Highest road in Oregon?   really?   Cloud Cap?
Nah!   though you *do* have the right to assert
  I mean   how good does a road have to be?

Never mind!
Get out of the car
      push a few tourists over the edge
            so there'll be more to *see*

Oh!   I'm sorry   just kidding   didn't mean it!
Will stop with just "Get out of the car," yeah

It's an oblong lake down there, my friend
Must have been an oblong blast that made it

Let's follow *those* guys!   see 'em?
They're heading for the topmost part over there
Let us walk in the pumice   up   crunching to them
      then carry on to whatever the crown possesses
            sobriety in charge   well, "in charge" is wrong
                  say only sobriety's a third companion
                  with proper footwear, even
                  mindful

How far one can go is anyone's guess
The clouds of Cloud Cap notwithstanding
      that word wanting to be a part of this
            the dome leaning with clean dirt like the playa
            as if the playa covers the high ground here
                        albeit not as finely
                        the pumice sand gritty
                        porous and giving

Where we saw the others go's not far
It will be an occasion   a stop   windily enhanced

There's a hologram of Yosemite floating here
Remember Clouds' Rest
            another respite for the wispy and the puffy

                    elevated to receive
                            the enhancement
                            of white ephemeral dancers

How about a little 'round the bend of the Cap?
We'll slightly dip down to accomplish this
Then   running out of space
        intrude the tangle of trees
            as if searching for a place to procreate
            and make a child of the summit
                        whose secret brambles are full of ideas
                            and memories of the *kama sutra*

There   concealed or not   might we cuddle
Or another word   more Hindu
        less amateur

We're not afraid of heights
Without fear do we go
        to contemplate dacite's   inertness   delicate
        wondering, "What's it all about, Alfie?"
A bad movie ending with celibacy

At any rate, too many syllables to our very own moans
We were looking for concealment
            and found a universe
                one that was happily clouded   occluded
                    if not partly or entirely vanished
                            at least what you meant by oblivion

The *way* you say that word with Scarlatti beginning
All the hundreds of his sonatas played in sequence
The precise order of their composition heard
        like our footsteps to the forest of Cloud Cap
        though not as *many* as the harpsichord's

Look, tell you what   one kiss may be enough
So exquisite   the rest might *fatally* unfold
        an altitude of love
            far beyond a National Park's capacity to impress

18. THE COOK REVISITED

It was tentative at first   but recognition came
Both of us remembering

It had been just a year ago
Our conversation then
       I had to feel my way along
         admitting I'd written about him
           being honest

I'd called the junction Diamond Lake
     though Diamond Lake was elsewhere
     sunning itself for the boaters and hikers

Diamond Lake *Junction* was austere
Sketchy   with a motel
    up and running
    but crowded with dvd's
      and the shelves of a buit-in store
               that was like a hoard

A wonderful dog searched your eyes
            and displayed its belly all day

A few bites into the burger
     I offered the cook my contact info
     and asked for his
He gave an address on the north-south highway
The one known as 97
I said I'd send him the story I'd written that he was in
     the one that began, "He *knew,* that cook at Diamond Lake"

This pleased him
He said he'd look forward to that

Later   travelling Chemult to Crescent
Turning into the geology of Big Hole

I found out *more* about the ship
the *Indianapolis* the cook had known of
a heavy cruiser
The new information?
Well, *Indianapolis* had brought the Bomb to Tinian
to be assembled and dropped

How could this learning get back in the story?

Hadn't the misery of the crew been sufficient telling?
When the ship took two torpedoes
and sank in minutes?
When sharks attacked the survivors?
When days passed full of insanity
before the belated rescue?

Or should the sin of "Little Boy" be added
his very own day in the sun   sun close-up
on the missing morning of August 6th, 1945?

Maybe it's better one tragedy at a time
Maybe it's better to make a third trip to the Junction
prime the coda as they did the Bomb
feed the *cook* for once   with preliminaries

But a third time I'd *also* know
if he'd known about the ship's earlier mission
the transport of atomic components

Then everything is known that can be known
And there is wondering
if some incredible karma obtained
and swept away the crew   many
witness reduced to mere survival

The cook and I could decide   or not
that ignorance is culpable
the whole ship unaware (
of what was in the hold

The cook and I could even enlist
Be a part of the United States Navy   year 2016

We're fit!   *he's* at attention *all* day
        and *I'm* wandering around in the land of volcanoes
        picking up and then discarding in-situ rocks

We'd make a hell of a team
                sharing Oregon with all our mates
This ain't over
And many wars later
        the singularity of the Bomb
                opens all bomb bays of the future
                begins any discussion of what is to be

We are positioned for lemonade
        in a spaceship bound for Andromeda
Thing is   there must never be another you-know-what
Never another second sun in the morning

I wish I knew if such fission or fusion is impossible
Or inevitable   completely
        ships sink
                and then a watery roulette
                and wondering

Who will end what's precarious?
Who will stay the torpedo?
Who will cancel the chain
        and see to all reaction?

19.   TWENTY THOUSAND YEARS AGO

Though it's certainly peaceful
And the slanting sunstar *insists* it is
        says all is well
                even as melancholy's redoubled
                                with p.m.'s fading
Something in the millennia whispers violence

What you'll see is disconnect
Big Hole wanting another explosion
        bigger than back then
            twenty thousand years ago

And so is witness made to perceive
A new baby   a brand new maar
        the principal volcano unfinished
            having *not* had its fill of steam explosions
Makes you want to be a warrior
Bring inside   bring into your being
                what blows the trees down
                    and causes the land to tremble

The pastorale before you has madness superimposed
"Don't forget about me!"
            shouted in the midst of remembrance

And have you already done so?
The outburst resolving itself
The bowl of Big Hole once more a too-serene eclogue.

There is no account prepared
There is no record at all
T. S. Elliot is ghosting a script
        but is yet undecided whether to tell
            and it's also unlikely
            he will do any weightlifting
For his is a basking brain steeped in a mysterious ennui

And it is vast as Big Hole's tree-filled contradictions

20.   FORT ROCK, BRIEFLY

There will not be a rim walk   not this time
No testing of the crack in the wall
        where it's possible to scramble

one level of the laminate stone
        to the next highest
        careful not to look down

There will only be the briefest assessment
A few tentative steps to see if it's still all there
        the Fort that's a Rock
        defensible for most of the circle of itself
                just the southeastern rampart gone

The southeast *welcoming*
        protection cashiered
            what you come to
            the breach made easy stepping stones

Though the flashlight's strong
        there is no temptation to go any further
        just as there's little incentive in line at the Gate
                    sometimes
And thus even Burning Man is put on hold
Preferance simply one's place in a queue

It's not really the time of day that discourages
There are all those knobby terraces
The Fort possesses   and tires the explorer
            fostering uncertainty
            high noon or early morn
                        makes no difference

Today the edifice evokes that other world
The city called Black Rock
        where one may never be as free as required
        the entire festival a tease
Being forced to stare at nirvana
            fully knowing nothing more
                        than approximate peace
                        a kind of mockery

All the more so for having a price
And dust   and rudeness
All the false steps possible *here*
        in the shadowy fort

where evil ancestors assert
      they are your very best friends   *really*

If heaven itself were a place that had an address
Then its mere physicality
     should make moot
         our professions of spiritual longing
See what you can of Fort Rock   without climbing

Let the sudden sage suffice for incense
           for a yet-to-be-named religion
Let the sharp stone silhouette
    defining possible   *impossible*
And so work the duality
     nothing is left of it
     yes or no   *all* the opposites

Nothing that could ever disturb one's serenity
    rushing into sanctuary
       bothering   agitating

All the noise gone that is Duality's only gift
A City that would set itself aside
    and broadcast Otherness
    despite atoms shared
      with the world beyond its perimeter
              orange   porous

Let me talk to that man over there
    busy loading brush into his pickup
Just forfeit the maar   and its ancient city plan
Question somebody   anybody at hand
    and he is
      pitching dead plants into his four-by-four

What should I ask him
    a parks employee   a goverment dude?

It's getting to be twilight
There's no time left   but I blurt out, "My friend!"
And he could be
    easily   a stranger   *that's best*

no history   revelations   knowledge of origins
family and family dogs
whether someone's seen service
                    or fled to Canada

Yes, who's done what
       that may never be forgiven
       no matter how much one may remonstrate

"My friend!"   (the one who *is* for a second,
                         unreservedly)
"I know Cow Cave over there behind Fort Rock
    know it's off-limits   except for the tours",
                       I began

And my good new friend said,
"Yes, that's right   and no tours when it's dry
     they don't want sparks to start a fire
     sparks from the undercarriage
         less traffic in summer   it's safer, so..."

We talked about the sandals they found
Talked about ages ago
     the excavation of the cave
         more a recess
         not *too* much shelter

It was called Cow Cave because the cattle like it
But also Fort Rock Cave for its proximity to the maar

Eleven thousand years ago
Millennia before Mazama blew
     Indians lived here at the edge of a lake
    and safely   a better Burning Man
       more like the festival's origins
       when the few
       the proud
       the Marines of a counter-culture
            frolicked on Baker Beach
           the shores of a larger,
          saltier lake of the Pacific

It was an inland *pluvial* body
Like others of the Great Basin
        the Ice Age just beginning to falter
            the high stands of fresh water

What abundance!   unwritten   barely imaginable!
What explanations the First Peoples found.
                    for what is found in science now
            the books that couldn't stop the planes
            and tanks   and worse

Now   the whole world is Africa
Where the hominid always starts in accounts
        and will spread to Space
        the latest cave   *shelter* even
                        from hideous oppressions

Wrongs so many   all is outwards directed
As if virgin deserts
        ours or Mars
            may make us virgins again
            living simply   frugally as BC Oregon
                        or as Pluto requires

"Here, let me give you a contact
        so you can get on board for the Cave," he said
                        and it was done

Fitfully   for my revery and drift
Not quite able to take it in
Still back there
        fashioning sandals by a very cold, clear lake
        its waves still eroding the southeast side of Fort Rock
            or *whatever* name it was known by
            storms accelerating the destruction

"Uh, thanks, mister!
There's so much discovery
        we'll need other lives and other times to do it"

"You're all right", he answered
            my good friend   good-natured

44

"Thanks!   I hope so"
        was the last he heard from me
                starting that counterintuitive engine

21.   CLOWNS

Parked
        in the surprisingly empty lot
                of non-existent Summer Lake

Wondering
        where, oh where were the people?
        why, oh why were hardly any Burners around?

But there *was* a yard sale
There *were* costumes and kids
                and much revelry despite the numbers

And rummaging quickly
        for I *had* to see the orange cat before I slept
            I found a clown costume hanging
            clean   its colors blue and black
            there was purple as well
                maybe other colors too

Thing was   I was instantly drawn
And it appeared to be a fit
    So   feeling decisive
        I removed the garment from the rest of the rack
        and began to ask questions
                entertaining as I went

Because Burning Man *flamboyance* had kicked in
Because I wanted *company*
Because an act is better than timidity
        and dispels those reasons for too much grieving

45

"That will be fun!" said the girl who was selling
"You're welcome to it!   c'mon, try it on
      but I can already tell it's perfect!
                              and those *buttons*."

"This is my first clown costume
      though *not* the first instance of clownishness!"

They called it a yard sale
The yard as big as the basin of Summer Lake
      and its fringe of sage and grasses
                              the nighttime energizing

"Sold!   but how do I...?   how does one...?
Wait a sec'   where's where you start the foot inside?
I mean *HELP!*
      I can't find a way to put my clown robe on!"

"Don't you worry!
Now stop fussing
      and let Meredith dress you
            she's the best   she'll help you out
                  leave everything to Meredith!"

And I did
      the yard sale loving all this performance
      the feigned confusion and exaggeration
Meredith inserting me into the gorgeous thing
Careful to get the pantaloon appropriate
      smoothing   spreading   adjusting
                              to the cheers the crowd

And suddenly   a new persona came
      my speech turning Barnum and Bailey
                              with gestures expansive!

Also   as if it were catching
      another guy had found his clown self
            synchronicity in charge
            the rack revealing a clown suit for *him*
                              as well

And he took it and wore it
And we were a clown team together
Rapid *repartee*   freestyling
        not missing a beat
        or hint
                we were unerring

"What are the chances?" someone observed
"Two clowns for one yard sale
        two guys   two novices   two *naturals!*"

"*Shoes!*" I demanded   "Give me shoes to go *with!*"

"Sure," said Meredith
        "how about these?"

They were weird
Lsd slippers   mostly yellow
        with hiccups of red and green polka dots
        the shoes seeming cardboard yet substantial
                                they also *fit!*
Or fit well enough for simply standing
        being seen   posing
                being on and off a playa stage

Some night or day of the week out there
When we rise to the occasion of gifting Polichinell
        and as much of Marcel as may be channeled
                with the help of circumstance

It is Today that critiques
                and Today that favors antics

So be it   we danced
        and set the night   if not on fire   nearly
And there was still the hot water of the tubs
Still Fred the orange cat to pet
                and the windy oblivion of early a.m.

The land here has come apart
And broken ground surrounds

The show is geology
       and *we* are geology's puppets
              in spite of creature comforts
              those cozy tents and sleeping bags

Prior to dreaming done   a routine is accomplished
Effortless   brotherly
In cardboard shoes
       and the robes of *jongleur*   jester
              the better threads of comedy

Let us see if Anna sees any glimmer long distance
       wearing her own court jester's cap
       remote-viewing the yard sale
       the children
              the playa lights swaying to manic revelry

It is arson trying to figure a way
       when cold, dry tinder had seemed to chill
"The End" had appeared
              before the title burst forth
              in noisy black-and-white
                     with music by Max Steiner
                     the movie not quite restored
                            and grainy

This is the technicolor version
       with blue   with purple
                     and mostly yellow shoes

The additional reds of my straight man clown
              reacting   all of us extras
              Les Enfants du Paradis
The remake bold
       in the shadows of uncertain diplomacy
                     and slow-motion warfare

22. THAT POOL AGAIN

It was unquestionably the best pool at the hot springs
The highest   the closest to its source

There is blind welcome
    six bathers
    no one sees   but *hears* in the dark
             everyone going to Burning Man

Talk turning to cancer
A girl who'd scared her father   but survived
    and going

A guy who once stood in his silver suit
So close to the flames that plastic flowed
    going back

A "virgin"   who
    when she was found out
    and while she splashed in the minerals
    someone said,
        "Don't tell the Greeters you're a virgin
                it's better!"

"Yeah, they'll pressure you to roll in the dust
                  as is the custom"
This from another invisible veteran
    the night like a gracious host
"And further   even if it's not your first time
        there's something to be said
        for staying pure and innocent"

Laughter in the pool

"Oh, and clean!" he concluded
    and challenged the company
        to be brand-new in Black Rock

23. THE UNNAMED LAVA HILL

How much trouble, my dears, to get on up there?
How much height above may be gained?

Well, we'd see   myself and those I love
     ascending in the sage and loose gravel
       the authority of semi-arid landscapes felt

The basalt argues millions of years and molten days
The option to flow
     the "hot spot" hot enough
         to inspire the lithosphere

We're not far from a favorite junction   31 and 395
But we are explorers   hard working
Anxious to see the land of early morning
                         and exercise liberty

We are a team left and right
The land protected by disuse
     no plans beyond pictures
     and serving the needs of hunger

There *is* no *power* abroad
And the Earth serves only Space and Time
All that may be found in the store of Heaven
     brought north/south/east   and west
     and sought as intangible treasure

It is a quick surmise we will leave no trace
Leave nothing but footprints there
       depressing the soil just inches at a time
         almost secretly
         everything still okay
         acceptable overland
             same as the jackrabbit's intent

Let us be happily sidelined

wandering supplemental wilderness
anywhere empty
Filling in the blank spaces with further vacancy

Each terrace a delicate recon
airy as the westerlies all over eastern Oregon
everyone pleased who found the time
and   in truth   to be there
meant an extra clock

It is a stagecoach atmospheric
no stops
no needs but constancy
and hearing the case for caresses
The winds are walking all over, like ourselves
on these essential ledges

And it feels close to the truth   travelling as gusts
Restless as science in the thrall of precise spirits

Turns out it wasn't any trouble at all
And the height above was *easy* altitude attained
was simply a gate
and the ghosts of four-wheel drive
their imprints reverting
in the brush of the ancient lakebed
gray clays interspersed

All this energy come to pass
like the exploits of astronauts
Thrust   this day   the ability to rise   remotely
No press or raw video feed
Gaining the unnamed lava hill on a budget of desire

Spread out   non-objective
A surveillance
a difference of hats
all else we can't control taking cover

And we saw it together   starting over
like a new approach to Chopin's f minor Fantasy

24. THE ABERT RIM

Always thought it was "Albert"   Albert Rim   Albert Lake
Then the dislexia cleared
        the fuzz resolved to "Abert"
        the name shortened
                the "l" gone camping with the clouds

What was left was still formidable
The Rim, massive   unclimbable
The Lake, undrinkable
Enough notice taken geology planted signs
                                ready with an explanation

Can you say, "fault block"?

Yeah, we get it
        things tilt and plunge
                and it takes a long time
                        though terms and science
                        seem to foreshorten
As if knowing why would diminish
While it made understandable the Rim   the Lake
        and   we are talked down from enormity

To make it grand again   walk *up*
        as far as the incline can take you
        to be steeply re-educated

BLM land   a bureau
                where you can ask what's not to like
Is it possible the government cares?

There's a good feeling
        a quarter of the way to the wall
                the last part   way up there
                the barrier prior to exit

The long-ago lava belichened
Green and maybe other colors too
        but still dark overall
                another planet embedded in our own!

When?
Don't ask   too many zeroes

It's said there was a "hot spot"
        that started   and travelled to Yellowstone

Great!
But it's one foot above the other
        and having a better grasp than the book's
                the brain reprieved
                on forty-five degrees of Abert
The consonant twelvth letter trying to return
                        trying to make "Albert" again

Making the effort   like me
And the more the Rim is accomplished
        the more Abert *Lake* is seen
                just inches deep
                        beyond the whiteness of drainage

A basin   the low point
Abert's opposites wanting metaphor
                        and example made

So for now   rest
                where it's level
Satisfied *another* could find a way
        to slip past the capstone
        of Oregon's continuation east

Far from family life
What does it make you
        to examine desolation
                overturn its pebbles
                        succumb to scented updrafts
                        en route to incompletion?

How will you explain the quietude of just eight years?
Your infinite age on the slopes of Abert?
The child it took to comprehend?
The zest
        of realizing no one probably has been here
        exactly slanting as this?

It's a college conceived in a dream
Where attendance means you're always late for class
        but the professor understands
                and adjusts the curriculum accordingly
            smiles and says   improbably:

"Now let's see what samples you've brought us
                                from Abert Rim!"

Though the class is philosophy...

25. THE PAISLEY LADY

She had a lot of questions
Maybe it was the license plates
        Paisley so very far from the southern quandary
                                of misfits

There *was* suspicion
But not enough to *not* sell coffee
And she seemed like someone who asked questions
                                anyway

Before the mocha
        she found out reasons   and built on those

"So you write?"
"Yes   the *caves* got written"
"Archaeologist?"
"Dilettante   I dabble   knew the caves were very old

and went on over
a *pretend* scientist, you might say!"

She paused   "Shall I make this a double?"
"Oh, yes!"

Then she began a sad story
        of misunderstandings and distrust
How Paisley's Caves had caused tension in the town
And grousing
How the students came to study the ancients
        and stayed and stayed
                the university wanting restrictions

"But they were *our* caves, too!" she said

The times were uneasy
The funny-named Chewaucan River still flowed
        in season
The saloon was still open
                yet a divide had occurred

She wasn't clear on how things stood
                today   the mocha perfect
But in the country
        things tended to stay standing
                though contentions are resolved
                                and relax a little

Her booth was out of place in pioneer lands
In a *good* way, though
The best of the City having an outlet in Paisley
        the name sounding kind of Sixties
                        in a non-Hippy setting

Already written was plenty on the caves
She'd receive it in time
She said she'd look forward to that
                wondering what an amateur's take could be
                a third eye, perhaps
                between professional townsfolk
                        and professional professors

She was certainly intrigued by the mess in the car
"In too much of a hurry, I'm afraid!"

She bought the explanation
        and since I was her first and *only* customer
            we continued the melting
                    every ice cube dissolved

She even thought I might fit in
The small town waited
        Paisley
        the family
                for that's what happens
                up and down eastern Oregon's vastness

There was Frenchglen   Plush   Adel
Many more
        where the truth comes out in public
        and stands around
And ranchers greet each other at a distance
            there being so much silence to break

We ended friendly   if matter-of-fact
And you sense once more
        a conversation needn't be strident to succeed

Even the "cave clash" she'd described
This was understated
And thereby   in some ironic way
                        more clearly understood

It was to be continued, therefore
            her and I
            and slowly
            our mutual desire
        when my haste caught up with her leisure

26. SUSAN

"Ask Susan!"
"I will   where *is* she?"
"Seek her over *there*   ask at the boutique
          she's around
          or *was*"

Two guys unloading bikes at a bike sales
Gerlach improper
          a museum's worth of wrecks   relics
          all of it swirling
Where is Susan who sells?

Ah!   there!
"Susan, let's look at your bikes, okay?
              a *small* bike
              please"
"Rent or buy?"
"Both   I mean *buy*!"
"Let's look"

We did
And there was a kid's   perfect!

"You can't fall *off*!" I explained
      "and a lock as well
        after twenty years of trying
                    no more 'gifting'
                    no more stolen bikes
Sell me a lock with letters"

It was done   great!
She said, "It's a Big City now   with Big City *crime*!"
"The Experiment has failed
              what do *you* do, Susan?"
"Teach"
"Aha!   and will you teach them not to *steal*?"
"I'm trying
      but after twenty years they made *me* a thief!"
"Why, then, I'll have to take you in..."

"Not just yet   I'll join you later for a ride
                                on my own matching kid's!"

27. AT THE GREETERS' STATION

Burning Man begins

The twenty-first for myself
        thirty-first for the founders
The Soviet Union was still around
        when Harvey brought that thing to the beach

And in '96
When I saw him on his motorcycle
        talking to a camera crew
                he was good company   strategic
                and there was comedy in what he said

Twenty years later
        two women Greeters want to know:
        'Are you a 'Virgin'?"

I went easy on them
The simple truth was impossible
The benefits   out of reach   like justice
The Greeters were volunteers
            play along
            let a gift be given
                            affability

You've no plans
        linger at the several tipis deployed
        promising to drive only five miles-an-hour
            watch the virgins rolling in the dust
                            as the gong is sounded
There's a way to stick around and be invisibly bizarre
        the art of stealth

no lives will be lost
        your documentary sonata well-tuned

The entire event is an awkward situation
Beautiful as the ladies were
        I wanted them to get some sleep
            the passions of disagreement dormant
            a necessary waste of time
Restorative   involuntary

There's a Greeters Camp
Just stay there   unstressed
The stick figure propped on Baker Beach
                    in distant San Francisco
        he would approve

Bring a nun to the desert and make her comfortable

28. AN EARTH GUARDIAN RECON

Go, then, to the Guardians
And see if the hot springs slots are filled
Anxious to secure another night on the *mountain*
    "Old Razorback" called

Please!   let Razorback be not taken!
Rather, may Trego Hot Springs have an opening
        the pool that's *near* to it
May the space to sign be empty
No volunteer as yet
Just a blank waiting on a wildcat's signature

If that much is accomplished
        then prepare an ascent   spotlit
            to the summit feathers
            and other Indian evidence
            the uncompeting artefacts

And there give thanks to the granite

First night   *dressed* for the occasion
                purple shirt and purple tie
                            still on the ballot of fashion

Burning Man will change your mind
Make research a dilettante's delight

First night   spent at Earth Guardians' bar
                all travelling done
Except Frank Herbert's *"travelling without moving..."*

There's a gong somewhere
            not the Greeters' single percussion stroke
            more a continuous summons
            instrument of the mind
                            proclaiming arrival
                            at the doors to Freedom
                        doors to Liberty
Black Rock itself a *giant* House of Doors evolved
The whole City as installation!

There's a table and chair at the Guardians
            but no one to take your name as yet
                    playa name   *real* name
It's after-hours   though the night is infancy
Secondary space   you can read

In the morning will you talk
Morning, find out who's guarding
        what *needs* guarding
A fast-forward not possible or even desirable
                            just safely landed on the playa
Safely past those sequential quotes
                on the long approach
Past the pennants   lurching to the Gate

You will ask on the morrow
Straight away   if Trego Hot Springs still exists
        needs soldiers
            needs keep-away

And press into palms gold coins of bribery

Not the crazed volunteer
        nor the fastest with slurred speech, even
            but an activist at least

You will say   with the sun around your shoulders,
"I want this:
        in the course of one day and night
        to be taken away
            to the minerals
            those that bubble from conservative depths
The crystals of the weathered pluton"

The week has hardly budged
Unlike the rest of the year
        the better solar realm of Nevada
            is already expanding the minutes and hours
            with the generosity of altered states

"You're....wearing....a.... *tie?*"
"Anything to get attention!"

And it was true
For I aspired to a *Shining* directed by Kubrick
        to be the kid
            or his dad
                in a haunted mansion

Oddly enough   it is Crater Lake Lodge   still
        like a psychic overlay
Stephen King finds something wrong
                            and writes about it
                        believes it
                        because he's an artist
                and insists

Maybe Shelley Duval is here
And she will enter Earth Guardians
            curious   incognito
            but not enough
I'll recognize   look up from my writing and say,

"How do you like it so far?"   just like Jack

There is something potent
        about this Earth Guardians lounge
        that's like a minimalist club
It has a *prelude* feel   with Timeout beginning
            just starting to break out of Limbo
                                and energize

The City is new
As organized as it will ever be
From now until Exodus *is* fall-apart improv
        lit by the "whoosh" of propane strangers
            who prefer anonymity
                like AA gone communal
                                gone intimate
                                lifelong

Funny   the first thing   now we're arrived:
        get the hell out of town
        to a lonely hot springs
Like a beautiful banishment's counter to acceptance

Self-imposed brooding to begin
            with immersion
                feet-first
                and tingling exceptional
                                Baptist
                                desires

29. REMEMBERING AT MINSTREL

You recall an imaginary proposal
Made in the presence of Deep Blue Lake
                        now Crater Lake called
And *write* it   ensconced in the camp with the piano

Still Monday
    the first day
        barely believing it
Once more
    health and finances
        have allowed this latest visit to Black Rock

The city entered like any other: stealthily
Delta, Utah
    where the inhabitants do not know
          the full extent of your injuries

The joke is Minstrel Camp has an extra "r"
      so that it's "Cramp" said
      "Cramp" lettered
        for all to see and remark

And   just as in the Guardians' den
            there's hardly anyone at all
        save the couple from Oakland
        talking fire
        fires in the dry brush
        confounding the fighters   tankers
California erupting

But there is still that proposal
Fresh   at the edge
    the love seat stable
    put in place with thoughts for marriage
Like decisions peaceful
Choice so simple it's the easiest of all

The river arriving its ocean all at once,
    after ancient springs
      you are thinking cool waters
The discussion fighting fire with friendly opinions

Will the terrorists take to the woods?
And when the dry season comes
    use accelerant   and cunning?
      use hands to set fires in the night

unobserved
        while a Santa Ana fans and consumes?

Hands were better used on an upright
One like this keyboard of Greg's
            which he tunes every day for Ragtime
It's red   all eighty-eight sounding
Even Chopin is possible
        the easy action permitting facility
        as if someone could get good at this
                            truly *rely* upon the fingers
"So, Oakland!"
"Yeah?"
"I'd rather *play* than watch, Oakland
    I mean be *activist* performer rather
        than sit on disaster's sidelines   just
            occupy what's possible artistically!

"May I take your picture   last minute
                    Tuesday about to happen?
May I call you 'Kids'?"

"We would ask you the *same*
By the way   this is my boss's daughter
                            how about *that!?*"
"Does the boss's daughter have a name?"
"It's 'Sharon'"
"A *playa* name?"
"Not yet   we'll see what she does out here
    a 'virgin' so to speak
            then name her for it
            the way the Indians called each other:
                    something based on behavior"

Sharon then said,
    "She who tickles when the sun goes down"

I feigned disapproval: "Such a name is too long
                    methinks 'Sharon of Oakland'
It's kind of..."   I gestured broadly
"Epic, don't you think?"

We agreed to become warriors
        and find out the psycho-thugs bent on arson
            before they begin
Give them lsd   and talk them out of jihad

"Yeah, they'll be saying, 'Look at all the colors!'
                        with no thoughts incendiary"

In Minstrel Cramp's performance tent
        the joke already starting to be old
            we bid each other *tentative* "goodnights"
            and only proposals survive

30. GREG IS TUNING

Greg is tuning   one string at a time   of *course*
In the quiet sun of a monastary morning
Minstrel Cramp awakening to repeated notes
Some forceful sonata needing no more than C sharp
        percussive
            like someone disbelieving the key was *possible*
                        and pouncing upon it *fortissimo!*

I won't disturb his tuning
            his upside-down aesthetic
            knowing it's all good   necessary
            knowing Greg

Half-stepwise he goes
Rising slowly to the treble in a thudding progression
And listening's a lesson given by an angry teacher
        introducing the student to *all* the keys
            before a first assignment
                and no possibility of a gold star

The bicycles that pass
        a water truck   an artcar out early

all who hear wish to study
convert his hammering to Chopin
take away the stutter
        cure it   and teach the *teacher* how!

The Cramp is still sleeping
Used to it   a very special staccato aubade

"Thank you, Greg, for your brash lullaby!   *go ahead!*"

By the end of the week
        he would invite me to *join*
        and I would search for a way to decline   politely
Camps are too hard
They are too much work
                structures up that must come down
                canvasses and poles
                    the heat
                    securing

Then   later   finally
        days after The End
        disassembly
        loading
        "MOOP" patrol

Oh, no!
Not *this* spectator!
        energy, energy, *Energy!!*
        and sacrifice!?
        Afghanistan!?
            rocket attacks!?
The learning curve has ended...
I'm channeling Chauncey Gardner, now
And like him I just like to watch
                    ("It's very *good*, Eve!")

"Greg" is a movie   twisting those pegs
        my laziness disguised
            after some off-screen exercise

I want to turn up the volume on this tuning

fought and died for
free speech so free   the conscience has no excuse
                                    is self-driving

The ultimate hero said to be modest
With cold symptoms
              staying in bed
Imagine the playa with box springs
                          and "Couldn't be happier!"

No injection site reaction
The inoculation was complaisance
It's so fine to recline
          the *executive* experience
                sort of a morning-after job training
                casual
But I will be younger   never mind
Younger than the Newbie at the Gate

Greg is tuning
And soon we'll hear sweet Scott Joplin's rags
          the up-tempo   the slow drag
                the *Mexican Serenade*
He knows 'em all!
                and so do we in his knowing

The time is ragged he keeps
Deliciously balanced
Gay Nineties sentiment
              pouring past the turn of the century

And the instructions to the piano player:
"Not too fast"   always
        as if to say,
          "Let us enjoy these good times   every day
                until the day the show does not go on
                until the *Titanic* goes down
                      and the world goes to war
                              with silly helmets on"

Deduct Greg and you'd have cramps for real
He is the President of Harmony

deserving of our vote   early morning
The guesswork is: just when will he finish?

Guesswork *also:* why is a Burning Man day so long?
It is long in a *good* way, though
        so it's not a question that complains
Just intense curiosity
How *do* those minutes expand no matter what you do?
Perhaps it's time's generous forgiveness for time wasted
Time's *pushback*, too
            and then we come to a principle that way

Do you love this idea?
        love   in the Land of Respect
            bordered by the Granite Range
            the other ranges God has shaped?

I am asking you to make it sacred
In the middle of the world's biggest party   it's easy
            with all this time
            ragtime too
Like charity sounding the music of the *Maple Leaf*
                        Elite Syncopations
                the margin of safety
                apparent

The preparatory jabs   a chromatic scale
    until approximate's resolved into acceptable pitch
Wanting *lyric* after the limbo
        of necessary   errant   percussion
        has sounded extreme *martellato*

That "going to war"
That Soviet toolbox opened by Shostakovich
        when the factories strove
            and the word "production"
            was never more *relentlessly* mechanical
Beyond the Urals and waiting for later
                    in desperate isolation

31. THE ARCHAEOLOGIST

One had to listen   and appreciate
In the misspaced hours, Tuesday
Waiting for the whole story of the caves he'd seen
        the historical uncertainties
        the best of the Bureau of Land Management

He'd said why he'd come to prefer the government
                                        to teaching
        and the Bureau had turned him loose in Nevada
            a careful plowman
            a jaeger

He recounted 1860
        the Pyramid Lake battles
            and wondered:
                just how long the Paiutes might have lasted
                    unmolested
Except for the occasional raiding
                        by other Amerindians

His narrative was lengthy
Kindred   I was thinking
How can I best make use of what he's saying?
What's the best *question* to ask?

I ventured Paisley
        and the Cow Cave at Fort Rock
            the better-off world of the Ice Age
When perversity was just a tribal tick
        the mannerisms of shamen
            in a changeless Great Basin
            its freshwater oceans inland   surrounded

Listen for their shouting   the testing for echoes
It was a planet's special province
A planet of its own

He said he'd been among the Nightingales
Had his field notes from dry Lake Winnemucca

Was Derby Dam for all time to divert the Truckee?
Though there had been an emergency
          it was so slow to unfold no one acted
                and Pyramid's sister lake was lost to us
                to the birds and the mud hens' scampering

No Supreme Court of the Sage consulted in the matter
"Do not enter"   the injunction
          "unless thousands of years are your thoughts!"

The archaeologist talked
          easy formality   as befit the topic
          "sustainability" a rather long word
                for simple aspiration   a sigh
                even losing heart for a moment

The sketch of what he'd spoken stretched over
As animal skin   to form a drum
To further resonate the outline
We touched on Fremont
          John C. Fremont   the explorer
          (how had he managed to be in so many places?)
                dragging artillery past camouflaged tribes
                who would feign hospitality
                    for the meager improvement
                                of beads and trinkets

Perhaps someone made a stirring speech
Why is it we cannot know?
That it's best archaeology's a blur   a tease?

Substance stays over the horizon and biased

You come away from Burning Man with conversations
          the most valuable experience
          that chance meeting
Timeout called in the middle of a movie by Fellini
Downtime   the director befuddled

I might be a criminal
      reforming with every tete-a-tete
Here's a voice
Listen as if it's NPR   but the science *only*
Lucid dreaming
     when   adjusting the dial
               the dream is changed
               the discussion gone native

We came to Sutcliffe
The town by the lake
      the little museum that was once there
      (what happened?   where'd it go?)
   the exhibits
   the ancient horse found
   spears and other artefacts

The archaeologist remembered
The displays' disappearance a transition
     like losing a culture all over again
        and there's no more shame
        just computer history

The morning's warmer   could it have a career till noon?
The spirit of the question!

The Earth Guardians have begun their day
They are wary
    inclined to doubt
       that these roller coaster times
       the rattle of guns
          will be good enough stewardship

32. THE SHARK CAR BY DAY

Without its red edges
    having no outline

being seen imperfect

There are two cities:
     sun-ravaged
     night-cocooned
            all travel interstellar

"Thank you, Shark, for all you do!"

It was *large*
A low-speed predator   ungainly
Shark that could be seen from afar
      the Sunday we waited for the Temple to burn
      camped in the rocks of a western terrace
           with spyglasses and binoculars

Miles away   yet the red lines were clear
In the art car collection *distinctive*
      strangely innocent
      as all the human race may be said to be that
               if allowance is made

There it is   in the Guardians' purview
At the start of a countdown
      to another temple it will help surround
        the machine age faking it
        until it can make it   somehow
In the nail-biting new century and beyond

A basking shark in the sunshine
Its sense of smell a mechanical possibility
The way too many syllables
      nevertheless say an instructive simplicity lurks

It's stopped
      as if *hesitant*
      unsure it has to keep moving to survive

If you don't return...
Oh, but you *will!*   to the open house that is our sea
      invisible
      for which real estate

is an alkali flat's apolitical expanse

And so will / return
       though I lose my life as *you* have
         a fossil being
           without power of its own

You can expect a frenzy
       and state of ersatz emergency
That which emerges from evolution
          and redly outlines what was

33. "STARDUST" WITH BLUE HAIR

We've always said we understand:
       revolution
       social change
          the difference made
          the positive mindset
The Great Unknown that is Utopia
Yours to keep   if only   if only

But a new pair of blue jeans
       what you started to say when I shut you up...

Let's go further
We will call you "Stardust"   and dye your hair blue
     dignity   maturity

The habitues of Minstrel Cramp number forty-seven
We are a means to your end
        the court informal
        what we can handle
And the jester says, "Earn points!   win prizes!"

Blue's the new royalty   the new You
    mobile   minstrel

blue immersion
relevance

We've always said we understood dynasties
But it's not what we *say*
Understood it's something to do with *us*

Our next move is adoration
good clear water
the perfect molecule

Let us hear the music of Chopin
the *Ballade*   G minor   the mystery Key
so Gypsy!
Play it so we hear it plainly
We're not mad with anyone   mid*night* or mid*noon*

Blue Stardust traveling the distance Infinity advises
to a place of answers
all you asked   and asked *for*
The day desire came
like an anxious technology
gambling unprecedented sums
on satisfaction
scientists
reconsidering everything

Ah!   blue minions of her revery!
World Wars explained calmly
a corner of Olympus set aside

We can have that debate about potential
Be spirited!
inclined to worship in pantheons
and win a Grecian title
have no idea of mortality

Is Zeus so scary you couldn't *talk* to him?
the bluest god of all
gone crazy with response?

She's taking piano lessons

standing there
    just listening   seconds at a time
        the way you're supposed to
        nearly doing nothing
            for   as long as the Ballade may last

Its scales and chords the aural equivalent of stardust
What constellation's turned to snow
                    and fallen on the minstrels?

Each audio cut rejoined
So that Chopin is seamless   outrageous
Greg's tuning in tandem with genius
        a professional staff of angels attending

The keys are colored blue
        the while sopranos are conjured
        lyrical   breakdown
The physical world has fallen apart
                too early for the future
                too *late* for stone tools
                            and living on the edge

Let your blue sky bend
And specify the darkness you would sever
        explaining the important part of the rainbow
        color that's an even number
        a digit derived from a brand new math
With braids positioned
            just so   in the watery night

A phenomenom of photons arrested
                            and jailed for a time
            perhaps all of us share the cell
            a trifle embarassed
                and bad-mouthing the drunks

Perhaps Stardust will make bail   make suggestions
Stanley Kubrick wants to meet her
        wear his *own* blue jeans for social change

It hasn't always been this way

Revelations   like oases found   far apart
                                           free-traded
The powerless aspire to at least a preview
        blue-haired
        the occidental zen-designed for peace
                        in spite of pestilence

We have always   Intrinsically   basically understood
But it made us lonely
Wanting to cuddle with someone blue
            maybe talk about social issues
            make repeated revolutions
In a playground full of G minor children

We're learning how
Learning what's next as minstrels
                    former courtships resumed
                    job markets wisely abandoned

We will manage
        paper-folding the brain
        whose origami will spread and be copied

Try and see it this way
Resting   trusting   hearing Country:
        "I'll be blue for you..."
Skirting the edge of fathomless depression
She is Stardust
        the star staying true to itself
            wait and see if there's any change
                        have and have-not sorcery

In the blackout culture
        a utility promises reawakening
                    the sizzling improvement felt

I can't believe we are doomed
And make such repairs to the psyche
            as she recommends
            at home and humid
            despite the dry air entering the shade structure

To master the red piano will be difficult
It is of huge concern whether Middle C will be found
So the minutes spent
         In touch with the instrument
                  are enhanced with powdery blue
                  swirling a variety of pixie dust
Who knew her talents were lifelong?!

No rain event is in the offing
We will end up desolate   but *happily* arid
         willing the Ice Age back

It looks like History will accept us
Send Stardust on ahead
                      second thoughts the same as first

All our friends to evacuate the cities
         be back in the Outback east
         with cramps and supplies
Adapting and dying *both*
The forty-seven doing all in their power

Someone's playing the drum
         with a secret intelligence such
               all within hearing ask,
               "What is that?"
And the answer happens:
                "Music of the future
                 informed by an I.Q. of thousands"

Music made of pure precision
Measuring harmony closely
A *behavior* of sound
         the red piano a pleasant fatality

You'll be using blue notes
You'll have to find them all
         play them all   on the red piano
               thinking how nice is Trego
               the Frog Pond
               the hot springs of Black Rock
                        where desire pools

77

Where you say such prayers as breathing and bathing

I'd always said I'd rebel
       though not being sure of making a difference
              while physics stays as is
              and I have Stardust to say,
                     "There, there!   let me make it better!
                            (and   be sure   I *will!*)"

34. A SPARKLE PONY SPILLS THE MOCHAS

"Greg, *please!*
Let me buy you a mocha!   what do you say?"

"Uh, sure!"
"Be right back!   keep tuning!"

The purple tie was getting attention
No one else in Center Camp had thought to wear one.
I liked the simplicity   the formality
It was a visual so *easy*
       yet out-of-doors charming
              the corporate tie conspicuous   anomalous
Well-dressed without trying

"Three mochas to travel!"
It shouldn't be hard
Just be careful   watch where you're going
       take a long time returning
              in the new day's bustle
                     mobile   non-geometrical

There is time   time away a half-hour's thought
       for the updating of dreams
              their paper cuts and criminal drift

He is tuning
He deserves a gift
     his is a theater of thrills

I am a doctor being careful   *three cups* careful!
Here we go
Center Camp is crowded   too bad
                   concentrate
                   continue
                   fighting sleep
         a trance state in broad daylight

Give me a hand, oh Guardians!
It's a struggle dream in the middle of Black Rock
We should talk about that
              the Trinity   the roots

Massachussetts tags along
Ages less than eight on the eastern seaboard
    way back
    the childhood channel
        it's odd   concurrent
           a rush of joy under all that's adult
The balancing act informed by the single-digit years

Telling the truth
And if truth has a ground zero
    this circus circle's the center for now
I will not change to survive

Consider it a domestic achievement:
The U.S.A. assembling culture on a *tabula rasa*

Though horror and shame engulf the Holy Lands
    lately there's collective escape
    minimal risk
The ticket's fine print
The possibility of death if one attends

Reputation is subsumed
      that portion of concern
      that seemed a paramount distraction

Let me stagger with the mochas
Get back to the Ragtime Master   not having spilled
Wander through a wholesome hysteria
        little tragedies
        tiny, really
                that stave off larger disasters

Visiting angels appearing
        who eschew their usual rounds to monitor youth

Oh!   watch where you're going!
The lines are long
        and we don't want to keep Greg waiting

The beginning of life
The end of life
Is there time to convert to Artur Rubenstein's faith?
                first love
                he was always a part
                of any piano lesson given

Ah!   there's the Poetry Stage
Magenta's platform
And there she free-styles
        through the adversity of dust
                hosting
                confessing her loves and fears

Be in her presence confirmed of free speech
        reinventing the words
        there are a lot of listeners today
Return to the stage
It is waiting on real life
                only a little disguised
                        with debt to appearance's sake

Amen!   all the time happy to be a spalpeen
        inter-generational
                laughing at "lack of purpose"

There's a joke taking place

What people do
        and it's funny because caprice was most of it

As real as possible: the sight of a praying mantis
                                        improbable
                        where did it come from?

These are not normal circumstances
Be on your way among bicycles
        the ongoing theme played
It's earlier Beijing before the smog
Watch it!
        let's have five minutes of anti-science
                gadzooks!   and gaga!

The mochas are stable
Still worth it   they'll arrive
        for I'm a waiter with ballet in my heart
        dancing past Playa Info
                Burning Man Information Radio
                    Earth Guardians again
                        the mochas *sloshing*
                                but contained

Lastly, dodging a golf cart
        going faster for sure
        than the five miles-an-hour posted
I'll say, "Hi, Greg!   look what I've brought you!"
Minstrel Cramp getting closer
        his notes had been a crescendo
            a lot to be proud of
            repeated: *sforzato*
                        attaca
                        non legato
                        heroic!

"Here you are!
And the lovely barrister volunteer who made it?
        she wants to meet you!

"Your happiness may depend on the whims of the gods
        but right now it's a mocha

every romantic endeavor   drunk down
   sincere heartbreak
   even happy-sad!"

At that moment a Sparkle Pony came
It was a pit stop she made
     peripheral   backgrounded yet astonishing

She rested   a hunter of the Truth
   adjusting her backpack
   the camel-bag
   the underlying layers
And it was evening
And then it was morning
And it was good   I mean, *she* was good!

She rested in proximity to the mochas on the table
   a table *rickety*   *unstable*
   where were kept the little notebooks in ink
And the Sparkle Pony did spill the brew
              it was an elbow   or a boot

"Oops!"   and the pages were doused
The sofa, the coverlet   the rug

"I'm sorry!"
"Oh, *baby!*"
"How 'bout I marry you!"
   she asked it while we cleaned
"Not just get more mochas   but take your hand in mine
     it's the least I can do!"

And she truly sparkled then   all caffeine forgotten

"Greg!   you're best man, let's go!
The piano's good
   leave it for now
     onward to the Temple for the nuptials!"

"What's wrong with right *here*
   in the aftermath of the mess I've made?"

And indeed it came to pass

35. CLOWN GIRL HELPING THE LINE MOVE

It is affinity   clown girl and clown *boy*

She knows the skill of a barker
        being who she is and how she gestures
                a volunteer clown to move the line along
                her Center Camp line
                where the pace may slow
                                and the coffee take time

And so she directs   with her clown body   my own
        uncostumed just now
                though Summer Lake's wardrobe waits in the trunk
It's just a matter of my dressing up
And turning extrovert as she
        letting *her* clown example suffice
                                for circus smarts

And she has it down
                like a shopping spree in No Man's Land

She is directing next in line as if they were last
A holiday to it   continuous   revival
The servers are waving in tandem
        clown girl in league
        a busy counter counting down
                        hot   and cold
                        her "ring" composed of body art
                                serpentine

By the time she's done
        her clown shift over
                Barnun, at least   if not Bailey   will take her
                makeup and all

to the next level of the show

Connecting those dots
Finding another planet
Too many people okay
    if there are enough clowns to go around

I am one   so is she   drest to kill the boredom
End the *torpor* of overcrowding
    when amusement may distract

Oh!   coffee keep pouring!
Progress as stimulant
She's funny   adorable as delusion
    when her art is solo panacea

Save my place   I'll be back
    having stepped into the suit of Summer Lake
      gotten at night
      when the multitudes had gone ahead
        to prepare a place in line

36. GEORGE THE GEOLOGIST

It was time   George will speak
His topic: playa dust!
    "What *is* that stuff?"
It's going to take awhile
The audience is large and there *will* be many questions

George is a big man
    and he looks like that comedian   Buddy Hackett
      a dead ringer
      where the joke is geology
        sand on the brain   sediments
The joke *explained*   flipping his charts

He's been given a mic full of feedback
        but he's found exactly where to stand to stop it
        and recite a perfumed fable
                proud of his research and ready for more

He's drilled   sifted   hammered   sorted
        living millions of years in a day
                and the sunlight's a spotlight slanting

His stage is the ages the Earth has known
Its acts are long and stars extinction's cast
        in a Permian tragedy
                and we're not supposed to know for sure
                it's left open to interpretation

George has returned to Burning Man
A retrospective mood prevailing
He revisits last year's propositions
        the parameters of Basin   of Range
        how all of it stretches ups and downs

He makes all those continents move again
Pronounces "terrane"
                careful to let you know the *spelling*
                and the homonym's difference
                                        "terrain"
And we are coming close to understanding the forces
        the planet's septillions of tons

He'll concentrate on dust today
Particle size
        microns involved
                composition
And after awhile
        on the way to comprehension
                the feel of How-and Why's upholstery

He was scanning the aeons
Running the movie of sedimentation
And just for the comfort of the narrative
                no one left
                the long minutes   fear of the future

Turns out the dust is safe   for awhile
With precautions   masks   goggles
        or even respirators

The dust is safe in small amounts
And if no one came to the playa to build
And no one came to tramp all around
        no powder would there be   no problem
            the *cracks* would be all
            the dried mud forever
                    the wind still invisible

There's a Burning Man not known anymore
        dustless   a few hundred San Franciscans
            the aficionados of Cacophany
            a singer of opera
                    guns with ammunition

George was still at it
"Now, the question is: 'How to remove?
                    how to get rid of this stuff?
                    whatcha' gonna' *do!?'*
It's ubiquitous!   it's gotten into *everything*
                            hasn't it?"

"So what's the answer?"

We were about to learn
        for he said, "May I have a volunteer?"
The crowd was reticent   shy, even
"You!   yes, young lady   if you please
        if you *don't please*
            I'm kidding
            could you help out?

"Wonderful!
Now we'll need a sample surface
Ah!   how about this table?   perfect!
        it's quite dusty, all right
Let us employ the vinegar   let us add the Calgon
                    the magic formula!

"Aha!   we've succeeded!
Look!   it's good as new
         all you need to remember: vinegar and Calgon!"

George was satisfied
The volunteer withdrew
She had proven deft with the spray bottle

Then George said he had an announcement
"Listen up, now
         after much consideration
         and soul-scrutiny
         after careful *reasoning*
                  I won't be back
This is the last time for me on the playa"

"But George, you can't!" was heard   "Why?"
There was disappointment   sadness
"It's not the *playa* dust, is it?"

"Oh, no no *no!*
         I've breathed plenty and never had issues"

"What, then?"

"School, *school!*   as in   going back to it
Finding out more
         being 'in the know'
         as much as 'the know' can teach
                  but I'll *miss* 'ya!"

There was applause
Appreciation   for he was very much loved
They would miss his quirky approach
         how the learning would stand out because of it
         as though it really is easier to remember
                  when what you're told
                  has made you smile

Perhaps he *was* Buddy Hackett
         or his twin brother talking

87

One day / would not return
The last festival yet unknown
I'll miss George
        hey, I'll miss *myself!*

His audience had gathered around the man
Wishing him success
        and hoping they'd see him sometime
In *geologic* time he's fired before he took the job
So jealous are the layers he spoke of
                all of the past trying to push him aside
                drown him in those shallow seas

But the time is now
And George shall be enjoyed to the fullest
        with autographs and best wishes expressed
        me *too*   / will not vanish today
It's too nice a day not to play and play   at immortality

The week obliging
        each day accordioning outwards
                to accommodate
                dreaming of endings so distant
                        they have no bearing on progress
                                personal or otherwise

Meanwhile   we all have George's geology to study
To take to heart
        and *moreover*
        we've learned to clean up after ourselves
And that's a *lot* for a single scientific Dad to instill!

37. BELGIQUE!

What a cool word is "Belgique"!
To not say someone's "Belgian"   but "Belgique"

To note the pleasure "Belgique" brings
"Ah!   you know!   you *knew!*"
"I guessed"
"Oui, tres bon!"

But then comes the hard part
        for no other French have I
        well, *en peu*
The accent's there   but the words are not
So it's "merveilleux!"and "regardez!"
                        and other simple exclamations

The country of Cesar Franck speaks *français*
There's a city there   Liege
        and the Germans once laid siege to it
                        how *could* they?!
                        what nerve!

Riding to Trego for the night shift
        the foreigners talk
                and are not so *very* foreign
I'm a Walloon, perhaps
Will they speak Flemish, too?

Bound for Trego be kind   be inclusive
                the van-talk to include "Belgique"
Remember *Les Beatitudes*
Remind them of their wonderful oratorio
        be the channeled choir and orchestra

What I need from you, *Belgique*
        is your nineteenth century
        your son gone to Paris
        to Sainte-Clotilde Basilica
                that organ   those duties
                that circle of like-minded musicians
                        D'Indy among them

In the time before jazz, cool jazz
                        a different aesthetic

This *Belgique* has occurred so often

it seems a disproportionate acquaintance
A small country whose citizens are tourists
                    and they don't stay home
                    but fan out to find me
                            the Franck *devotee*
                            at Burning Man

Or at the high pass above Ouray, Colorado
Where those motorcycles landed
And a man and a woman said,
        "Oui!   we are *Belgique!*"
            their French a dialect, actually

And you had asked
        as if it were Black Rock,
            "May I take your picture, please?"

It would be nice to have *Belgique* overnight
Camping out at Trego
        in the shadow of Old Razorback
        the mountain that's my heart's desire
But *Belgique* will be going elsewhere
To another hot spring   Double Hot Spring
        the one that's truly dangerous
                            that's *not* for soaking

I may enjoy their company till just past the rails
        for only the ride together
        when the driver must be careful
            scanning north and south for a train
            and its nearly sudden   silent approach
Hard to see as reasons why this ongoing synchronicity
                            this *Belgique*

And is it really a "Low Country"?
Medium low, maybe   there's Holland alongside
Let's see... The Netherlands   where's the Zuiderzee?
        how long will the dykes hold?
            the World Court pass sentence on the Globe?
What is The Hague, exactly?
                city that takes an article to say
                the least part of speech made important

Belgique!
A melancholy
        certain music
                a Symphony in D Minor
                Franck's "note of notes" evoking "finis"
                                        music of The End

All of Belgium's tourists reminding us:
"There *is* a place to go
        though it's never *easy* to go there
                and always a good thing done badly

And whenever they're encountered
        invitation is made   the same
        the symphony first heard in Spokane, Washington
                that beckoning to teenage sadness
                when   so early   were later days surmised

Just saying *"Belgique"*   the music starts
Those very chromatic measures

Perhaps Dutch may be needed   another language
Dutch in places it's spoken
                        or at least imagined

Antwerp skip   jewelry ignored   won't need it
Even if the Shane Company gifts you
                        with its entire inventory
                        of hard and stony
Terror reflected   and glittering
Spontaneous stones returned
                        though wistfully

The challenge is *Belgique*
It's nice   one's attention being sought
        soon the continent
                perhaps to tour
                soon making all possible amends
                even if those to whom amends are made
                can recall no offense

The Belgians are luminous
        creatures on fire   for all their civility
        European revolutions a candy they'd quit
        and the magic show of post-modern sensibilities
            trembles uncertainly
                au naturel
                    in the presence of glaring jihadis

There's one last mission
Get me to the Church of Invisibility   on time
Expenses paid, maybe
        everything *assisted*
        no questions asked

For by the time *Belgique* has brought me there
        no condition may be met or known
            can be a hunch
            it will be time
A crease in the morning that wasn't there before

The absolute lesson promised
            by the first piano teacher
            the marine
        who instructed
        "you're scratching the surface, my friend!"

The surface will be left behind
Jostling   fighting for posterity
Step back!
        I've been working in the dark
            when it was time for a vacation in the light

The crosshairs of birthplace   shifting.
        to another place
            still a part of the world
            but only as long as the occasion of asking

The formal request made to enter
            a Portal of the adjective *Belgique*
Where noise dies down to whispered texts
        perfectly understood
            a different decision than any before

wisdom gone to bed where it belongs

38. TREGO

When you say goodbye
    will the paradise you seek be enough?
    and will forgetfulness be a part of it?
    will you say, "Take me home" the first day of it?

Trego is enough
Its waters and radio   in the night
Every place you go
    I'll call you from right here
        the so-so pool *perfect*
        no amenities
The road divides with self-esteem
            Trego just a ditch

A hot spring made elongate   abruptly encountered
The safety of the people is at stake

I am speaking to you
Let's start   no budget   no audience or charity
When you say goodbye
    will the evidence suggest you mean to stay?

Thermal surrender
The desert advertises interior places
    you'll be safe
        the people find oasis

The thrill of the train!   so close!   hugely metallic!
And when the silence returns
    it's as if there'd been some research on cacophany
    lasting as long as the boxcars' graffitied rumble
        the ground pulsing with thesis
            the minutes are given degrees

Your scholarship is needed
In the unburdened wilderness
            there is no outside control
            because *all* is outside
                and no one is missing

I am placing my feet in spite of war
The water's Arabian
Nevada will accommodate Lawrence
        the Bedouin
            Prince Faisal's resignation
                the rising of a crescent moon
                            in a wireless world

Let's talk about your sad "Adieu"
We have to go slowly into nirvana
        it's so different
                Keep straight
                I think it's east
And tell me: when you get there   will you know?

It's the Great Basin
Who knew *that?*   and when did they know it?

More research
There is no government here but geology
Its stronghold is vast
        no journalists
            the story's too old

Trego   soothing   mysterious source
When getting started's the way you'll stay
        dissolved in the seconds
                sloshing lengthwise   environmental

Call it the afterlife   Later   beyond Beyond is previewed
An agreement comprised of pledges

The waters are radical
        breaking news put back together
                so the wildlife is unannounced   random

Will you sanction the well?
Put sorceress pressure upon?
When you say "Farewell" it will be easier, then
        quickly tested for ecstasy
                implicit bathing
                        supremely immersed
                        in a powerful contentment
                        prearranged by friendly spirits

Take me home to this suburb of Burning Man
        the nearly "Empty Quarter" of reformed Islam
Swordless   in moonlight *full*
The crescent advanced to bright wholeness
                while I wait
                        embryonic myself
                                for your return

39. FALSE SUMMITS

Though Razorback is just one mountain
        its granite's still divided
        a bachelor peak

There is time to learn those rock gardens
        as if in a charter school of erosion
Study Latin by flashlight
Resting
        half-public
                half-private
A sequence of planets   false summits to reach

Or a series of countries
Each loftier in the dimmed-down twilight
Reasons to be happy
        Hollywood in the Thirties
                accepted for what it has been

I'm a young man climbing for Sahra   for Capra
        the mask of the Feathered Serpent worn
The ridge is like a program seen
Repeats run on an ancient Philco
                black-and-white in the night

The first footsteps historic
        as if it is the Moon
        the false summits *there*
                too near in the airless sky

Go hungry to the top
Past the lower platforms' weather of sage
Save the food
        be alert as a linebacker on an uphill field
                        determined

The hot spring was left to Barry'
He'll monitor
        asleep   his subconscious sufficient
Trego is safe
        the while Razorback is just-like-that
                        a deep trance state
Gigantic imaginings whose random monuments are strewn

Third reconnaissance   instances
A molecular level
My spotlight's a bright ghost
        on its own   visiting anthropomorphic forms
                concave granite coming apart
                those millions of years ended   insecure

Otherwise wealthy
A region of stone windows
        made   in crumbling
                to be as simple as they can possibly be
                        entirely lost

The weathering's instructive
        each course's completion   deceptive learning
        on the up-and-down mountain that remembers last year
                like an earlier-in-the day thing

You're here as a promise
Someone else wanted this ascent *also*
    and Sahra will hear of this solo
                      of Paiute artefacts left

She will know the night as well
This one   comprised of trekker sense
           greater and lesser fears assuaged
Ambition's retrofit
When Razorback's X-rayed spine
     is template for a monstrous stegosaurus
        his stepping-stone body   conglomorate

The effort is faith
The single mile was *expecting* the mountaineer
     and told its creatures you were coming on time
     through the warm winds
        of Black Rock's summer evening
        to enjoy a timeshare of all the outdoors
Longing   one summit at a time
              to be acquainted thoroughly

An English mile
So very uneven you cried for the level lakebed again
     even as love for the mountain increased
          and strengthened the pilgrim

Daniel Higgs
His *Mouth of Union* challenge
     not as the world has seen it till now

Place your hands upon the granite's crystals
Dark and light   an *extensive* precision
     the sculpture right where it is
     played like a piano
     a plutonic sonata with false endings
          its fermatas unmistakable

The mentor is stone
Be like it
     so that affairs of the heart are all the more desired

There is nothing neutral at altitude
Nothing dangerous done in this moment's certainty

---

40. THE FOX

On the anniversary of the first climb
On a near enough day to twenty years ago
        when Burning Man was new to me
On the summit of Razorback   renamed Sahra's Mountain
            shine the spotlight down

Point the beam at Black Rock City
Others will see it   off-and-on   from far away
        a signal
        it will be a little mystery
            "What's *that?*"

Perhaps newlyweds at the perimeter
Resting from their bike ride into the deep playa
Married at the Man
            they'd left to be alone
                "What's *that?!*   it's like a beacon!"

It will be a portent
            the harmonies of Faure transmitted
Moses not needing to come on down
Just leaning on the tablets jammed on high
        reclining on the flat encrypted surface

Facing away from achievement
Facing east towards Dry Peak
Wondering about the rest of Sahra's
            all the granite gone to sleep untrod

There is the same way to go   back
        being able to tell her now

that she's been here after all   as planned

And it was easy
          not planned *too* much
                    like the study of music
                    just find yourself at a keyboard
                                             in love with touch

Return   already scripted
          with a free ticket to descend
The sky close to vanishing
The seeing-eye light seeing everything backwards
The bass after too much treble
          a pastorale turned to shadows
                    a chiaroscuro in the Indian night

There will be the medicinal waters of Trego to enjoy
Keep going   leave the sculpture a little at a time
          careful past the big rocks

But we're not alone!
There are eyes
          at the limit of the spotlight's theater
                    its purview

There has to be a creature
          the eyes of marriage taking good care
          the first day not over   still anarchic

Whatever it is   it is staying
A wayside nocturnal
          closer   slower   please shine again!
                    let me see you!
                    don't run!

What *are* you?
A fox?   here?   is it possible?
So shy you never show yourself
          but the brightness in hand has captivated
                    your small body tranced and staring

Tawny   as delicate as imagination has made it

Every feature   fine-lined adorable
Our fox for as long as possible
Don't move!
      I am nothing human
      having vanished in the glare
And the orange fox sees only a great light   irresistible
A moral overwhelming the animal kingdom

The eyes are black
      and so amazed it must evolve on the spot
             getting ahead in slow motion
             enforced by five hundred candles

Hypnosis makes a circle
Don't move   be the sun
      for the fox thinks it's daytime
      daylight that strode down the mountain
                    to be a feral   private star

Take possession of exquisite coloration
Our fox's nose is petite   supernatural
             aristocratic
             nuzzling the night air for answers

Stay still!
Our lovely fox is in thrall to the light
      my incremental pirouette keeps it mainly motionless
             in a tractor beam of tough love
Shh!   no noise!
Boots in place or the spell is broken!

Did you want to say something?
Me, too   but not even whispers
      otherwise you're gone
      telepathy only!

"Where's Sahra?"
"Oh, she'll be along"

Our beautiful orange, tan and white hallucination *keep*
Like vows to continue
Good!   it's circling

almost completely
now completely!

Yes   and it was unafraid for once.
And departed finally
        slowly   exalted
            still glancing back
            transfixed!

And it has taken twenty years

41.   WHERE IS THE SLEEPING BAG?

So where-oh where is the wonderful sleeping bag?!
        the one that's good down to zero
        the *warm* one
        the heavy cocoon you crawl into   grateful?

It had been lain in the scrub
        before the mountain was attempted
Stashed in a place, to be tired in   after
When you're "home alone" with the quiet radio playing

How is it missing in such a small camp?
Is there hearsay?
Any witness?

My friend who was all alone   I will ask
        was there a patrol when I was gone?
        someone zealous to Leave No Trace
            who could have captured the bag
            and the supplies left   thinking "abandoned"?

One's steps are faster   looking
Faster *finding*
        trying to find
            starting to repeat   to retrace the search

the same ground gone over
                        as if this can make it appear

Trego Springs spirits have taken it!

"Barry, did anyone come?
Barry!   wake up!   was there some patrol?
        anyone at all asking questions?   BLM?   Others?"

I remembered headlights seen
From the high ridge   double comets on reconnaissance
        and the stillness had intensified then

Taking time to think it through
        yes!   it must have been Enforcement's overreach
        the untended sleeping bag
        flung in the bed of the official four-by-four
                                and driven away

Must have happened that way
But wait!   there's a campfire   low voices
        a database of intimate talk
            a man and wife wondering what's wrong
            why the agitation

"Excuse me   I know it's three o'clock in the morning
                and I'm ruining your tryst   apologies
But did you guys see anything?
I mean, there was a sleeping bag   go ahead
        please say   because it's gone   gone!"

"Your sleeping bag?"
"How awful!"

Their fire was delicate   wavering
        like the questions, dammit!
        the mystery
But I leave them alone
Tell myself to shut up   go away

They can't help and their politeness unnerves
Their concern makes it worse

102

what had I seen?
what had *Barry* seen?
the happy interrupted couple?
Oh!   approximate observance!

In a thesaurus   how many ways to ask?
In the small clearing that's Trego's acre
            how many hiding places possible?

Look again!
Keep searching!   Keep going!   serve the panic!
It cannot be it's vanished
And then Bobby Vee begins to sing
        "Take Good Care of my Baby"
        the early Sixties trying to help
            living dangerously through the decades
                to calm   make us see reason
                and how unlikely the loss

Just stop
And stop asking questions
Work together with Bobby
            take good care of your personal religion
            that despair be not interwoven with sage
For despair is a drug
        not one of choice
        but good enough for addiction

The cocoon's disappearance   triggering
Grander frustration   cancer induced
        being sick of the show
            you'll go after the director and producer

Stop!
Just stop, *please!*
Be friends with yourself again!
Do not mind dying as you didn't age eight
        shooting with sticks
        being shot and crumpling   *artfully*
            the way children fall down
                with exquisite pretending

103

The very best acting
The next world immediate
The child's *acceptance*
        a perfect mockery of adult terror

Stop for the caps and the pistols
        and   lingering appreciatively
                        notice the sleeping bag lain!
                        see it once more as you left it!
In preparation for age eight and the Age of Bobby Vee

It was confusion
A strange disorientation
        you'd been on strike from sanity
        on strike as zombie such
        the search had been a blind one
                        in spite of five hundred candles

And the search ended
        brought no relief
                seeing how easy it was to be lost

42. THE CUDDLE PUDDLE

The Cuddle Puddle waited   tented
A white strategy of shelter
        with animals   stuffed
        tigers, bears
                "Oh, my!" strewn
The contents of story books dumped softly

It's going to be fun!
Find the power animal and flop   cuddle   chill
        be unconscious at noon
                gnostic with respect to oblivion
                the unsettling City *forgotten* as you doze

Even the surprise speaker can't keep you awake
        and stays peripheral
In the Realm of Letch
            subliminal stripes and markings
            lucid dreaming the day away
                                a cozy cuddle

Step over the fence
For the Puddle is enclosed
        unleaking Doctor Seuss and other menageries

Cuddle Puddle had come recommended
Always the best way to get around
        you go where they say
                remembering nothing else
"Can't miss it!   look for the big white tent!"

I did   and alone-together within I went
        where a dacoit may find a refuge
The truth is there's another world in the world
        where even reputations may be mended

You move quickly to huddle in the Puddle
Laying low in the cushions   defeat averted
        with only fair questions asked
                        off the subject of sim

Say "Hi!"   being joined by others of your kind
            definitely so
            bizarre as bisnaga
        the cactus consumed for its desert memories
The spectators subsumed in participatory carnival
Deserved   as any number is beholden to googol

Bought into fantasia
        with confident *recreational* conspiracies
        explored with no pressure to take action
Pet the lion   the adjoining giraffe sprawled
Home security gained in a vasty lakebed

Say "Hello!" to J.J.   just arrived
        ah!   from Belgium, yet!

105

Told 'ya'   for what goes on is ongoing theory
Belgique once more
        and will the Low Country feel as good
                        as the Cuddle Puddle?

Lay as in "now I lay me down"
                in its European zoo   also pliant
                and a giving taxidermy
A bed of pets   outsized   of the Serengeti
And ironic security is found

"J.J.   think about it
A warm and fuzzy rumpus
        right here
        right now
Where inanimate objects purr and roar
And bleat as sheep unshorn
                the contents
                        of letters written by Kindergarten
Addressed to hospice in block, alphabetical script
        no one turned away"

"Outstanding!" says J.J.
"I need to bring my wife
        gift her
                with what she hasn't been getting from me
                the gentle word since we arrived"

I answered   unsure of your whereabouts, my love
Answered
        thinking of my own unfeeling
"yeah, go find her, good idea!
The perfect make-up and reconciliation!
Exit the stage of struggle
        and go into these wings   peacefully
        with arms around each other and these surrogates
                clutching substantial straws"

To Cuddle's to embrace
The Puddle a go-for-broke pool
        an etesian barely stirring the canopy
                its free delivery like a phase of barter

Blowing over
        like reputations improved with dispersal

The bear's the best pillow
                and his replications hereabouts
                multiply the presents
                        of a summer's Christmas
                                gone wild   yet silent, too

Yes, bring the girlfriends and wives
Make it a surprise
        like good behavior at the biggest party in the universe
        eschewing the hateable prisons
                the vexations of politics
                        yet accepting this
                        the big box of animal presents
                                not minding their miraculous enclosure
Someone say if it's not copied, surely
        from Eden's square pastures of adorables

And it is unnecessary to rush out
        it's not "Wait until I tell Amanda!"
        but "She already knows to come here"

Another lecture's beginning
Syllables only
        like the sounds of the first days and weeks heard
        we graduate to crib
                and its Shakespeare   downsized
                to superficial cuts and owees

Sunken J.J. cannot raise himself
The sofa puma a deep containment
I'm not much better   draped over the hippo
                and just as lazy for sure

43. THE MORMONS AND OTHER NEIGHBORS

They were ritual shot glasses
And Steve was proposing strong whiskey in the camp

All of us   celebrating arrival!
It's what one does   first off
We were the Magnificent Seven
        and we hadn't been asked yet
                to save the village from bullies

We were fresh from bumper-to-bumper
        and any rescue's a toast
                before teaching the bandits a lesson
                    spinal alignment while we clink
                    whoops!
                    except for me with the water glass!

There was the guy with the red truck
        his wife
        two girlfriends
                and the Mormons...
Wait a minute!
Why am I the only teetolaler?
This wasn't adding up
        until the Mormons explained
                        the Scrabble word "titular"

There were other wheels turning than doctrine
        so great   a religion's reimagined
                        that will keep America going

It's nice out here on the edge of town
        with all that extra playa to walk
        at the radial of 5:15 and the outer ring
The last letter pronounced with reverence

The "Walk-In Camping" would be better
However there's the noise of 2 o'clock then
The lakebed throbbing
        the beats bouncing you and your bedding

all night

Fact is   Burning Man's all about the graveyard
The shift that favors a party befitting

No, the only zone
        that makes allowance for the day shift
                is right here
                in this company of the Outer World
                where it's dusty, sure
                                but silent when it counts

Every one of us agreed
And there was a second round
        of their whiskey and my water
                to *seal* our agreement

The sketch of each neighbor's not possible just now
        except to say my camp mates were smart
        were savvy
                talking trucks and practicality
Smartly married   or just best friends
And it mattered
        the teasing and playful boasting

Had I canvassed a thousand for compatible neighbors
        I couldn't do as well as these exceptional tourists
                and I'm just glad to be here
                with modest satisfaction
                        sturdy shelter
                                and well-nigh indestructible shade

44. THE FAERIE GWENDOLYN

The Chopin she heard
The Chopin she *taught*
She was the Faerie Gwendolyn

She said there'd be a car rally at Furniture Car Camp
"Come over!   here's where!"   and she scribbled

We had a great discussion
        student pieces
                how to instruct
                    how to *improvise*
It was a crescendo and cadenza
The best of emergency
        when talking is swift   mutual
        when we seize on synchronicity

She'd been playing
        playing the very same piece that *I'd* been
                the famous "Alla Turca" of Mozart
                I'd just finished the Rondo
Mozart poking fun at the Ottomans

And the Faerie Gwendolyn had played it *here*
        at Minstrel, even
A Major's clanging finale to K.331
The fingers with fluttery adrenalin *flying*

She also loved Chopin
        that *Fantasie-Impromptu* of four-against-three
        the left hand tested for finger independence

Yet another "lake port" and haven
This lovely Minstrel place   and fortuity!

"A car rally?"
"Oh, yes!   *furniture* cars!
    there'll be a fashion show also
            you must stop by, please do!"
"Of course!"

Then she joked
"Oh, my God!   I mean   *hold on!*
I musn't let my enthusiasm turn into online gushing!"
"I don't mind   will there really be a rally?"
"Yeah!   *then* I teach 'em to *count!*   and teach the *touch!*"

"You truly of the Faerie Kingdom?   are you?"
"Oh, yes!   and my students are learning the faerie arts
        delicate extravagance
        all the harmonies of the zephyrs
Airy expression   then the roar of the engines!
The checkered flags produced
        their black-and-white
            the first principle of art displayed
            as Contrast
                waving Chopin
                    and hot rods
                        past the finish!"

45. ARGENTINA

He seemed a *gaucho*
        and his girl was dressed in taffeta

They were South American class
        with a quiet elegance
        as if they reminisced
        as if their memories included former lives
As *Peninsulares* at large in the New World
And it was Madrid that spoke in praise of Iberia
            even as they ranged about the *pampas*

Of course he played the guitar
And of course she danced
        a family of two determined to keep it that way
            always on the verge of children
            but dissuaded by a strange aristocracy

In their presence Buenos Aires happened
        the city rehearsing the future of the tango

There was a ring
The diamond up late as they were

well past the midnight's tolling
Years in the night
                between the western and the eastern sun

Their demeanor
        was like the unplanned tease of a hoary religion
                making random comebacks
And their Spanish is summons, an alternate *Carmen*
        where Bizet has relented
        and allowed Jose his happiness
                the matador just a moot acquaintance
                heavy-duty opera gone to sleep
                with a glossy magazine in its lap

Also   in the Argentines' presence
        one wishes to make an effort to collect
                get what they have
                for now and later
                        or whenever pokiness overtakes

Learn the guitar like Segovia
And play as much as may be easy at a time

Dance the tango for stamina
                those days that are simply erroneous
                        and be reacquainted with life

46. GREG'S DAUGHTER WILL ARRIVE

Greg's daughter will arrive
The girl so busy she works in three fields
The story so intriguing   we'll just *have* to meet her!

And be *reminded*
        of University days in Seattle
        when   in a fugue state I wandered the campus
        trying to channel the entire student body

Preternatural in the aisles of the Suzzallo Library
My hand lightly brushing the bindings
         absorbing entire contents
         as fast as a fast walk can manage

Full brain
     full life
          puberty raging
               full stop

When Greg's wonderful daughter gets to Burning Man
     she'll be asked where and how she went right
     when I was so wrong   and *blissfully* so

The answer will come as it always does
Like the pranks played on parents
                         that turn into careers

47. CRATER LAKE SAX

There was a summer sax starting
Improv like a series of shiny questions
     the answers competitive
     Truth taking time
          for there's not a lot to do

Here are families moved
     and living far from home cities
          hunkered down safe at the Lodge
          having left town and followed the wail
               the sax a-piping all the way

Wanting to believe the Pied Imperative's summons
His notes for jazz banknotes exchanged
Clear air's culture upheld like higher pitches
     those hundreds of eighths   sixteenths
                    and their doublings thereafter

Summer of 2016
The smart year embracing the others
        having made an actual *decision* to do so

The sax is elitist   mirthful
"Therefore" it seems to say
        "Therefore, I am secret forever
        yet broadcast soul in the mountains
                commanding the Alps to resound
                    with countless jazz
                        the beat beyond its measures"
And   as endless wishes are made
        with coins and paper dollars
                imagination's adopted
The saxaphone case filling
Thirty days and nights so far

Unbelievably   the all-new Crater's in quotes
        new as any incarnation can make it
        the ancient explosion an ephemeral "poof"
After all we knew
                    now it's just the sun
                    the sax
            late morning
            present tense

Let's get some stair climbing done, why don't we?
Be up and down   as the jazz scales instruct
Geology marginalized
        so that the Earth is thought of as bluesy
            its zillions of years forgotten

The sax player's like an Eveready
The patio appreciates
        applauds its collective security

Sax solo   maximum strength
His is a-coming back to be himself
He wears suede
        his life goes right
                brunch will be improvised

a quicksilver salad

48. THE SEARCH FOR DAILY STEPS

Well, it's Burning Man
But it's also time to make a search

Stairs must be found
        stairs to basically stay in shape
There will be steps that will be right
And steps that will be wrong
                        for the sake of exercise, go!

Seek them out!   the sooner the better
        for the playa's very flat
        and the mountains too far to go
                    each morning   noon   and night

There are platforms   two-storeys   three
There are ladders
        but they take too long
            and it looks too weird
            to be up and be down them
                            for no obvious reason
And there are stairs *crowded* where the dancing is

It will take some time but it *will* happen
Hit the streets   looking
The kid's bike is fun
        you collide, you can't fall

Go for it!   head for the music
        the big sound at two and ten o'clock
Keep an eye out for lookouts   the observation posts
            anything high
            and how to get up there

It's Tuesday   there's time
In the past there were stairs at the Man   still are
The *Temple* has flights
And once   an industrial-strength tower served
          that stood at least ten storeys
               a skeletal summary of all things urban

Yes, the art on the open playa has helped
                         and might be useful again

The game is keeping the doctor away
The game is paying homage
          to age eight
               Infinity's year
                    let's find it!

And then you *do!*
A magnificent ramp   "PANORAMA" called
          it's *perfect!*
          it's *right!*

The home of Slinky races run
You'll have to *share* the stairs
          but that's all right
               you can even play *yourself*
               between sets of eight floors at a time

The Slinkies are rainbows pushed
          from the forty-fifth step shoved over
Best of all
          with all the Slinky competition going on
               no one takes notice of all your trudging
                    it's like being invisible
                    in a socially acceptable way

And so, as the many Slinkies slink downwards
          flexing their rainbow springs
               the quota stairs are done
               one by one till noon
               and a subtle sun that made the white sky warm

When it was over and there was nothing left to do

I found something better than the stairs
                              I found Anya to talk to
          someone who understood
          the stairs
          and much else besides
And we talked in the early p.m.
Enough to know we were kindred

Odd   how, in the roar of the world's biggest party
          a simple conversation's the take-away
          and certainly *One Step Beyond*

49. CRATER LAKE DOG SHOW

It didn't last long
Is twenty seconds long?

There were only two dogs
A tan one and a gray one
What breeds they are I think I know
          they mostly look like mongrels, though
Be Robert Frost for a third of a minute
              he won't mind
                  while my books fill up with snow
It may be summer   so what?

There's a family, of course   a *fabulous* fam!
I'm sure Bob Wiley would love them
          same number of people, too

Oh!   I forgot   Dad's the psychiatrist
And they've come not to Lake Winnipesaukee
          but to Lake Crater   I mean Crater Lake

Where's Mom?
There are three girls
              the one on the right is Anna for sure

but Siggy is missing
           the kid who wouldn't or couldn't dive

But I digress and it isn't fair to fans of that movie
I won't make further fun
           but wait   I haven't really made fun
              just taken time to allude
                to Bill Murray   Richard Dreyfuss
                and the incomparable Julie Hagerty
It's praise of a sort

But this scene is a twenty seconds dog show
The puppies of Frost in bright sun
           very tonguey, too
           very on-display
The gray one is kerchiefed
The *tan* one, I mean the *golden*—
No!   what color *is* it that colors that I.Q.?!

Who will win?
        what award is right?
                where are the medals kept?
Oh, I just happen to have them myself!
But which *dog* is to get one?
                they haven't done any tricks, either

Two dogs diverged in a fine yellow morning breeze
I could choose the one less grown
           and that could make the difference
           all of it   they *are* very different
                          as *I* am quite different

Be nice to this family
It's just twenty seconds
           don't start asking questions
           don't dote too much on their pets
           don't tell them where you're going
Save Burning Man
              there isn't time
              and they might not understand

They're a very nice family   and I am not nice

118

They won't find out, will they?   Robert?
        not in twenty *seconds?!*
        hope they don't

The gray one's drooling
Its tongue is very pink
                and the other's black nose is shining
        You need to choose   have you chosen already?

Let the grooming decide
Let hands-on be the judge
                let adorability settle it

They're knockoffs somehow
        copies
        but how, exactly   and *why*
                and why it should matter   well...
Whatever originals there are
It's better not knowing
I'm a copy as well
                and copy Frost with extreme prejudice

What does it mean?
Why is Bill mad at me?   and Richard?
        Julie!   I didn't mean it
                you're my favorite comedienne
                Saturday Night Live and way beyond!

"*Good fences make good neighbors!*" I quoted
"What?" asked Dad
"You guys are sitting on the wall!"
"So what?"
"Oops!   I meant to say something *else*...
        we're more-or-less all on the same side
        er, of the wall, actually!   hah-hah!
        of course, if we were on the *other* side
                that is, the *crater* side.
                well, we couldn't be, could we?
                that's why the wall, I mean Frost's fence
It keeps us from falling in, I mean *down!*
So we're not neighbors so much
                as one not-so-big family!"

And then we laughed and laughed and laughed
    so hard the dogs started barking
        and I chose the gray one with the pink tongue
        for its bark that was kind of a whine

Not unlike a certain very needy mental patient
                                    name of Bob

50. "WHO TOLD YOU TO CLIMB UP THERE?"

Regardless of the accusations made:
    that he was irresponsible
    that he was selfish
        told lies
        and didn't treat his employees well
Alphonse was going up!

"Who told you to climb up there?"
    this from a business associate
"I do these things to get even with my critics"
"And how, exactly?
        Climbing Garfield Peak accomplishes that?"
Alphonse paused as he was setting out
"Can't say how, *exactly*   *your* adverb
    but yes   trust me   I feel the getting even!"

"Ah!   well, I'll see you for lunch, then
Don't sprain an ankle!"

So Alphonse went up
He had Mount Scott in his sights
    the high point of Cloud Cap
        distant Thielson
        Llao Rock   closer   opposite Garfield
He let the prominence of Hillman Peak
And then the Watchman   let all he saw *erase*

120

Below was the Phantom
The Ship that stayed in a port of pumice
Below was the Wizard
        well, the Wizard's "hat"

All in his mind as well
        stashed and protecting
            he felt he could express himself
                to the bees   and other beings

He'd brought an old-fashioned altimeter along
                eschewing electronics
He stared at the readings: feet and meters
        slightly annoyed with Napoleon
            for complicating measurement
            if he lost at Waterloo
                could *we* not lose his invention?

Alphonse needed to know how high he was
But he also wished he were one of the First People
        not caring

Garfield!   it was cool and comfortable
He thought about tomorrow   and telling the truth
He'd start with his wife
        disabusing her of a certain belief she held
                that she didn't matter anymore

He wouldn't just *say* she does
        he'd demonstrate affection
            try to recall a few of her favorite things
            and *splurge*

He wasn't watching and tripped on a root
"Damned government!" he thought
        "must have been a lazy day for trail maintenance!
        harrumph!"

It was a "harrumph!" somewhat unconvincing, though
He said his "harrumph!" self-consciously
        but Alphonse was alone

Alphonse's "harrumph!"
was a *private* "harrumph!"

He recalled the question, "Who told you to climb it?"
"No one," he now said aloud
He was suddenly uncertain
though he couldn't say exactly why

He fingered the gewgaw
the trinket chain around his neck
The answer was always a show   something showy
he showed it to the Universe

Garfield intimidated
it seemed dangerous
even though thousands thought it was no big deal

Did he think he'd fall off the edge?
No   the trail was safe
Unless, in a suicidal way,
he were to launch himself from a ledge
take himself totally out of context
No, it was a spiritual fear
a free-floating anxiety

He pretended   alone   he'd been institutionalized
He pretended as he ascended
he would be taking advice
advice from the families   the couples
the lean and mean and seasoned
also on the mountain

But he wouldn't be acting on it
He'd pretend
and *also* pretend it was *stairs* he climbed
to the summit of an American president
He wondered if Garfield was one of the four
Those presidents shot   killed
he tried to remember

Again   he took in the all-around
the terrible cobalt

the serrated bowl of the Crater

Alphonse had made it into the *New York Times*
He thought the attention to be unwarranted
    it was certainly unwanted
    the morning edition had upset him
        had been unflattering
        his affairs were now public
His *business* affairs   not his cheating
But his conduct was being questioned

He tripped again
    he hadn't learned his lesson:
        look down as well as out!
            "Curses!" growled Alphonse

Ethically   the problem was simple
He'd never known a "bottom"
    not even music had led him to morality

These cliffs were his to roam   his "getting even"
He'd leave the trail   get good and lost
    well, he knew the place completely
    it might have to be at *night* he got lost
It was his human right to disappear

He picked himself up
    brushed off the dust
                "I'm going to be more careful
                each tumble's a metaphor
                    I don't wish to contemplate"

And then Alphonse asked the sunny day a question
"Did someone tell me to climb this?   *Really?*"
He thought there might have been someone after all
    someone ancient
        someone who had another name for the Lake
It had not been a *command* to go up
But the voice was powerful

So he realized as much
    broke out of the offhand explanation

the reason given his friend
        his excuse
                and he entered a fairy tale
                started up within it

Though he'd been to the top at least twice before
        it seemed totally uncharted
                a beautiful illusion!

If he later told someone of this singular ascent
        the listener might ask,"What happened next?"
                ask it at every turn
And Alphonse might be unable to say

Garfield Peak seemed to be every summit ever seen
And a mastermind presided
        one who brick-and-mortared
                all the heights and depths of outdoors
                cemented, too, the planet's plains

The IQ required was that of Infinity's brain
Still, Alphonse, as he plodded, was too much in denial
There was no epiphany
                he didn't have it in him
                the "bottom line" was keeping him down

His business and pleasure blending such
        the Pure Land of true insight was blurry indeed

"Don't sprain your ankle!"   his friend's admonition
He'd concentrate on that
                as he rose   incrementally
                and finally, he joined the crowd at the top
                        where picnics had begun
Where there was no more President to go to
Where someone blew a horn in triumph

For Alphonse, it was the next new thing that mattered
        and he strolled about before returning
Regardless, he would treat the world the same
        and   as before   still wonder why it was
                he never seemed to get even

124

51. UNION, WATCHMAN, HILLMAN

A partial scan
     Union   Watchman   Hillman
        there are *more*, of course
And ancient tremors still tremble the stone

In the arc of three summits only
The blue is the same pale cutout acquisition
        of violence imagined
           the best kind
A cosmic day care's purview begun

Union   semi-distant
    the bygone
    the volcanic throat
A snatch of Rio de Janeiro
      looking quite plutonic
        though it's the later component
          of an absurd, igneous happening

Think round   *roundabout*
The summit of Garfield Peak the pivot point
Though only part of the scene is considered
    let Union, The Watchman and Hillman
    let those peaks be a blue-gray triptych
Just a *portion* of three-sixty's degrees
      not needing police or having any problems
          besides blind geology

I think you're *right*, my darling companion!
Your ballet never-ending!
We should go some distance to all three
    as if we were coming back
    a   symbology to it

Imagine Crater Lake gone dry
    if you should ever really vanish
      but there is no sickness
      in this carefully unlocked Oregon
Heart of Union   heart of The Watchman

Heart of *Hillman*   the highest

And I didn't know that
        until you opened the books that said so
        and also said you would dance
            like a beautiful technology
                resolving science and love at once

52. KEEPING THE PEACE

Soon there will be a new year
        one like no other
            and we will be changed then
            and we will talk about things differently
            2017

Thank you so much, 2016!
For being such a fine prelude year to '17, the last
And standing on the summit of Garfield Peak
        with others of your kind
            observe the perimeter of Crater Lake
            your whole life in relief
Albeit treeless · and misleadingly tremendous

I'll be honest
        it may be a five-star horizon
            but the autobiography hath dimmed
                and made bluish all detail

It is keeping the peace   though barely   everywhere
A guitar dispatched to lend credence to your surroundings

A peace kept by that other blue
        fresh azure   2016   2017   and counting

53. WHEN I FIRST ASKED YOUR NAME

There was a diagonal to it
    the picture split and hung twice
But who was the blue and who pumice-tan
           could not be determined

When I first asked your name
    was when the canvass suffered tearing
      and divided along some mutual fault
        that would be a sharing dangerous

Some portion of loveliness
Held in reserve for later
    for argument's sake
      for industrial relations
        for two-timing
          for Never's "n" sound resolve

I'd wear a wig
    if I thought this would convince you I'd changed
      from the diagonal learning of your name
      and those "few things straight"

These are Crater Lake daydreams
    saved for the nights and worse twilights

"We're sorry," says the Blue   and bright rocks
Right then   the big surprise on purpose
        that landscapes intend
        begin to impart
         and then renege on

It's like, "Wait a minute!"
And the minute fractures
    or breeds millennia   keen disappointments
    sprouting strange names in history

What's so funny?
    Oh, the Brady Bunch to a ghost town gone
      sleeping on top of a stove in winter

When I first asked your name
        the diagonal answered
                "Tear along the lines of permanence"
And then had a question of its own
        "How ragged do you want it?"

"With or without jewels   we will stay awhile"
"What *kills* us will make us stronger"
                    what is your meaning, my love?
                    what is your meaning?

Drinking   shooting   and gambling
        what the west has in store
                Oregon's only National Park
Even Burning Man
        well, *especially* Burning Man
                will test our pioneer affection absolutely

When I first asked your name
        it could have been Tombstone
That's OK   the corral has a certain appeal
And Doc Holliday's illness
        is already my own familiar cough

Think how to rip   and then *do* it
                realistic
                oddly, forward-looking
Ready to interfere in the King's business
Or the Queen's
        wherever they hide
        and whatever they're up to
                        in the name of tyranny

You and I
        the founders of a new country
                        of stress and striving

54. VANISHED LAKE MEDITATION

Certain doors were closed now
Retired are those Ice Age vistas
    except in the overheated compartments
                                    of nostalgia
                bursting with ersatz substitution
       and refusing the present

As though we have time travelled forward
      from the ancient lake
         inexplicably displaced
            so that which was cold and deep blue
         in *one* breath
              has not survived the next
And a sense of bewilderment is added to the rest

So real were the waves and indigen canoes!
Now we can't find it
      like the puzzled infant
         that is looking everywhere
         whose mother, even
         is not sufficient finding

Let the truth of these miles around
      welcome birds back
The avifauna *then*
      in commotion above the Great Basin
         filling so fast
         it might be a true bowl brimming

In this timeout   pretend the pluvial lakes are rising!
And anything can happen!
In the Land of Directions,
     the drafty sage scents the hours
     set aside for the ages to persuade us:
Having once happened it always is happening
Having once existed it always exists *unquestionably*

Each of us allowed this
      like a confidence kept

one's vision permitted long distance
The lava's uplands' endless terraces
Temporal decomposition   and displacement
        like that ice ball once in Black Rock
        and those clocks embedded within
              melting longevity
              do remember   1997

20,000 BCE   *common* era   *before* common
Years in common
        peak realizations
              being at large   in reserve   ·
              one's steps are conservative consecutive

Milankovich   his cycles
Earth's orbit to elongate
        in accordance with Newton
              his theory tantalizing
                    as unseasonable rain

And even with the full advantage of science
        the late Pleistocene's a mood swing
                          one that qualified

If you're intent on wishing still
Wish Gaia to reveal what we've wanted all along
              at all costs
              clarity
              the transparency of virgin lands
Industry's scuff marks delayed   on hold
Like the nights after Shelley's immemorial afternoons
        redly tinged by the light of Prometheus   ·
        and long-running revolutionary thought

The power to stop the good numbers of Infinity's calendar
They do not advance
        but find out an eight
              and wait upon Saturn's quantum deceptions

I want it to be winter at least
A winter. that will make the age a little easier to find
        this was what I want:

130

a season opened like blinds
            have friends over to discuss details
            the full house of a windy lakebed
Partake of spiritual energy   that brings a solatium
      the planet autopsied

The universe is a House of Doors
Like the Burning Man masterpiece of *1996*
Our industry will be directed
      the closed doors of Summer Lake
            all the inland seas approached
                  and their handles turned gently

And the enemies of ecology
      will lose power and nothing deserve but scorn
One must experience the danger of thinking differently
            being *alone* being enough

Noticing the exact pastels of this semi-arid homeland
A stage set for the camels and early horses
      for zoolatry

I have lived as the *smilidon*
            known the stare of the short-faced bear
                  the entirety of megafauna's corral
And told the hunters to turn back
Retrace their steps to the tundra
            "There's nothing here   nothing to see
                        nothing you'd want"

Ah!   and three-legged Fred
      the tabby in the lobby of Summer Lake Hot Springs
            remembers to purr
            and put pleasure ahead of too much wistful

Please, that winter now   if it cannot be then!
Winter in the notches of September's days
      of walking out   while this is possible
            beelining these immensities
                  like a game of going straight
                  after the crimes of the hominid
The species in search of so much acceptance and validity

destruction is the answer

This will not be a screed
Even a recital of wrongs is false witness
        the baby blaming itself for crying

The plan is to retrieve an idea
And this will be enough   resolution that's millennial

Go to the high ground
        those basalt cupboards and attics
                those remarkable shorelines
Learning Spanish along the way
                the words for
                caution, *cuidado*
                danger, *peligro*

Because old movies are playing
The Treasure of Pancho Villa
        the film that begins with the end
                and goes back
                and shows how Gilbert Roland
                        came to be fighting for his life

There is the treasure of Time itself
Let's fight for *that*
        in a shoot'em up pulsing
                with environmental imperatives
                        going back to work
                        when the work is good   and plentiful

"Cuidado!"
No sprains!
Watch the feet are well-placed
        so that there's *routine* to the dance
                in the scrub and dark scree slope
John Doe wanders in the shadow of Abert
Such a good kid being bad
        easily distracted
                wanting to swim in the Ice Age
                a loved one unloving all but prehistory

Being drawn to Egypt
And much more besides pyramids
    when their construction was remedy
    for too much loneliness   no money   no *time*

The lake is now a fragrance
      audited   waded into
      a scatchy expance
      exactly what happens
Ground cover's blue-and-grey embrace
          happily entitled consultation

Nature's numbers added   subtracted
    till its Golden Mean is arrived at
    suddenly appearing
        a peace of consequence
         and thought to have vanished

55. FURNITURE CAR RALLY CAMP FOUND

Would there be a fashion show here?   Gwen?
What shall I say
    that may be said to be the first thing said?
That I will rally with the ralliers
    because someone who plays Mozart
    the same Rondo as *moi*
    who said,"Come to our fashion show!
        at Furniture Car Rally Camp!"
      and gave very specific coordinates
      for the show.
        the location an o'clock radial
        and one of those curving streets
        the curving *just* discernable?

YES!   I should say *that* first thing
And keep going
    the same way Black Rock City keeps us going

And Gwendolyn it was   who knew that Mozart
Who was acquainted with the sendup
      of traveling Turkish bands
            in the streets of Vienna
                  his making fun because he *could*
                  because Islam had failed to take the city
Way back in the day

Sing it *a capella* on the way to the furniture
Hum it!   croon it!   such a fine Mozart tune!
      a soloist arriving ahead of time
She'd said 4
But hell, "playa time!"
            4 is early is late

Ah!
Found is the checkered domain!
      those flags   the "finishing" touch
May I discuss the squares?
      the little black-and-white sqares
            like a Forties movie trying to materialize?

I'm ready   the camp is found
And a question forms: "The Faerie Gwendolyn?"
"Ah, yes!
      let's see...
      I saw her earlier...
      she was here...
            hmmm...
            there's her tent...
                  you want a drink?"   a question back

"Maybe   maybe today I'll start drinking again
After thirty-five years!"

Naw, just continue   searching and inquiring
Feeling more and more welcome
      for the Furniture Car Rally Camp was friendly
            look around
            it's actually *tidy!*
                  with a spiffy red chair   a blue one

134

and other candy colorations

And what's that furry fuzzy pole a part of?
What pink purpose?
        why, it's a piece of furniture   *motorized*
Mobile   like the Radio Flyer wagon
                        with the ladybug theme
                        and bug-eyed staring

But wait, there's more
There's *fashion* as promised
An obvious carpet   scarlet
                        the ramp

It's 4:40 and overcast
And there will be a fashion show after all
        with wedding-white arches
        and veils
        the pavilion from which contestants pour
White, a pleasing counterpoint to Libertine momentum
Whose banner's waving invitation
                three gold stars and strange stripes!

56. CLOUDY AND WINDY

It is August 29th between ten and twelve
And the morning is a comprehensive brightening
        an eclogue conceived in the heart of prehistory

Take a memo:
            the administration of eastern Oregon
            is the guidance of clouds and wind!   .

Lori back there in Paiseley
        said she'd come from San Jose
        come to this streetless, carless land
Gaining just enough latitude

to empty the continent
gangsters gone
opera and ballet

How miraculous then is an "old-school", radio
tuned to just about anything
even the ads seem cozy 1948

Lori has chosen well
And her espresso was perfect
all of San Jose that's required
a whole metropolis compressed
strained   aromatic

Twenty miles down the road
you haven't left
geology's tables and chairs *everywhere*
but going unrecorded
the depth and width of these lava plains

What a lovely house it is, Lori!
What a morning you began
as Paisley's spokesperson
clear and precise
pure information
yet warmly imparted
The beautiful timing of serendipity
When no one's early   no one's late

Wonder if the town has a gildhall
is old-fashioned enough for that

Add sugar and stir
The takeaway's a confidence
that says there's no obstruction
fences   parcels
all of that receding geometry
existing in the memory   barely

While these clouds are cushioning
And the deep air gusts and rattles old iron
the gates of would-be rangeland

136

While this is possible
        and *makes* possible a better August 29th
                        than ever, before

57. WHAT'S IN THE SCAN CONTAINED TWO
    SYLLABLES

It bears repeating: Abert
Three junipers and a slope
                with words

That you should be with me here!
In spite of your desire to just read your newest mystery

Perhaps the beautiful mystery of Abert's uplift?
Maybe all the aspects of incline
        and the upper barrier's prohibition
        that final wall
        what six hundred feet *above* is like!
                how elevation makes us see as giants

See *far*   a better map   with clouds and wind
I am looking for authors qualified to see all   know all
Who would accept a commission
        to say even the least about this country
                and still arrive at a pure bucolic
                the Pure Land of Buddhist imagination
                        found
                        where Elsewhere's persuasions
                                would have it

I would say to those writers,
"Welcome to the show!"
        and welcome, too, to increased peril
                the world at large an equalizing planet

Plan how to remain calm in the face of lawlessness
For all the comforts of this Third Millennium
At its inception *disorder*
          and it floods in   like replenished lakes
                              to inundate our prospects

From high on Abert's palisade
                with the junipers twisting
                dancing in the updrafts
It bears repeating that you chose to be together

You arrived like a cyber sorceress
          to rewire the Miocene
                calibrate the "hot spot"
                that even now seethes beneath Yellowstone

Having traveled there from hereabouts
          make it Steens
          Steens Mountain   your *own* birthplace
                                    and province

58. SAGE IN THE GULLY   WITH ROCKS

To see with painters' eyes
          this is my desire
                still descending the narrow gully
                      where scrub has found its roots
                                          in the rocks
                              masking safety
                      and balance

If one would not be a cripple
Then each step is posture
                the briefest pause

And one may be said to be motionless
That extreme caution

138

                that springs from solitude's witness
For the hidden boulders will shift
        tilt
        be dislodged   and seesaw with peril

    Such is the scree   its large-scale shuffle
                              no repose in the angle
    The flatness of the highway devoutly to be wished for

On *purpose* have we come
        to review the decades
        from a hillside of broken rock
              where a peace prize is in the offing
It will be different than other awards
Silver-stemmed and crackling
            like the brush
            with the wind moving it

And there   out there   the dark green "islands"
        spaced in the white ingress to Lake Abert
              impossible lily pads waiting for thunder
              the false lake further on
              knee-shallow

It is all a democracy
Every feature to vote going forward
Every landform having its portrait

And where we have been
        beyond volcanic buildings
            is like a homestead made invisible
            a *specific* event
                        in the history of Strange

Safety is here   though the boulders move
        perhaps for the first time in ten thousand years

59. GRANITE PEAK'S SHADOWED SUMMIT

Being due west
    well-positioned
    with no health problems

Being late in the day   a Monday, an *August* Monday

Granite Peak is suddenly shadowed
The summit *only* darkened
        the region so hard-won that immemorial day
            once
                when the last steps had been taken
                                with disbelief

That day when the mountain stopped being higher
        and came to a stop
        an agreement
            so far and no farther
Both Black Rock and Smoke Creek deserts assessed
                        from the standpoint of conquest

Oh, but call it something else!
The wealth of nine thousand feet and more
                    when it's three-sixty   all sides
                    and comedy all alone
                        that critics would love
                        though their laughter destroy

That day of ascent   that began and ended in the dark
            but was spotlit between
It was like a job fought for   the *high* ground
You're an employee of the mountain
        and even *now*
            with a shadow up there

Laid off, perhaps
And who   in passing by in late afternoon
            make it six o'clock
            the hour of the shroud
                that qualifies achievement

                    throws doubt
                        like a shawl
                            about the edifice

The lower parts still alight
        as if bright ambition knew its paths
Be in the show
Draw to affection   the warmth of stone in the sun

It had been key
        to find ways around the ramparts
            the abutments
                the concentrations of juniper
                            crowding stiffly
It was *memory* you needed
Knowing safe passage depends
        on seeing forwards   backwards
        imagining return
            though one's quest is fierce with going on!

It needs translation   being on the level
A principle   where the struggle below
                is just as acute as what is above
And climbing Granite Peak is then an equilibrium sought

The mountain's blond where the clouds stay clear of it
And this close
        the central triangle has retreated
        Granite's familiar profile
            bested by the bulk of foreground

There are still routes on standby   trails to other tops
Wagon Tire's one
            caches of water in secret places left

Waiting for a next time
        next century   prior to dawn as before
        with a long approach through the sage
            the sun rising as you do
                up the soft sand to ridges chosen carefully

Yes, and carefully going into cracks and grooves!

to access the ledges
        enjoying salmon cans
        raisins
        plain bread and water
            like a happy prisoner
            till height has made you free
                and warden of rustic battlements

Prepared to grant amnesty to any would-be inmates
        of a mountain so massive
            it pulls you over
            as if your wheels were not aligned
                or gravity is different
                in the presence of an asteroid's mass
                    added to the crust
                                the *Earth's* crust

But call it something else for once
Find a word big enough   bigger than "granite"

Meanwhile, stay stopped due west
        thinking of Franz Liszt's symphonic poems
                thinking of the *Faust Symphony*
Barely performable
As Granite Peak is *just* climbable!

And a measure of that vastness may be an easier task
        is easier   with Liszt's concurrent reckoning
        the orchestra well-tuned
                for chromatic slipping and sliding
                        about the main key's harmony

So much is the same, aloft
The batholith's soft sand
            is both delay and reassurance
                "All is well   and all *will* be well
                                    in the garden"

Being There, of course
Like some augmentation of experience
        one that matches the stepwise progressions
                                of Faust

Where downfall's accompanied by exaltation
All the time praying, actually
        the soul being easily discovered
              among random erosions of the wind and rain
              ruins *easily* anthropomorphized

Being late in the day   *melancholia* will visit
        because the past simply won't stay in place
        but travel as I have
              the vacant road to Gerlach

Try to get to the side of the mountain opposite
Beyond Bruno Selmi's ranch
        the right turn to Smoke Creek
              Bloody Point
        where you want to ask someone:
              "What happened here that was bloody?
                 and could it happen again?"

And sadness will try to follow
        past the enterprise of Planet X
All its bowls and vases   artwork's island
Dry in Lake Lahontan's imaginary miles
Romanticism stalks   insubstantial yet compelling

Dangerous beauty
        like the exact shape of a cloud
        or a killer's intentions   settled on
              by agreement with the conscience

The color of the western wall
        that may or may not be a word in all of Space
                              to pronounce as protest

From the road
        and feeling healthy enough to be truthful
              say it's a courtroom
              for Liszt says so   long-distant
His nineteenth century lectured to   subpoenaed, even

I see the benches   the dock   the jury box
And know some assessment will be made a verdict

The Law will ascend
        follow lines of reason
        arguments
                like the first attempts
                        to call a summit one's home

Those many trials before it was done
                        and *where* it was done
                                and conclusion reached

Even now, Granite Peak dares the traveller
        to go cross country to Burning Man
                        instead of driving around southwards

There is just something about all that igneous rock
Makes you want to go that way: across
        get to know the country close *up*
        invade the cinemascope nationwide's contained
And walking there is touring the country
        prior to the Gate   the Greeters
                the long ride through alkaline dust
                                at ten miles-an-hour, max

But that's a patience that's easy
        if you've come down from the heights
                a private Moses
                speaking in tongues to vacant Nevada
Becoming rich without trying
Angels with gifts for the hospital of open air

Would the shadow wait for me?
The dark diadem wait   until its shelter's my own?

Let the cloud stay close
        while I test a new staff
                in transit to meet you again, glorious crest!
                your pluton both abyssmal and exalted!

60. EARTH GUARDIANS: THE NEW CONFIGURATION!

To appreciate the change
      one would have had to have been
                            coming around
                            for awhile

The Guardians have rearranged their benches
It's like someone perused the Four Directions
      and decided *north's* the one
         so the benches were pivoted
                   from east-facing

I liked the way it was before
But I like *everything* that is before
     the year 1996
      but then you *knew* that, didn't you?
Why are you looking at me in that tone of voice?

Oh, it's such a nice day, though!
Whiteouts?
        love 'em!
        and we know how to dress for them, don't we?

The kerchief, that's right
And if the whiteout should escalate
     there's that special mask
And if it *really* blows up   then   the *respirator!*
                       it's all good!

Ah!
I see you have discovered the Alternative Energy Zone
I mean Demo Garden
     let's be down with that, yeah!

There's a guy been running around
     says he's been trying to get permission
     permission to operate
Says to get ready
It won't be long   he almost has it together

he'll be cooking solar
not enough to satisfy your hunger
but hey, it ain't the point!

Someone's gone to a lot of trouble
and color's been added
I see crimson   there's a purple table cloth
It all looks very promising

All the bicycles in the dust are swarming
some purpose, perhaps
They are more than mere passersby
but their objective is obscure

If you've seen the Guardians' schedule of events
The lineup is intriguing
what *appeals*, my darling?
and just what on Earth
are those Earth Guardians up to
really?

Just hold me   *"hold me, my sweet baby dear..."*
As Chicago Rose sang so beautifully
At the week's inception
it's still your love I seek
and not too much more
well, at least you're listening
just now   on a Tuesday

May we not simply sit on a northward-facing bench
and be happily perplexed by it all

61. BMIR'S CAVE OF THE WINDS

It's BMIR's cave of the winds
Those air waves in and out

Burning Man Information Radio can be a park
        but it's barter, too
                the state has so little to say
                and the federal

Blow it out!   94.5 fm!
The cave of the station
        filled with hangers-on   next up
                the interviews
                public service announcements
                live performances

Here in the supernatural desert
        all through the day and night
Colorado on the playa wafts
                the subterranean
                        brought to the surface
                        taken to the next level
Launch us forward after the backwards culture
                                        of reaction

So BMIR is an up-and-running cavern
        where information's a breeze
                and DJs are docents for fm by the hour
                each a version of fireside   the chats
The Twenty-First Century listening

There's a golf cart parked   a messenger?
                                a Ranger's call?

Keep believing
        if not in volunteering, exactly
        then   in *spectating*
                for even that is participation
Observing and exploring Cave of the Winds radio
Making official a vicarious spelunking
                        blind you could do it!

And once inside   speak into the mic
                among stalactites and stalagmites
                it's all thrown together
                        equipment   Cheetos   diet colas
                                        haphazard

The stalls of a ramshackle souk are entrances
Have you heard of this place?
Or are you so new
        you've never known its broadcast draft?

Perhaps the Reverend Billy's next on the air
And that's *his* golf cart there   a "Holy Cow!" he rides

I'm wearing morning clothes to the Studio of the Winds
        prepared to pay a fee of caring enough
            to listen to my beloved Colorado
            its winds like envoy spirits

62. HAWAIIAN MANNEQUIN

He's dancing in a blue robe
His head is round   well-placed
He has an audience
        a witness   recording his dance
                        that is *Hawaiian* for sure
            the undulating hands
            one side of his body
            then the other

Oh, yeah!
He's Hawaiian all right
        but he's also a mannequin dressed
                        whether he's real is moot

It's a Jack-in-the-box look of "Aloha"
        and he's definitely wavy
            what you'd see right off the plane
            with leis draped

But he's *here!*   right here in that blue robe
Call it a cape

And his proximity to radio   the world of BMIR
        makes us suspect he's somehow an artefact
            a weird consequence of the station's operation
Information Radio having brought him to life

The future of window shopping   *showcase* A1
Generic Hawaiian
        and the girl in the halter kindly rewards his hula
                by showing him her iPad
                wherein he's captured
                    proof he exists   no worries
And those mannequin eyes are wide with gratitude

His shiny black hair is like a thin toupee
And recalls the Mayor of Munchkin Fashion
Robo-Jack   Kama'aina at large in Black Rock

And now the girl is at his side for more impromptu snaps
        for more proof
            being "at your service" expanded
                to beautiful blue daydreams
                acquired in the course of random interests

Modern dance is tested for its Polynesian possibilities
Rounder heads!   a business opportunity
                    adorned with indigo
                    see how scary that is
                        before you buy
                        but heck, why *not?!*

It's a lovable investment

Whatever we're talking about
        the galaxy will take it away with rotation
            every two hundred and twenty million years
            around the Center
That's how long it takes for the sun to make a circuit
And surely   the Hawaiin mannequin?
        well, he will not survive

He's good enough to be permanent, though

The girl as well   both are deserving
        so let's include her
        allow her expert youth a perfect freedom
            like a window
                that lets you look for a Hawaiian Cosmos

The *serendipity* of their being seen together
Talking to each other in a language that changes
            each second
                in the presence of technology

Would there be a purchase?   what price?
Starting very high-end
        and then cheapening to affordable
            and finally part of the "Gift Economy"
The gifted is dancing
A blue-caped superhero
                    master of the dust

63. CENTER CAMP, EARLY AFTERNOON ON A TUESDAY

The space seems especially white
        the overhead is a canvass bleached
            stretched to perfection
                a perforated thing
                such that   even though it *shelters*
                        suntan lotion's required
Did they actually think it would be too dark in there?

Who's come here today?   how many?

How utterly *different* it all is from the early parachutes!
        they were always looking somewhat military olive
        you'd watch them billow and be blown about
            while resting on hay bales
                satisfied the country of horses and cows

had come to Burning Man

And pretending to be a ranch hand, that was easy
You were a *lazy* version, that's all
        paid to be a layabout
        in a revery of work simulation
            Ben Cartwright and the boys letting you slide

I ask myself again, "Who has come here today?
                                to 2016's tent?"

There is an assortment of hats
            black top hats
            the straw
            the derby
            the caps
                animal heads

There's awkwardness here and there
And there is also all-conquering confidence
And the miscellany drifts
        in and out of the Center of things

I'm wanting to be wrapped in L.A. exotica
        be seen as fashionable
            or perhaps even timeless
            where we are now   where we were *then*

But if a culture based on gravity's attempted
Where gravity is made model citizen
        gravity as faith   this Center Camp, too
A force of nature needing acolytes
            even if Revolution is continuous
            (that song, "Imagine"...)

Burning Man has gone International
        that *had* been a lark of San Franciscan Dada
            the collective whims of Cacophany
                                slipping into renown

Center Camp's like a partially painted canvass
        in motion

the oils a movie
running past a projectionist's quitting time
the reels tireless   the sprockets sure
The artist painting each frame
of a soundless documentary
as fast as possible
the voice-over mercifully absent

Crazy liberals!
Crazy rednecks!
sandwiched
An open-and-shut case of split-mindedness
in a new Fellini

Maybe a novel's just started over yonder
where a girl in red is writing
Having come to the Center
instead of things falling apart
they fell into place   and she's begun

And there beneath the pennants
Two attorneys have agreed to get married
and consider other professions than the Law
body sculpting a surprising future
when the devil may be a customer for good

Is it a gathering?
Or a gang of voters
aggressively determined to nominate an effigy?

I know this is another planet found
and terraformed
revenge taken   for the aliens did resist

Okay, okay!
I'll stop   I'm in a better mood than what I said
and delight in all of it   *every* detail!
Making sure to ask first before any pictures
Two of the astronauts consent
He's taller than she is   but
they said there would be sex in Space
even if *she* was taller than *him*

Is this digression?
Of course!   Burning Man is that, *entirely*
                    enough to have to start all over

64. IN THE COFFEE LINE

There's a lot going on in the coffee line
You wouldn't think so   but it's true
And the craving
         the *craving for mocha!*   that's the least of it

History is here
            insinuating itself
            even in the most informal situations

All is "go-to"   the term   the adjective
         the minimum discriptor needed

"Go-to"   the ubiquitous
And I'd go to anyone in the line
         or *about* to be in line
         or having already *been* in line
Beginning with a stranger
            who's suddenly as favorite
            as the most-loved member
                of an extended family of thousands

The one never hated   and
A conversation start that's ongoing
         where you'd both left off
            last year   or ten years   or *twenty*

So that much is accomplished
The exchange a series of haiku
            brevity that flows
            from what's familiar   even heartfelt

Is that Larry Harvey over there?
Though he's insisted he doesn't exist?

There'd been a *sign* that said he didn't   once
          prominent   a placard   one of many
                    wisdom on the way in and driving slowly

There he is
          a sighting to be left alone
                    even his groupies have learned respect
Yeah, what if he just wants to be in line, too?
Just wants to be a virgin
          who's made to roll in the dust
                              at the Greeters Station?

Hah!
Can't have that!   the media beg!
          they want to be all over it, of course
                    the Organization!
                    the nature of Fame requires this!

It's impossible he should return to beginnings
Baker Beach, San Francisco
          an eight-foot Man assembled
                    that's what you have out there   outsized
                    today's giant

Innocence depends on the newcomer
          even as business tentacles probe the perimeter
          looking for a way

"Oh, shut up!"
                    what you tell yourself
                    reasonably sure
                         that Burning Man is safe from the money

And now the line is moving again that was stalled
The orders were confused, perhaps
We're all truckers at heart
          waiting our turn at the scale
                    having given up on luxury

the open road has brought us here
                    to the biggest truck stop of all

I'm laughing at the Left *and* the Right, though
Thinking it's kind of like Copernicus
        saying things that ended Earth-centered

Both political persuasions
        like the convolutions of the epicycles
                circles within circles
                    and then they're demolished
                Copernicus
                Brahe
                Kepler
                Newton
                        Einstein...

But wait, there's *more*   there will always be more!
Any thought to have a qualified sequel
        Infinity's peremptory demands

And   to get to the End will mean mutability
Humpty-Dumpty happy to fall
        daily press briefings   retractions and corrections
        recitals of mistakes
                false physics exposed
Years ago renounced in trials by fire   non-stop
No one taken seriously!
        no, not at all   it's best

Kind of leaves things open
        working against ourselves in a *good* way
                getting in line for revision
                for mocha that's the same as that
Stimulating   the next new thing a fishing expedition
                        for more of the same
                        a certain paradox involved
                        thereby obtained

We're closer
And the volunteers are volunteering at a *very* high level!
Just look at 'em!   the *energy!* $E = mc^2$

155

Somebody said, "Can't-stop-'im Steve!"
        but I couldn't accept the compliment
        it was simply proximity
        being close to the counter
                and the busy ones behind it
                those servers calling out
And it's catching   you yourself are enthused as well
                        perhaps for all time

Long ago a dancer said as much
        "Energy begets energy!"

There are newspapers to read
                the *Beacon* is one
                        there are others
And since the beginning   almost   *Piss Clear*

For a long time we read it
And when it was over   all the issues were collected
        saved for a book

And all this stuff's online
        there's no rush, really
                it's all archived in the communal mind

Pretend the line's a line for work
And the rag you read's *The Revolutionary Worker*

Pretend it's Moscow   waiting on rations
        queueing for basics
        in a deep-down Depression
                some city lost in the Thirties

"Where's your identity card?"
"Are your papers in order!?"

"Oh, yes! *The Black Rock Gazette*
        yes, my paper's in order
                all the latest   all spelled out
                we can *share!*"

This is the ultimate "go-to"
A counter aproned purple, red and yellow
        an abbreviated rainbow

And history   a partial story
     just enough to make us wary despite the revels

65. RIGHT THIS WAY!

There's Playa Info   red-flagged
     the noisy whale
         then you're through the pale, cubist gate

Right *this* way's the Center Camp
Not exactly a *camp*   but surely the center

They've red-flagged the Info
     is there danger in knowing?

Don't answer!   not yet   get bearings, first
Scout beyond the whale
     having heard its songs
         be done with fads and learn to concentrate
         want what's readable
There's a craze for every act of the hominid

The installation art   that's the best!
The delicate arch
     that reminds me of the portal in a *Star Trek*
     "The City on the Edge of Forever"
         was it Harlan Ellison's script?   yes!
         that most Shakespearian of all the Treks!
When "Bones" freaked out and entered the past by mistake
     and the others had had to find him...

The whale's made us sensible
     and a threshold's resisted

its pale facets *suspect* planes
fashioned by a wizard
Though the bright sun would disabuse us
of his occult doings

There's no angle wide enough
to be sure of the picture
And a primal fear from Hollywood flows
made of alcohol and cocaine

How far back would we have to go
to get a script unfueled by drugs?
Playa Info at once!
discover the power of their oracle to determine!

And if questions may go beyond the orange
The plastic webbing
of the known world of Black Rock City
See if there's a *farther* perimeter   scout this

I think that even if we trekked to Dry Peak
we'd still be part of a purvue
and beholden to Playa Info
George Washington's dose of laudanum taken

Be the president of a country
one acre in extent
forecasting prosperity
for anyone happening to immigrate there

The view is fair
And from this vantage   go ahead
and find out the artistry
of secret kingdoms and queendoms
in plain sight

Do link these elements!
Joining whalesong to songs of discovery
Everyone wins with connection
excellence   is where we begin

And I will do that   right here in the present tense

What confidence is possible!
    in the gateway, ultimately
    in the whale's diving deep and turnaround
        its songs and oceanic compass!

Playa Knowledge gained that becomes a fever
A wind that follows you around
Years and years at once   all the info that's required
    to survive not only *this* desert
            but the worst of the Afar Triangle
            where salt is mined and transported
            in triple digits of parchment
The land like combustible paperwork

There are bikes in the foreground
With forethought
        the principle of "right this way" is applied
            to a cubist embellishment of gateway

There is no longer any danger
        or if there is
            there are candles for later
            when this blazing day settles down
                    to stars' first punctuations
                    that teach concentration
And how it may be a craze long-lasting

Outside the box of Burning Man's empire
Winging to Dry Peak, to plant a red flag

66. THE WHALE (CONTINUED)

It is closer now
The cetacean   the see-through whale

The one that didn't like the land enough to stay dry
    and so returned to the sea

while the returning was good

What *did* you look like then, whale?
As *land* animal, I mean
Did you sing?
        or was that only later
        when the fathoms let your singing carry?
Was that the reason you resubmerged?   went back?

Oh, there are bones in the earth that ask all this
Or even say what's what
        the bones put together by laughing paleontologists
"How can this *be?*"
"What the hell?!"

It had learned to crawl but preferred to swim
        and *migrate* of course
        pole-to-equator-to-pole   to prove it could be done

The whale at the start of the avenue to Burning Man
Magnificent!   and it swoops down
        plunging
        as if from the surface of an ocean of air
            to be at our depth and holding our breath
                        oh, lovely consequence!

There is an inspection in progress
Singly and in small groups, they stop by
        the big art of the whale to measure
            and maybe climb   if that is possible
            climb in the *mind*

They come to see the structure of beauty
And whether anything of Jonah may be discerned

Come to see if its heart beats with more than an l.e.d's pulse

It is a physical sculpture
        wavering   with a hologram's ghostly version of itself
            in the ink of the night was the whale's pen dipped
            to make some kind of sense
                of perfume and oil lamps

We've seen and heard its literature at large
Those lyrics transmitted and wanted
        like emotions
        after monomania's enterprise of blank stares

"Transcend" is just two syllables of a verb   transitive
Trying to accomplish liquidation
        one way or another

Love come 'round to arid places
        the whale's dives like repeated baptisms
        with watery dialogue
        a birthright adjusted
        for the denser medium of seawater

What have we done so far?
A *better* question is: what will *now* be done?
What could ensure this creature survives
        and only goes away
        when Evolution sees fit
        and has prepared its next lifeform carefully
        leisurely   with any improvement guranteed

Perhaps the whale crawls back on land
There's always *that*
        whatever takes time will take you away
                                                that's the key

Though it seems improbable
        on the "Be Here Now" planet
        so rushing forward in the dark
        it is easy to die
        without appreciation *of dying!*

The whale is closer now   we've approached
There's time   millions of years

And the artwork before us says, "Use it all!"
        use it so that multiple moments
                        add up to certainty

The Universe once more believes in its creation
        as if additional security measures had been taken
                when "All is One" seemed insufficient awareness
If you even accidentally doubt   then safety succumbs

Fly, oh whale!
Neither sea or land is your home!
The *air* is your artspace
        be lightly molecular
                like the best of illusions
                        and travel this sky
                        farther than prediction

67.   WAITING TO BE AUTHORIZED

They're less glamorous in daylight
Those artcars waiting to be authorized
        certified   approved   licensed   inspected
                then sent on their way in the sun

Sent roving
Allowed their freedom at five miles-an-hour
        out there ships of state
                going island to island
                where art has rafted   but

First, always, questions and tags to be acquired
So they are waiting
                the Department of Mutant Vehicles is open

We're just so thrilled!
        there aren't so very many
        let us make our own inspection   uninterrupted
                have a good look at them all!

The one with gray paint   yikes!
Like a colorless nomination

a mobile campaign   looking governmental

A gray bus with a second deck like a covered wagon
        the color of climate denial
        a gunmetal look
It's either time dispended
                or the best of land battleship
                or police/community relations
                                hoping for neutrality

It is an *unattended* artcar
As if someone grew tired of waiting
        and turned the waiting into walking   away
                perhaps to champion
                the rights of special needs

And there's gray as Finality
The color of Entropy
        that summarizes ending   *and* starting
                and where Eternity's shingle proclaims:
                "Access Denied"

So the future's a limited rectangular transport
Walk on   what else, being multi-generational?

Ah!   the little silver runabout
                has a go-kart's dimensions
How nifty are its lines
        like a comma gone crazy with punctuation!
                or a transportation committee of one
                whose learning curve
                        takes it everywhere
                                the study of language requires

It's an important role
With grammar covering lots of ground
        the old-fashioned way   *didactic*

Flip it *over*   and it simply *is*   the same
        though inverted, still a pause
                        paused *now*   and patient

And there, a goat!
Or *trying* to be that, I guess
    one that desired gold and got it
    though everybody had said, basically
      "No!"   "Nix!"

As though a Dr. Seuss would rhyme the request:
    "No, nix, you may not have it
    you may not be of gold   *no tricks!*"

But the goat did succeed
With stairs to the hoard
    to precious controls and spectacular horns
      whatever you want
For the goat is on the children's side
      and   lobbies in the desert for "All Aboard!"

The ubiquitous orange cones are clashing with all else
Orange compromised in being thus trapped
    in a utilitarian nightmare of solid geometry
      and it is our mission to remove them
        and forego their dubious usefulness

Explain those cones, someone!
Be reasonable!   do orange cones belong in our dreams?
    and are they really a fit
      with the concept of Radical Self-Reliance?

Let's meanwhile continue to explore the wait
And fictionally award and authorize *ourselves*
Take a look   approve of   certify   license
    and thoroughly inspect what's here
    so hopefully in line   and courteous

Ah!   a hammock hangs
    frontside a boxy and *foreboding* mutant
    dark as Darth Vader
      in his oversized helmet
        dreaming of sequels
        and cloning, of course

A red smudge   like a morbid afterthought

suspenseful   dangerous-appearing

I am wanting that peril now and always
        as it says those things I am wanting to say
        with the attitudes demanded
                in short   the wherewithal to keep it real

Did I ever tell you that?   give it tags?
Leave hints for you?

Leave it for now
        the Pac-Man behind the nightshade shuttle
                remembers me
                and stirs with an appetite

Been seen so often it's a game of keep-away
"Eat well and prosper!"
        Spock's other, *unknown* saying
This Pac-Man's a street cleaner
                blue-eyed, with brushes
                and he needs sundown to go to work
                        looks raised for inspection
                        good luck

Get to steppin'   there's more
There's always more at Burning Man
        and that's so you'll never complain!

There's a diaphanous see-through mermaid
        whose banner body's mastered duality
                and wants to share its secret

What about the saucer?
There's always a saucer   this one's lipstick-pink
The aliens running around as if it's acceptable to do so
        when to do so takes away all the mystique

Shouldn't the UFO's stay debatable?   spurious?
Always in need of more convincing data?
Do they have to be a pink fact with room for two
        a cliché on cruise control?

Okay, I take it back!
　　　if they'll let me squeeze in
　　　　　a third passenger to go along
　　　　　in a grounded spaceship
　　　　　　　　　　here to take over

Quick!
The dragon!　　*gold* again　　golden artcars!
　　　a popular bullion
Wonder just what this dragon can do
Sleek, if unglamorous
　　　shiny, though inert

A menace still in need of approval
　　　　　the dragon waits
　　　　　they *all* wait
　　　　　　　to be authorized myths

68. HOUSE CAR

It had every year in its design
A gray-black transport that was also a house

It had the look of a cabin and generations gone by
　　　where children learned　　and learned to walk

The projections　　the *horns* that were a part of it
　　　grew out of all proportion to upbringing, however

Or it's reclusivity on wheels
An old man's bungalow
　　　drab with stylish bitterness
　　　　　and overhead of hermit longings

There's a definite Burning Man aesthetic
　　　one that includes such whimsy as the house car
　　　　　with its almost baroque conceits

Pride has placed those symbols   that filigree
        that no space should be forgotten
                                unembroidered
And the good graffiti for the culture is scrawled

The gables and wooden beams seem carefully adjoined
Oddly   there's a sundial's tilted table in front
        like a useless cowcatcher
Is it a broken component?
                once level?   once functional?
                when we might have played cards
                or danced Ponchielli's "Hours" away?

Creatures of the hull
        with tentacles of Microsoft
Well-established denizens of night-and-day clubs
Who could blame us?
Would the world be better without us?

It was time for the morellos   gifted at Center Camp
        those sour cherries saved for this inspection tour
                the blood flows faster
                creation's requisite fluid

Ultimate Mad Max
        Mel Gibson's ride   powered by wrath
                the end result of financial crises
                poorly managed

Black-and-gray like an earthy pessimism
Test its transmission   check the expiration date
Talk about everything with those others aboard

Is this a form of Vietnam, crouched for aggression?
        going to get even?
Don't bring it up
        no post-war courtship could ever make it right
                                or should

The images flood like idolatry
The patterned exterior

an accomplishment worthy of the best sci-fi
So give them a pass
"After We're Gone" is the message
    the Future carried about as a fancy casket

It is not going to be easy
    Little House on the Playa the dark side of the *Prairie*
        no, not easy   we could talk about that
        pick *any* war
        The First *World* War   *that one*
        get it right   understand

Stay in the teens of the last century
    till it's clear
    as Margaret MacMillan said
        it was the *War that Ended Peace*

I think it looks like this beast
And profits from morbidity start
No matter how you carry yourself
    its farewell wagon has plans for you
        and   strangely   your honesty assures it

69. PINK AND PURPLE ARE A VERY HAPPY COUPLE

Pink and purple are the colors worn
The happy couple's decided on tutus
    though it's doubtful any ballet will happen

"This is a movie!
    you can move!
        go!   *that's* it!
That will work and work well in the edit"

White hats and coffee cups
    be my friends for five minutes, I beg
        any *longer* than that

and my defects of character will be apparent

So far they *are* friendly
        as friendly as pink and purple can get
                with pains and pleasures shared
All of our intro is focused on a handshake
Twenty years of acquaintance found in a first grip

If we could do that every time
If just meeting is a meeting *recalled*
        in later dealings
                those dealings are then freshly conceived
Like any child of a truly happy couple!

70. GEORGE IN RECITAL

I'll quote him
It's historical   he won't be back
        so this is for the record
                just some of what he said for the last time

He's discussing the valley
        as he calls the basin of the Black Rock Desert
He's letting us know how hard
                        how *approximate*   is geology
                        let's listen...

"A difficult thing
        to try to work out for just one period
        let alone for *all* of geologic time
                those multiple sources of sediment
                they're all so screwed up

"Why is there a playa?
Because this is a dry lakebed
        of the former glacial Lake Lahontan

"The multiple 'high stands'   lake shores of yesteryear
        you see them along the valley wall
                as you come in   from Reno or wherever
The white mineral coating the lava rocks?
        that is *calcite*"

I was the one who'd cried, "Mic him!"
Else George's recital would have stayed a silent movie
        a moot assessment
                unfit for the record

Bravo, George!

71. HIS AUDIENCE, HIS STUDENTS, OF A TEMPORARY ACADEMY

His audience, his students, of a temporary academy
George wrapping up and schmoozing with his fans

Mixing, so he's a student *himself*
        a little rebellious
                with respect to the strictness of science
Maybe he'd like to shortcut   cut to the chase
        without a geologist's magnifying glass
                                        or ruler
                                        or any tool at *all*

Maybe that's why he's going back to school
To recapture the thrill of underage
        when what's proscribed
        is all the more likely to be tried

World is ending   work is ending
                at least work done that's tedium
                geology's career

It's better back in class

a class like this one
still facing one way together
        as if George's talk had a unified momentum
        and kept them rapt past its conclusion

72. WHAT'S BEFORE US

It's just not going to happen
Razorback   the island mountain
        not so much a razor when seen from the north
        rather   a rounded bulk
        reminiscent of a hill   call it Sahra's *Hill* also
            looks easy to ascend
                    you're going to just walk up
                        to see hills-on-hills
                                slowly roughening to jagged

And that is what is not going to happen
This being said on the level   before *any* hill
        before the effort's made
            and any height above is known

It's a task until it starts
When   no sooner the incline is found
        those lower parts
            where bikes have been and been tested
                            there's an easing

No sooner the first footfalls are accomplished
        "task" changes to "Thank God this is happening!"
            again, gradual
            a satisfaction unknown for too long

With six o'clock Tuesday p.m. chiming
And the van that brought us here
        to the base of the mountain   returning
Recrossing the always dangerous railroad tracks

when a train's approach
                    may be as silent
                    as the rest of the desert
It seems a Rachmaninoff Land

A place where sadness sits down
Has room
            and it is thought that lonely whistles blowing
                are just not necessary

What's before us also is sage's salon
Ghosts of the Gold Rush rushing about
            their transparent horses and cattle restless
                    the wind back and forth
                        talking of last night
                        before it's even happened
Though the sun was impatient to be gone

Trego's ditch is still hot and cold
            with a soothing now-and-later feel
A volcanic twilight
Deep down finding surface expression
            for those who would channel pioneers for a day
                who themselves are too busy with survival
                    to bother with a mountain
                        tossing out names at the most

It's a place to shout it out
Discover thought once more
            and what it means
                    to experience cause and effect in the words
                    or I devolve to spontaneous ululation
Finding oneself in a strange chant
                    that's sideways to spoken language

These are debutante dunes in the vicinity
Uneven   as befits a coming out that is awkward
            when a debutante balks at the whole idea

And looking at Razorback
            lofty as ever   and less luminous each moment
                I remember a radio studio once

There was a man who sang *Une source*
A song of origins   that from which inspiration arose
    I think it was a river

Trego is *my source*   the waters *calming*
This is the moment
        your own
                immensity approving like a crowd
                an automatic multitude
                    rubber-stamping freedom for the ages

When you are comfortable
        in granite sand
                and crumbling structures
Because where you are is where you live
                always drawn to out-of-the-way
                believing in its therapy

The time machine is flawless and holds many mirrors

Perfection's at large
        reminiscing mightily
                and it may allow ascent after all

If I say, "I can't wait!" you'll understand, won't you?
The one who waits for all good things
        spirit   shaman
        whoever you are and may be
                in this future we enjoy
                looking around the corners of the Black Rock

Nature unmasked and waiting, too
There will be a fox up there
        "Call it a premonition,"
                as Morbius did on the Forbidden Planet
                    when he warned the others of danger

But *here* is danger desired

73. TELEPHOTO

It was important to understand what was possible
And   looking out long distance
        look out for yourself at sunset
                        with a telephoto mind

That the scan might contain a detailed profile
        and be right, left and all around
                while there's something to see
                and Dry Peak still has color
                        the palest burnt umber
The softest regime of twilight
                        that is yet authoritative

Where is your family?
But understand what's possible this minute
When the mountain called King Lear
        in the Jackson Range
                lends restorative sleep
                        beginning to be invisible

The horizon's a prompt to fantasy
A fall-apart beauty
                to go with listening to emptiness

You're thinking *close-up* also
        a well-run passion
        what's important this evening
                begun before it's dark enough
                        to be called the night

And close-up of contentment
To undertake what you may
        deciding conditions were right

The mix of ground cover and stone
                an appreciable zen
Listen to the women   your mother making sense
                        as always

This is what is said
        for a third time on Razorback elicits a discussion
            of wilderness now   wilderness to come
                those millions of years

The landscape's correct
        makes "clearer the words of the tribe..."
Like telephoto, his words are sharpening! oh, Mallarmé!
The skyline is stripped of further metaphor!

This far up it's easier
The panorama's all   visible and indivisible
                always, we're going to be
                    always *here*
                    with the sunstar disappearing
            that gave color to the Granite Range
            and the distant Fox Range, too

The sky is arrested
Blue escorted into violet depth
        the happy prison of Earth shadow

The means to sustain oneself
        are given scent and substance
            questions to ask are forming
                        with each footstep found

Questions for the *summit* of tombstone plutonic
For each platform of the climb
        where surprising flatness
                is not fully understood
                or even acknowledged

What an inner sanctum might be fashioned!
        tunneling in secret
                till a mountain fastness is ready
                and confirmed
                    as a Hall of the Mountain King!

For when one wishes to retreat from telephoto
        and hide in the heart of Razorback
                where   perhaps   a piano hides too

175

Yes! a Bosendorfer Imperial Grand
          brought in for the purpose of earnest study
          the complete works of Scriabin
          how his sonatas would resonate
                    there in the stone!

Celebrating wrap-around
          the colors adored by that composer
          those colors coming and *going*
                    and each day differently!

They'd be easy to say with the keys
                    the full spectrum of black and white

74. SUMMIT SHOW

It was there, of course: the highest rock
There is nothing farther but the unknown
          the southern continuation of the ridge
                    something we'll saved for later
                    that would be a dangerous descent

An Indian banner fluttered
There were sticks bound together
          like the makings for a little tipi

Be a voice
Be sure of *this:*
          the spirits want you to sing to them!
                    sing with *approximate* rhythm
                    doing exactly what a metronome cannot

Call it a kind of research   spiritual
You're worried about nothing
The fabric's loose.   and blowing like a woven protest
And symbols allude
          they seem like familiar designs

what pottery alleges   and baskets

Is it a wrap that's whipping about?
A blanket?
        go closer
                experience the temptation to remove
                make it a keepsake

Experience the coveting
        even as your chanting builds
                you would privatize
                        take away the talisman

It turns out theft is moved forward
So that the banner's safe
                        and your thief's hands
                        grasp at open air
                later   suddenly
                the mountain climbed already
        so that you cannot do it   steal
Time and occasion deferred

A cross not Christian undulates secrecy aloft
Black-and-white-and-red
        the hands of a watch to unwind
                being expectant
                waiting on a paradigm shift
New and Old have collided
And the lights of the city
        are a galaxy's worth of gravity
        a crowd-size semblance of disorder

Shine the light, then!
Faraway but communal
        "spooky action at a distance..."
                adversarial, even
As if a wanna' be star fitfully signalled
Lonely for the constellations of the town
                                that is disc-like
                                        a party wheel

Be a mystery!

A temporary lighthouse made operational
        desert ships to guide in the deep playa below

Let the interval of our knowing suffice
A winking and blinking that's a vector
        one of limited duration
                inexplicable as the pleasures of ecstasy

Once there'd been a storm seen from this very summit
It was then a land of cloud shadow
        the clouds moving eastward with *lightning*, too
                and the moon going west
And a memorable fear had quickened the pace
Descent was hurried   "Get off the ridge!"
        too exposed
                not wishing to risk the bolts
Surrendering to caution though luck is all there is

Even so, such weather is prayed for
                        as one would for anything rare

You've brought a radio again
        investing in the long waves
        reflecting
                how is it possible
                that listeners to "Coast-to-Coast"
                        actually *believe* its assertions?

Still, it's *lovely* to listen in the summer night
        with peanut butter   crackers   and peaches
And you find once more the granite chair
        so excellent   just the right incline
                you rest
                lie back in comfort
                        to contemplate moon landings
                        your weight one-sixth the usual
The stone cool and conforming

Is there still time for Mars?
Oh, if only the machines are willing!

And think of Venus

and what it would take to terraform

She is there, of course
The best goddess you have ever channeled!
With what ease have you acquired her persona!
And what *trials* you have made of simple courtship
        that could not be an ordinary romance

She is that queen
        beyond whom there *is* no further royalty
        and certainly no contest   a trance
Whoever enters will understand
        be it Tannhäuser
        myself

But in love with you   living *through* you
        there is singing of approximate opera
        and alliance made with guests of Beauty

Though the West is in decline   the *Old* West persists
        in grown-up Nevada
        at the edge of its cities it starts
        and is as it once was
        Razorback and its haunted summit
one of that era's surprising props
its walls not worried too much

There *has* been a collapse of expectations
        and nothing   else is known of redemption

There's no enthusiasm for a paradise world
        for what could be if the soul's set free
It was never Intelligent Design
But the patterns of the swatch of cloth up there
        make moot the proposition
        straightforward and flapping
        in the glare of my spotlight

And illumining the banner
        is like a caressing of the Truth
        you notice how energizing is acceptance
        all sideshows in abeyance

What I wish to talk about
What's *interesting* here
    in the middle of the night
        up and down this peak
            are the answers to questions
                unique to this landscape
The dollar being worthless in the wilderness

Thank you, Great Spirit of a gloriously alien religion!
The cities made you inaccessible   remote
    even coming here
    one's timing's off
        the seeker's gifted with obscurity

This is why   coming close to this banner
    in the atlas of the world
        there is so much desire to take it
        bring it back
        bring it *elsewhere*
For I would covet the inexplicable
                doing worse than improving

There would be no rebuke
The Universe has allowed for all possibilities already

It stays in place   that I might stay sad at least
    though in some way undeterred

The show has begun
The main show prepared for conception
That birth
    that ticket assigning a seat
        in the eighth decade since

The Basin-and-Range of Nevada's made allowance
    and twists the facts of Civilization to suit
        our sickness
        to become an epidemic of kindness

There's a blackout for now
    with gentle chants *sympathetic* to our quest

the clear waters of springs' urging
            insight's authenticity
Thoughts intensely familiar
            yet fresh as the westerlies   arriving Sahra's Peak

A balm of wisdom
        that one may never parse
                beyond knowing someone cares

75.   THE HOLOGRAM CITY

You *can* make this up
It's science fiction already established
                        and taken over the valley
                            the high-tech conclusion
                            to low-tech's life span

A time to call a city an illusion   a *projection*
Vision right *now*
        like a pre-owned future
        it radiates recycled blue-and-purple
And its white lights are a tarnished purity
                        what God left out of the Plan

It's better this way   for it's a town we understand
        curving 'round the playa
                with secrets secular
Who is not persuaded geometry is sufficient beauty?
Islam was sure
        and entered into a *surfeit* of glorious design!

From the top of Razorback Mountain
        bring the Hologram City closer
            with 10-power binoculars   all you have
It isn't Palomar Observatory but see what you may see
                    uncertainly
                    unsteadily

                        the better to imagine
                        Plato's "forms"
                what was intended
            like a show
            the edit
        the final cut of near supernatural activity

Three months ago they came
Laid it out   all the streets
        shooting guns in the sun   uncostumed
        being sure the day would come
                when all their hard work was electrified

Agitation strove for a foothold in all this
Consolidated carnival instincts
            the whole world arriving
            after the fashion of representative wizardry

The Hologram City is indirect
        coming to the fore like a ghostly cyber flow
And it flutters in the glass
                    ensemble's streaks beheld

And indoctrination by shamen
        gone incognito   even to themselves
            in the spaces
            between the lamps
                of Black Rock's galaxy grid
    The comets kicked out in parabolas
                        and very hopeful of returning

The city is a transparency
        held in place through the efforts of Isaac Azimov
        preparing "jumps" to Trantor
            the Center
                the Eye of the Foundation

Nice way to get around when you think about it
In a *Fifties* kind of way   *"I get around..."*   that song
        so improbable, make that impossible

Is it dangerous down there?

A double exposure.
        how the overlap of lights
                coexists with Nature's dark
Close Encounters of the first   second   third kind
                                and counting

Counting to the stars   and
                what it would take to get to them
It *could* be done even now   Knowing what we know
Though after forty thousand years
                        the crew might certainly tire

And we're already asleep   even now
No need to knock us out for the sake of arriving
        Proxima Centauri and its super-Earth
                or anything else that may be found
Uh, slow down...
If it's a *planet* we wish to find
                        what's wrong with right *here?*

The hologram
        like a dream of Frank Herbert's
        when a Third Stage Guild Navigator travels
        travels without moving
                just by "folding Space" with all that spice
                        outstanding!

David Lynch, you are forgiven
You made me believe it!
        Jose Ferrer looking worried
                by the threats made to his person
                as Emperor

I'm a baby up here
        fresh from ultrasound
And *look!*
        mothers and fathers of all persuasions
                vie to raise me
An infant of this nightscape
                yet strong enough to bargain with owls

The glowy hologram's my crib

Asking for help is the hardest thing
       the desert would disseize
       but the city   like a flower   sustains
          needs met

It's blue-and-white sploshed down
       with hints of a purple identity
          and colors   *all* the colors
          publish themselves
             and *annex* their light to the light of ages
Like a down payment on Infinity's spectrum

Gravity's a constant
       that Unified Theory cannot embrace
And Gaia pulls   like a vow to continue   in place
Open up to all possibilities
How time machines are nothing more
          than knowing the force that attracts
          is the same *now*
             as it was in any epoch of BCE

Nobody's *died*, even!   started!   ever *finished!*
The front and backyards of yester were extended
       wherever the world went

We do not require a map to see the sandlot planet
Only walk like a child
          oblivious of the north   the south
             the east and the west
So that "lost" is the begging and every step taken
          till you come to the Hologram City
                   bewitched
                   bemadamed
                by the night's cold currents

It's time to set aside the fears of first grade
The anxiety you knew   and discerned in others

Obsessed with the circus
       summon Ray Bradbury
       as a guide
          so that additional chapters of *Wicked* appear

Point to the city, now
        a sorcerer casting a spell on *illusion*
            living in Pretend World
            the Real World is safe
                        and continues

Thinking it could disappear
Wink out of the gray terrain
        like the Donner Party   starved

Only the new millennium has promised immortality
        promised plenty despite oppression
                epiphanies in all the *wastelands*
Has wished everyone good luck
Has warded off extreme danger
                        banished slim chances

Let there be music where none is heard
Despite voices saying,"You have to get out of here!"
        no one moves
        and brass symphonies sound
                quite determined
                    like hard fighting with headlines later

The night is very entertaining
        even with one's eyes closed
The right question is:
                "What exactly are you doing?"
            and if you cannot answer
                    then just turn up the volume
                        on discord and anti-science

It is immediately depressing to depart from the Now
        that which has been your friend and advocate

I am happy to behold the dappled distance
The heart of a techno displacement
Hear the Cosmic Sounding Line strummed!
        single-stringed
        like a Chinese impulse
                unleashed by the pentatonic scale

185

Write it down we have experimented
        here in the desert
                whole cities planned in a few short days

I've made good on a pledge to Sahra
That I'd climb here
        the mountain that's news and authority
            whose editorials define fantasia   relief
                            the cessation of pain

And the strenuous effort required is a *welcome* trek
        that updates resolve
                stabilizes despair
                    allows its composite vexations
                        to be culled   one-by-one
                            until there's a summit
                            and nothing higher

With housing costs being so exorbitant
        a home on Razorback is smart
        Smart and Final like a reassuring ad

The Hologram City spread out
            like a blue-and-white executive action taken
                        by countless angels

76. WEDNESDAY'S LAMPLIGHTERS PRECEDED
BY CORDWOOD

With Brubeck in the background
        and cordwood in the foreground
                it comes to pass the Lamplighters pass
On a Wednesday   the *only* Wednesday
        of a week in play
2016's version of the festival

Festival?   yes, after a *fashion* of festival

But truly, this is a "Praise the Lord!" version
         as many lords — oh, and ladies, too —
                  as would fill all of England with importance
                  an *elitist* crew

They have left   in the lurch   those other celebrations
The ones with too much to do in too little time
What drains and enervates
         and we needed non-profit to recover
         that is why this *tabula rasa*

Now, in fading Wednesday
         the volunteers file
                  looking liturgical in their gowns
                  a Passion Play   Act 3
                  the journey to Golgotha
                           with those beams on their shoulders
The horizontal part of the cross bourne
With lanterns

Multiple saviors enroute to dubious salvation

But this isn't really fair, is it?
Someone must light the streetlights of Burning Man
         the ubiquitous kerosene hanging
Never mind there are now far brighter lights in town
Sights the early Nineties never imagined
Forget   that the lamps' feeble light is barely a glow
                  there they go

Dutifully   into a dusty twilight.   devoted they go
         each an acolyte of olden days and lesser bling
                  even the color of fire seems old fashioned

The cordwood's stacked against the chill
Moot kindling gathered
         for survivors   two seconds from nearby RVs

And fires are attended by voyeurs
         but never mind, this is not a complaint
                  the buildings are collapsing
                           that held the idols

We're left with brand-new nervous systems
        systematically destructive
        but in a good way

It's nice to be in a state of flux
Brubeck's to blame
            for bulging and denting the meters of music
            going 7/8 and 5/4
                when he *could* have taken it easy

Oddity's triumphed
Oddity is growing
        barely anything's repeated
            it will even transpire class warfare erupts
            and White Ocean be polluted 2017
                with envy and zealotry

In the high times of early Black Rock
When the arch humor of The Cacophony Society was
And opera was sung by a solo soprano
        White Ocean's experience of vandalism
            sabotage accomplished by Burning Man
            by fellow citizens, even   well
It would have been barely imaginable

The White Ocean's DJ extravaganza
        its beautiful dancing   tremendous sound
        opposed!   rebelled against!
        cables cut!   water, lots of it, emptied!
        doors to trailers glued shut!   hell, yeah!

Can't help seeing the progression
The change   it may be entropy starting   next year

So light the lamps of course
            conservative   right of radical
            a serious,
                but by no means deleterious,
                slowing down a bit

So that "radical inclusion" means more than the latest
        the latest being sold beyond barter and gifting

Warm yourself
        satisfied the firelight
            the oldest lumen
                sends imagination nicely along
Dave is accompanying   the heart in tandem

The ensemble the same teamwork that makes work easy
        and then we know better
            what to do in emergencies
                late night
                any night the fascists take over
                    and have to be removed
                    any way possible

Drives me out of my mind   the *vigilance* required
Let's watch them till they're gone
        the cordwood ready
        to fire the burn barrels set up

Watch all unfold   slow-motioning the scene to suit
Acting out   in concert   vicarious
            in the Christ cloth
            fire at the hem
All transactions pursued with passion
Right choices   wrong
        and the rest of the spectrum of decisions

But there is mainly one resolution Wednesday
        with the sun downing
        stay   or go   and it's "Stay!"
            the deciding factor neither background lamps
            nor foreground cord
Rather a screwball post placed and gosh!   what *is* it?

A metallic, coppery-zincky kind of weather vane
        still something *else*, though
                skinny   balletic
            coils on a base of bamboo
And a "Billion Bunny March" sign attached

Screen everything!   see what's unintended in 9/8 time.

77. TWO CAMPS, TWO CONCEPTS

Two camps
Two concepts

Say they're refugees
And say anything else

That they're "Burners"
                    the latest term ·
                    for those who come here

Two kinds of refugees
Syrian   San Franciscan
        we're scanning the Voodoo Lounge
        and the Minstrels

Pretend they correspond
                    Voodoo   the UN's emergency
                    Minstrel, less stressed
                        just the City's refuseniks
                            serenading passersby
                            with the possibility
                                        of music for all

Voodoo working to spell the tyrants
            cultural aberration
                conservatism packaged
                    for a run at world domination

Minstrels   the purloined calm

Let a Caribbean imprimatur learn of Exile
And consider how dolls may be brought to bear
            on injustice
                    and after that   magic a rescue

Here   on the Esplanade
            cranes are ready to roll out of the crane pool
                to lift and enliven versions of migration
                and confront one another

I'm empty-handed
Compelled *to* store interpretations the old-fashioned way
        through later recollection
                downloading what's left of biological storage

But the best computer there is   *hand*-held
The best nano to come might end *confused*
        perplexed by the new century's screams
        their manyness and loca

And I think it's the very *sight* of tents
        that tells the 'why' of this obsession
                just *starting* another Burning Man day
                or later   stopping en route to some art
                                that is shining at noon

The canopies that rise and fall and billow
They commence to instill associations
        and longing for explanatory Voodoo   and minstrels
        for *connection*

Everything is seen
Everything is slowing down
        haste is turned to ordinary walking
        and *less* than that: a standstill
As if we're somewhere between a muse and a shaman

Time be a friend   and, *if* a friend
        allow a central quiet
        before the home stretch of conclusion

You have a right to conjure   *shh!*
The Cosmos whispers!   right here on Rod's Road!
Vacancy filled in
        with white-and-red checkered cloth
                magenta, yellow and black used well
Streamers   shelter
A small-sized hub of karma   centered with libations

It's calling!   inviting!   with its pale yellow logo
        but the bar is empty

only invisible mathematics at work
                              to make things right
                              large and small

And you know the voodoo's *strongest* on its own
        most intense then
                the furnishings
                      the carpet
                      charged
Those same trillions of dollars you hear tell of
                        having no power to purchase here

Refugees, you are welcome!
        to Unity's empathy
        the caves of the homeland
Be subsumed in ionized hospitality!

For whatever reason
No, for *every* reason
        two camps are adjacent relevance   balance
And to all that ragtime, jazz and cajun say, "Amen!"
As if a portion of Mardi Gras happened
        and the manufacturer's warranty had run out
                              on prim and proper

The way we want it?
Something like minstrels   and the Planet of Voodoo
Enlightenment sifted
        drifting like the oh-so-fine sand and silt so dry
              alkaline to your liking
              between white-outs   tan-outs

Let us think about a better world
        given these two camps' creative example
        after their conceptual energy
                        for it's crazy to do otherwise

Be sane   or we're not coming back to life *and*
        the 9-11 Towers
                won't reassemble their collapsible floors

Let there be discussion

Talk to me in a chosen language
Say what we truly need to know

78. IT CAME FROM... *SEATTLE!*

It came from Seattle!

But *wait!*   it *was* Seattle!
All of it in a hawk-car and beak-bus joined

They brought Puget Sound
        the Space Needle
                brought the box the Needle *came* in
                        brought Chief Seattle *himself!*

All of it all the way south and east
A rain-mobile subject to breakdowns and downpours

They brought Lake Union
        Lake Sammamish
                Mercer Island
                        brought the Floating Bridge aboard

It's all there and jostling for room
With a collective totem heart
        beating north-by-northwest
        in the winds

They even brought a little Longfellow along
        his "forest primeval"
                what's left of it
                a tally of timber
                a green account kept track of   travelling

Forty miles-an-hour, no faster, into arid Oregon
Into the spaces of summer   with hot springs
        its fresh water added to alkaline flats

Yes, it came from Seattle   all of Seattle on board
And it may never return

But if it ever does
        it will have brought something back
        the other way going
                Burning Man having hitched a ride!

79. THOSE CRANES AND WHAT THEY'VE SEEN

The immune system weakens with age, right?
Whatever   but don't bring it up   it's a party
It's not only early age
        but early in the week, still

And *further*
Do not move about like one of those large cranes
        cranes that barely swivel
        and which have been known to crumple suddenly
                in cities   well,
                anywhere the wind goes gusting

Their work is mostly done
Though they'll be positioned later   en masse
        when the privileged few
                can see Burning Man's apotheosis
                and be high up
                        higher than *he* is
The utilitarian's exalted   its uses exhaustive!

Someday *I'll* take a ride in the crane!
Be uplifted myself   jackknifed
        slow motion unfolded

We'd be a mixed crowd   like this party
Infrastructure and jet set

DPW·   for whom *nothing's* too fantastical
        and we'd all be red-eyed
        waiting on combustion
        the fires' furious tornadoes!
                counterclockwise in the dust
                as if they'd rewind the entertainment!

There'd be sandwiches and booze up there
The crane operator *careful*

Why are we yelling right now?
Oh!   the party, of *course!*
Pretend this is the way brains work   look around!
        together we are   with drinks spilling
                cranes not a part of things for the moment
                though always they have something to offer
                and may be quickly summoned

The party's like parole
        where the reason for your incarceration
                                cannot be recalled
                                only guessed at
                        but strangely
                you're sure that someone here may know

"Oh, there's sushi!
How unexpected!   thank you!   is it safe, really?
        it *looks* okay..."

If this is lucid dreaming
        she'll let me kiss her
                the Ukrainian drest in folk attire

Where else but Black Rock City
        may one discover someone
                from a faraway country
        working in a field you've never heard of?·

In perfect safety you converse   over olives
Over carrots and celery
        the Burning Man to-do list lengthening

In the party's corners
        an evening edition of daytime flirting
But the imagery of cranes returns
And come to think of it, they're right over *there*
                        part of the party, actually

Glad I came costumed
        my own crane motions   moot
            lots of things are happening
            it's wonderful!   it's Roman!
They're immune to confusion
And thinking clearly in spite of drugs
                    a kind of cold-turkey consciousness

"Really, you shouldn't have!" I said to Ukraine
        she was gifting me with homemade custard
"I certainly *should, should, should!*"

So many friends and so little time to learn their bios
        "oh, well"conclusions

Epicenter of a counter culture   *flourish!*
Continue on
        unhindered by conservative thought
                        what's saved for later

The splendid improv here gives the lie to assumption
Shows to be false a proposition: too liberal, too bad...
Can the untethered mind be made practical?
        or would it get too askew like the crane in a gale
                    lifting I-beams wrongly?

The finishing touch eludes, though
Can't settle   like the Sixties   adrift
So that we ourselves
        doing and wrongly unaware
            fail to swerve when danger's head-on

"Hi!   how many is this?"
"What?"
"How many Burns?   how many times?"
"Uh, well, er, ah – that's 'need to know'"

"But I need"
"To know?   oh, well   lost count
       hey, meet the bartender!
             he's the only one not inebriated!"
"Really?"
"Yes, our designated thinker
             his responsibilities are many"
"For instance?"
"Cranes, for instance
       he's a crane operator
             figures if he imbibes he'll forget   you know
             lose his touch, maybe
                   and the crane would plunge"
"Got it   and got *synchronicity* too
       between the raw fish morsels
       I was seeing those cranes over there
                         imagining what *they've* seen"
"Funny you should say that"
"Oh   why?"
"I'd been trying earlier to explain that word to the camp cook
       but it was too noisy!"

Noise...
"I'm immune   noise and everything else"

Immune   no swivelling
       the crane subsumed in techno
             the party like a battery
             to power whatever age is desired

That first step must take you beyond or take you nowhere
Building in the dark a breakable highrise

Privilege is simply *being* here
       and borrowing a little from Hippie belonging
             the question, "How 'bout a beer?" *unasked* still

80. THREE WICKER WOMEN LONGING FOR RUM AND COCA-COLA

Given how precarious will be existence
And how always are boundaries overstepped
The gray creatures
        silhouetted in twilight's sky
          will lead
         like three wicker women
           robed for effect
Their combustible bosoms are reassuring

They are straw "wilis" from ballet   and spindly
    with longings mysterious
    but it's affordable danger
       their attention drawn
         to the "Rum and Coca-Cola" wagon
           weaving and veering

They're dressed in dyed pima
Outsized togetherness
    with twigs a semblance of sign language
             broken meter waving

Talk a story concerning life in the forest
And then that forest transplanted
    growing
    enwrapped
Having the power to adapt to catchy tunes wafting

The boombox nears
The better to serenade the installation
    which *does* have a name
       the artist has assigned one
       something to do with trees   I've forgotten
Who remembers all that's desired?

Yet the work has slipped the bonds of any title
And teeters   provocative
    a full *range* of suggestion

The artist set in motion
        these trees   anthroform yearning
            for the sound of this music
Though instinct insists they've been here for years
They look brand-new   and just arrived the Artery
                            the open playa
                being spirits everywhere

Who's making a case for Immortals?
It's really simple
Look upon their forms as argument
        for Legend's common cause with Fate
            with their capital letters and capitol cities
            in the clouds of childhood

Some stormy fantasy-morning of one's youth
Seeing landscapes in the sky
        placing trees like these witches three
                that may thrive and have dominion

There was no hesitancy
        populating the cumulonimbus
            no castle could sink
                but effortless drift
                abiding the jet stream

The music is *Rum and Coca-Cola*
Arriving to enliven
        and the pleasure of the wicker women is obvious!
        they would annex
            and take captive
                the crowd of revellers aboard the artcar!

Take it all   and give back supernatural ability
            the pulse of folk-consciousness
            crackling
            kindling omniscience
                broadcasting as open-air hospital
                bed rest in desert breezes
Whatever ails you to steal away
        and pester other climes

It's a good thing!
A quirky juxtaposition
But just as in dreams
        when symbols aren't compatible
        yet a deeper bond is possible
                and protects those most vulnerable students
                    of magic's delicate branches

What exactly do you see in silhouette   so eerie?
Cousins of the baobab
        the formal wear of bundled sticks

The artcar has accelerated
        traveling a little zigzag above the posted
        but slow enough to stymie Doppler
            whose effects are reserved
                                for trains of the realm

And louder voices continue
"Rum and Coca-Cola, sipping..."
        the young soloist
                the trio of hoary hags
                    going for a composite womanhood
A synthesis to sound the notes of all-inclusive
The cycle's stages immediate
Dark clouds   light skies
        so joined that remembrance is moot

What becomes a poplar or stays a twig

Music's sent the wheel away
            to seek karma that's commensurate
            and is not to be disturbed or detained

It might be a single Siren's at large
        with alcoholic subterfuge and wary
She makes her appeal   in the downtime of impressions

Please let us simplify slumber such
        it's the waking dream
The Masonic order of E Flat Major
        Mozart's key to the secret society

This time it's women holding rites
Their own *Magic Flute*   in three-part harmony mostly
        maybe a Sarastra instead of a Sarastro
        exalted juvenile lady of olly olly oxen free
        loosely guiding   head-on

Drink the rum and Coca-Cola
There's nothing A.A. can do, don't worry!
Living in Pretend World
                    the Real World is safe

Clear enunciation has the trees swaying   "participatory"
        that word with so many syllables
            saying it is enough
            one doesn't have to actually participate
Unless it's to take an inventory of branches and twigs
And while you're at it   count the rings   knots
                                and grafts, if any

Divert the attention of the lead singer
        Karaoking to a bygone hit parade
            out   if not on the town
            at least on its outskirts   swishing crazily
                in concert with forests come to life

Science is waiting on a ceremony worthy of its high IQ
Build   manage   join us now!
We wish to hear your voices swell
        to a choral version of a mixed drink
            in a country of dreams

We have travelled a highway wide as Nevada
        no agenda
            just an appetite for doom honoring loved ones
There is no resistance
And the desert articulates a solitude inherent
        though a party's in progress
        roving to equivalent togetherness

That party's best that's a little bit lonely
                    revelers try harder to be civil

                         welcoming cobwebbed trunks
                                and mobile roots

How far is it to Burning Man?
Far as all the roads there are
        when you may chance upon a runaway surrender
            like tumblers of a safe   and safe journey
            cascading

No traffic, no problem
You might remember to signal
        otherwise you're good to go
                anywhere the rum and Coke can take you

Though I'm nescient
        this is such a teachable moment
                        I'm liable to learn

Oh, witches!
        wilis!
                Druid dames!
Own the stitching of the day and the night!
                        waltzing at the edges

No rain will fall
It is rampaging youth   a harvest
The artcar's arrived and pirouettes about
        it wants stop-motion
                and being joyous in a studio of fading light

The trees' capes are compelling   appealing
A *trio*   an incitant   albeit gray, august
Their triple threat informed by lighthearted abundance
        of rum and Coca-Cola combined
        and combining ancient and whatever else

And the wicker women longed
                for just that refreshment

81. WITH ORANGE, STRETCHED

With orange, stretched with wonder
       the strangest color played out as swings
      thin as the early years   no *seats*, even
    pencil lines crossing   recrossing
         a cat's cradle in the dusk
All triangles possible   being a sketch having fun
       with its very own geometry

Have mercy, Pythagoras!
The children have gone
    having other desires that are a thicker orange
    substantial   brighter

This   *outline* of a place has more than orange
And as the day dies down
       pale green   and even blue accompany
      each color flashing
    scintillations
Without which those spidery strands go unseen
    for their meager width required strobes

The swings were *intention*
String theory only
    and no seats   to complete the attraction

I want to click a microphone
    and broadcast
    the playground's warranty may have expired
      and become a theory of mere amusement
     a delicate trapeze
      cross-hatched with benign

There has never been a better time
    to study fiber optic nerves stretched taut
Lines like the lines from Here to There
That spoked medieval maps
        with those serpents in the sea
Gossamer's measure of distance a microcosmic web
    waiting on some sort of entangling interaction

Welcome to the show
　　　that qualifies as diagram
　　　　　breaking the law of the pendulum
　　　　　in lacking a clapper
So its weightless gravity will not play a part
But think differently
Strumming the unnamed instrument　　pulsing palely

A fluttery impromptu
　　　　　or the heartbeat of sprites displayed

On encountering minimalist art
　　you want to reduce the transactions
　　　　the to-do lists
　　　　　　all the oughts and shoulds
　　　　　　　all of *storage*
　　　　　　　　the inventory of toys
Counting the hours we'd rather create
Counting coup when no one is there

You want to halt the Five Million Year Plan
The conquest of Space
　　　the memorization of religious tomes
　　　　being terrified of outcomes
　　　　　the pursuit of high school skinny

And if it's Mozart you would play　　"Keep it simple, stupid!"
The A.A. takeaway echoing
　　the braincase meant for marbles *only*
　　the uses of the "purie"
　　　the flick of the thumb brought to bear

Let arguments cease
And "No fair!" be unnecessary protest
　　for orange and friends　　(blue and green)
　　　they've agreed　　stretched
　　　and connected
　　　　downsized the installation's medium
Its substance narrowed to piano wire
　　　　waiting on a pantomime recital

Espirito santo
So finely spun is its enchantment
                         Espagnol will be invoked
                         the charge that language has
                    and which lends holy thoughts

Was it well-financed?
Did the Organization see to it
       make sure the installation got built?
Exactly what was said?
Is the artist friends with Larry Harvey?

Oh-oh!   he doesn't exist
Burning Man has said so
       once   on entering   the sign was neatly printed
             no question about it

The answer's like a tungsten filament   winking
Bleak neon concept:
       the fact that atoms get excited
             does not require more than this example

Electro-luminescence!   wonderful!
The heart-and-soul of Black Rock
       a strangeness so moving a craving develops
       enjoyment like a proof of some heaven

Pretend this austere suggestion
       was made to Amerindian spirits   weakly
             then it's hard to know who or what
Could BC have fashioned this?

If it's simple enough   the mind will succeed.
Community will
       grandfather
             grandmother
All the great, great, great, greats relevant

There's a secret kept but I'll tell you what it is, yes
The truth is it's sometimes said by all
The *desert* is the reason this city's set up
The lakebed   its edges   those lonely summits

205

How the playa seems stretched as well
        like a drumhead to bounce us
                throb in time to those flashing lines
                swing lines   the nominated frequency

The "trampoline" is flat
                but what's the profile below the silt?
                what's under that hard-baked mud?
Unknown   because it's "need-to-know"

And we're bare and barren   an isosceles thicket
Think it through
        gently as geometry can go
                your theorems doted upon
                crib proofs   no tears
Just baby talk in the dimming day
The pastels leaching so that color's a conception

Orange stretched   and blue and green
        monastary hues
        that some happy monk has made and saved
                signalling that shimmer!

Will he speak, his needles and pins aglow?
Can he come out and play?
Strict candy connecting the shortest distance found
                it is an ode to vacancy

There's no app to make "sense" of it
All the better
        part of the reason for sticking around

The way I read it
        the swing is encrypted
                colored toothpicks
                        from a pincushion haystack
I think their several gleams will catch on
Raise IQs   our brain waves to be in synch
                                with the flutter

Do you wish to see it?

you'll see
        see it solo if you prefer
        there's less pressure to approve
                                    or disapprove
And emptiness may better whisper
        its sweet neon nothings
                an art installation amusingly overreaching

Still no seats
Still a minimal privacy
                and two-second seance
Orange a truth
        and blue and green some kind of common sense
        stretched to the brittle breaking point

Keeping it tight   like a bible of three words only

Choose carefully the colors
        that will follow *their* recitation
                spare as these monkey bars
                        one side ghost of square
A scintillating wannabe playground

Sketch mind, stretch mind
        in charge just enough
                to hold it all together
                        no key required beyond kind intentions

82. LITTLE HOUSE

Too small for any politics, really
But there's actually *more* than one little house
        and they are charmingly steepled
                        the pyramids topping off

Their pointy roofs are head room
        for pointy *heads* perhaps

or dunce caps

They're drastically miniature
                penthouse properties
                there was zero discussion
        the CEOs moved in
Huts of high finance
            with executives *still* thinking big
                        yet confined to a doghouse

We're talking modest digs and their darkened doorways
The little house   or houses
        has   or *had*
        no discernable address   or addresses

Think "clump"   clump *of*   yeah
There are little windows
        diamond-shaped
            the square rotated slightly

A voice
"Come forward!"
        not exactly a command
        or an invitation
Once you *say* that   *anyone* says that   decide
        hypnosis?

There's something Russian about all this
Or Polish
        pertaining to Belarus
            or Ukraine
One of those East European places

Has to do with the construction
Those planks   the boards aligned
It seems the smallest peasant church
        its chapels join for prayers in tandem
            Russian Old Believers
            one to a cubicle
                to process the infinite Information Age

Here's the thing:

the installation's specific
though its evocations are many

Is it too late in the day to stay?
One night   no wake-up

Could be a baby opera house
A *reductio ad absurdum*
        divas sequestered
                no frills
                no rehearsals

Gnomes there be!
Little people full of purpose
            obsessed with privacy
How comfortable in there?
Never mind   think cozy   cozy
That's what we want to feel
        what we really wish to be
        even if it's war
                with bad guys everywhere
                    charming their enemies

It's a fact the dwellings attract
And Hobbits hope to enter into
They are very friendly   wanting shelter
        uninterested in any Tolkien plot
        when they might be trying to save Middle Earth
All they want to do is cuddle
No story need unfold that involves a ring

"Where's the property manager?"
            the question asked
            of a man who seemed to have access
Someone who may have knowledge of the cubicles

"You're looking at him   and *he's* looking at *you!*"
"*Speak* then, and tell us of the hovels"
"They speak for themselves   they've made the news!"

One could not help being drawn to the house or houses
It was announced that time would no longer flow forwards

but backwards
so that "next time" would be "recent" instead

The goal was to observe the *building* of the little house
Or   houses
see the pre-existing condition of construction

Someone *else* said, "You'll need a ratchet for that..."
And there was silence   uncanny   supernatural

I thought of Crimson Rose   all the art she's seen
How she could get anything done   *really*   it's true
She could have hynotized Stalin
I can still see her ballet
high on the famous wooden figure
Burning Man before he burns down

Hold on!   "Rosie"of the Artery   the go-to angel!
Bet you helped with little house
or houses
Gave assistance   helped position and raise
As you made easier my own efforts in 2001
two weeks before the Towers fell in New York City

And it was a cozy house /&/ made as well
Called "Psyche's Windows"
the structure was an octagon
a gazebo with fabric   and a bed
and lots of fiber optics glowing
There was a piano nearby
A giant spool   sofas and armchairs
music, too
Rachmaninoff's *Vespers*

A place to go after all else had failed
A home for Psyche after being banished to the wasteland
for the fault of gazing at Eros
the Windows' *raison d'etre*
but no one turned away

83. IN THE BMIR HAMMOCK

It was a lot more than a simple sling
Once in the hammock and swaying
And the soothing broadcast underway
        the experience became
        "If only *this* were the week, it's enough"
Information pouring out of the station
                like a soporific happening
                            zen-designed

Such was the hammock's suspended belief
        that waking dreams began
                and were successive   overlapping
                    abeyance combining wonderfully

With the baritone drone of the DJ
        introducing   commenting   complaining
        conferring with very special guests

And those who lounge
        or stroll
                or are in and out
They enjoy a certain levitation

Radio is like that sometimes
Disembodied   pure invention
        an experience of the astral
                one's significant other a cocoon of sound
                all economic theories forgotten

And closing our eyes
        a hammock gifts bluish-purple
        a watery darkness that's a meditation's oasis

There is no *news* in the hammock, either
No Russia   no USA
        and all other borders
                become the scribble of strands of yarn
                unravelling a loose signature

International   yet the province of the mind
                                    and all its skyrockets
            part of the story   *and*
                there are many parts

How lucky there's thought
And that Burning Man Information Radio is a serendipity
        one that's a gentle rocking
            and feeling you're good at something at last
                like capturing leprechauns

Not even budgeting one's time
                the *hours* fill your fifteen minutes of fame!

There was just that hammock
        when poetry was no longer desired
        when it was seen enough had been said already
There'd been a surfeit of all else as well

No tension   no violence
And the shade was good
        those others present
                    not close to anything serious
                    a guileless demeanor   endearing
And we are all enclosed in a sound-nest of many timbres

Do you *really* think you'll be able to leave?
 So damn comfortable?
It's what you bought the *ticket* for!

Pretend this intimate setting's a brand new family
        well-met in the Congo
                or wherever hammocks are strung
                    anywhere it's pennyless by *choice*
                                    by *design*

A locus where *stringendo* and *largo* are combined
C'mon!   the basics are musical!
        though treble and bass are absent parameters
Musical even if the sharps and flats are missing

It all starts   *everything* starts   with a pattern

212

For me it was the pattern of a flowered wall
        when the nursery first came into focus
        and eyesight began its long journey to cataracts
Odd that a waterfall's conflated with failure

Is the relationship real?
And might a one-year-old contemplate "fetal alcohol"?
            can we leave "syndrome" out of it?
How about *everything* out of it!

The BMIR hammock's enough reunion with infancy
A soft crib and no complaints
        certainly no tantrums

Or think this is AWOL from reform school
                once they learned of the bomb plot

Drink some water
        because there is that voice again...
            "You must drink again!"
For dehydration is possible
                even if there isn't a thirst
                the word you need to learn: "water"
Remember, you're a baby and need to find out

But to bestir oneself!
The bottle's in the backpack
        the backpack's draped   out-of-reach
Okay!   "Yes!" to the Playa Voice!
                that's always, *always* there
                            everyone hears it

Think of all the other things the Voice is telling us to do
        besides *"Drink...drink"*
Especially in camp   reminding us of chores, errands
It's like that list come to life and giving orders
        the list compiled   pre-Burning Man
            the list always added to

"Water! you...must...drink!"
And now   careful not to lose the hammock
        abruptly spring

snatch the green Gatorade
and as quickly flop back
the hammock still your own

Once more swaying
listen some more   new technology the topic
BMIR informing

You let the sandwich proffered put you to sleep
The snack gifted by a brand-new friend
The radio will govern a lucid *dream* of the new technology

On waking
you discover you've powered a spaceship
first interstellar craft to reach the Capella system
The guest is gone and the station's playing jazz
Jazz like Dave's piano played in Medina
Medina, Ohio   how long have I known him?
so *many* songs he's written!

Medina, where his smart poodle ran
on the spacious suburban lawn
And there's not much difference
The desert jazz is near to his own
He had a big reach
and easily found his way through the changes
it was mostly ten notes at a time
all ten fingers

Essential questions   beautifully unanswered
Extraordinary heat told to wait till later
At the end of the hammock's hour   some PSAs
those public service announcements, *oh!*
there have been quite enough of those

Never mind!   leave it alone!
Our happiness and sadness needs no attention!
no bulletin!
serendipity's subsidy
what's slung and enjoyed
entirely suspended
utterly instant   and *staying* that way

214

84. THE "BABY" STORY RECOUNTED

The story would be told again
This time to a radio audience
It's fun to be on-air at least once per Event
    and easy enough, too
       five minutes on a mic   that's all you need!

The story has morphed in the telling
Has changed a little at a time with repeats
      what year it was is forgotten

No, wait!   Caravanserai   *that* Burning Man
2014   just two years ago
    and I volunteered for something

"Put on this orange shirt
    it means you'll be staff, sort of
      you'll stand out
      you'll be out*standing!*
The gig is: let no bicycles into the souk"

Souk?   that was the Arab market
        centered as circumference
        the iconic wooden statue
             surrounded

They were insistent
"Keep the bicycles back
    Burning Man must stand alone
      no traffic   they walk   *got it?*"

We had gotten it
My friend had also volunteered
    and we'd reported   been assigned
"Guard here, guard there
      nobody passes on wheels   that's the deal"

Ah, it's all coming back
So just climb the stairs and enter the studio   BMIR
    relate what happened

the DJ's interested and eager to have you

A song finishes   he introduces and cues
My earphones are snug and I find myself talking
        a little nervous   but the nerves would help
        94.5   it was time to tell them
        it went as follows, sort of

"When my friend and I arrived the souk
        there were other orange shirts
                and no bicycles got through
The shift was four hours
The late hours   but not the early

"The only thing I'd ever volunteered for
                        after the hot springs patrol
I'm just not a volunteer type, that's all
But this had been enjoyable

"The night was not cold
        and my friend was pleased I'd joined him out there
The job was easy   no bicycles
And there was that very tall Man
                standing in the ambient glow

"Presently, a couple appeared
They'd been riding this double bike carriage thing
They were parked at the edge
        and there was what seemed a bundle in the back
        it looked like a kind of papoose
        was that a baby, perchance?
                        I was totally intrigued

"I approached
'Hey, guys!   I apprecite your not bringing the bike in
        but, uh, just out of curiosity   is that an infant?'

"They smiled
The guy goes, 'Right! the lateness of the hour
        Oh, I know what you're thinking
        bring a baby out here in the middle of the night?
        with dust devils prowling?

216

and is that the best choice?"

"I waited

"'Don't worry,' he said   'it's a robot baby from China!
The latest model newborn from the People's Republic
          no, really!   fills a need
          the elderly and the not-so-elderly
      sometimes they just miss having a baby around
      but they don't want to be changing diapers!'

"I gasped, 'What?   for real?!   you kidding?'
I looked   the guy said, 'No, not kidding!'
          and I continued looking
          it had very pale blue eyes, whatever it was

"The husband and 'father' went on
'Very high tech!'
          and his wife added,
          'We're still learning all the things it can do
              superb programming!'

"'Oh, my!   but that's realistic!   it burped!'
          I marvelled, starting to believe for the first time
'Go ahead, say something   talk baby talk
          it's voice-activated'
So I went 'Koochy-koochy!'
And sure enough it turned its little head
          and the eyes seemed to look right at me
                              and even twinkled!
                        'Jeez!' I said

"'Now pinch those cheeks,' the woman said
'You'll find they feel just like an actual baby's'
I did   and she was right   the thing even smiled!

"Minutes had gone by
          what an accomplishment
              I knew Burning Man had its techy-nerds
              but this baby was off-the-hook
I stared some more and played with the machine

"And then   and then...
        I suddenly turned to the couple
            'That's, uh, that's a   er, uh...'
They smiled   with unabashed mischief
        as they heard me ask
            slowly   haltingly
                'Uh, that's a real baby, *isn't* it?'

"Then there was laughter   *uproarious* mirth!
Oh, they got me, all right
        and their child even joined in   going 'Goo-goo!'
                and making other silly noises

"We parted eventually
They were quite satisfied with the joke, of course
I said, 'Very amusing   you guys are good
        you really put one over!   *yikes!*'
We waved goodbye and I resumed the guarding

"But after experiencing their excellent deception
        I was determined to fool someone myself
                and I waited
Waited for the spaciest Space Cadet to wander by
It didn't take long!

"'How's it going, dude?'
'Awesome!' came the reply
        he was definitely oblivious
                you could tell he'd believe anything
                            with those dilated eyes

"'Bet you're wondering why the crowd,' I said
He wondered   '*Yeah*, there's sure a lot of people here!'
'Well, it's like this
        I'm here to help with crowd *control*
        becase the Man is going to *walk* tonight!'
'He *is?*'
'*Oh*, yeah!'
'Really?'
'Really!'
'That's so awesome   when?   when?!'

218

'I paused and gazed up
                    at the highest Burning Man ever
                    precarious assemblage!
And then gestured grandly
'When, you ask?   soon, soon
        they are working on the gyros
                wouldn't want him to fall *over* or anything!
                you can understand that!'
'Oh, for sure!'

"So we're on Playa Time   it's whenever they're ready'
'Wow!   well, *where's* he gonna' go, dude?'
'Ah!   a ranger told me he'd walk around the souk
        you Know, maybe once or twice
                in a big circle
                        then return to his usual spot'

"The Kid was impressed
'That's going to be so fantastic!
        do I have time to tell my camp?'
'Maybe,' I said
        'but there's no certainty
                might be five minutes from now
                or five hours   Playa Time
Maybe if you're quick
                how far away are your friends?'

"He had to think hard about that   and then
'Oh, yeah!   Snowflake Village, *that's* where we are'
'Well, that's right on the Esplanade
        worst case   you don't make it back
                you can see the show from *there*
                then, too,
                in case the stabilizing gyroscopes fail
                        and the Man falls over
                                you'd be safe!'

"He looked relieved
'Oh, boy!   thanks for the clue, I mean, the heads-up!
        I can't wait to tell the others
                funny, though   it wasn't in the... in the
                what do you call it?'

'Schedule?'
'Yeah, schedule   why wasn't it in there?"

"'No, no   it's supposed to be a surprise'
'Well it sure is!' he said   and vanished
      before I could tell him otherwise
                              from what he'd heard

"Disappeared misinformed
      my bad
            no   my good BMIR broadcast!
Go and do likewise
Not just April Fool's
      but fools of all the months

'And let our jesters be a geneology of pranks
                        extending to ultimate entropy"

85. THE GREEN TRIPLE-DECKER BUS

"The green triple-decker is tilting   it *is!*   Look!
It's not?   well, it *seems* to be
Yes   maybe it's only sagging one side
      some struts, some springs
      some suspension gone   but it's undoubted

"Is it safe?   look, before we board   answer *that*"
"Don't look at me in that tone of voice!"
"The bus is bent to starboard
      sure you want to ride this thing?
            to the junkyard?
                  to recycling?   oh, all right"

"Yeah, that's more *like* it!   hop on
            there are worse ways to come to grief
            we'll find out where the bus is going
The very impressive green triple-decker!

220

"Changed my mind, it's 'No'"
"Why?"
"If everyone shifts to the sagging side we're over for sure!
This means a lot to you, right?   I give up
        let's do this, you win
            we're still going
            I'm getting on!"

"By the way, there are girls
        never mind that other stuff you're worried about
            we'll save 'em when the thing tips over
            won't *that* be fun!
Maybe we can let you drive"

"You know, all this desert's made me mad, I tell you
        made me want a forest of cedars to enjoy
                            and all that shade
This is like an arid London   a London *vanished*
        except for this green triple-decker"

"And let us not forget the pianist, Michelangeli
Lost in the *Brahms-Paganini Variatons*
        we were listening   just last night
            we heard him practicing
            captives wondering how he did it
By the time he'd mastered all the tricks
                    your London town was deserted"

"Yes, we'd learned the *Variations*, too
Playing them slower, of course
There was nothing but the word of the teacher to go by
        bye-and-bye
            we'd gone from beginners to virtuosi
                by the time a new sunny day arrived"

"The music's made us ready to ride
We're prepared for the leaning green triple-decker bus
        the mechanic will come along
            be given a place of honor
                with all his tools aboard *and* his assistants

"Oh, *ponderous* transport!
I've brought some grapes for us
        green ones
                special for you
Try not to think we're taking chances
        though it's three storeys careening
        five miles-an-hour is all we go
                        stopping   starting
                        no ticket is required"

"But wait a sec!
This is your *dream* we're in
The one you described
        the bus built by your nuncle
                yes, that's what you called him
                with that extra 'n' hanging around
                        sure to mislead

"And it's green like you said
How did it go from a dream to this
        unless we're *all* in your dream
                that's recurrent   obviously
                shouldn't we all be in bed?
                        everyone in sight?
                        should it not be bedtime at least?"

"I don't know   but interesting hypothesis...
Quick!   the camera for evidence
        the light's just right!"

"Hey, take a video as well, why don't you?"

"I'm hearing my grandfather exclaim,
        'Gallblast-it!
        if that isn't the doggondest contraption *ever!*
                never saw the like, nossir!'"

"He wasn't really that stereotypical, was he?"
"Not really   he might just have said,
        'So where we goin', kid?'
                        not that he'd join us"

222

"*We'll* join us!
The Dream Team now boarding rickety UK
          the same that barely survived the Germans
               now banished to the wasteland
                                   of public transit
                              green
                         and breaking down"

"And it's lonely despite the crowding, don't you think?
All aboard the imperial wreck!
          tokens real and imagined clinking
               their non-precious metal
                         falling down, down, down"

"And *what* has become of the 'motah cah'?"
"Aw, let the English *ahdvertise!*"

86. RANGERS, STAIRS AND ART

Well, they're droning, those Rangers
Droning   and drowning
          in the airwaves' watery medium

It's Ranger radio talk
          their updates   their pleas   their weather

Meanwhile, stairs are whispering,
               "Find me and climb me"
                    they seem to crowd in
                         taking over the mind
And those endless public service announcements
          are just a lot of background gibberish

Stairs!   where *are* you?
Stairs for the cardio-vascular deity
There *must* be floors around
          just as there is art around

and ready for the camera

Stairs and art
Be on the lookout
        getting what you wish for
            the essentials
            and no laptops   no costumes   no drugs

Just the Salvador Dali plain
                and all habits unplugged
Months every minute of this beautiful concentration

Get going
        and pay no attention to China
            though its pentatonic scale got your number!

87. THE MAN AMONG THE MANNEKINS

It was more than a story and not made up

There is a year to it: 2003
A neighbor girl has said
        there'd been a man who'd died
        died at Burning Man once

She was matter-of-fact
            or rather   she did not go on-and-on
            did not speculate too much
        like what would make a better Mexico
        or how about USA?
And yet she was very empathetic

It concerned mannekins
The story was mannekins as art installation
        and a man among them
                he'd hung himself with the rest
                and was not discovered till later

Someone said it was Art
        Metropolitan even
                but that was a hard sell

Was it some sort of posthumous promotion?
A bid for a life extended?
        a sustainable protest?

It *was* planned   certainly radical
                        certainly self-expression

The Internet will say it all
There'll be a name
        in the Big Book of Burning Man he's noted
        can we say, "In the annals..."?
His name   all that's known   what might have been

What to make of it today depends on a campmate
It is *her* account that matters
Her minimum outline that lets him live some more
        imagination's way

In this case history fails   the story's too strange
The actual event too perverse
                        distracting
And his art, if his suicide was that
        will be abstracted and sold as a mannekin is sold

He might have said:
"No matter what I do, I love you so much
        and I am proud of you   all of you
        I wanted to change
        and now I have
In ways that were impossible while I lived
Lived a life that was closed in both directions
        past and future
        the weather reports were always storms"

He was on top of his agenda
And he planned beyond detection
        macabre   evil

a cartoonish impulse
A *New Yorker* cartoon
One page away from the drawing of a church
        with would-be churchgoers
                gathered to read a sign that says,
                                    "closed for the holidays"

So he's secular in death
Listeners do not meddle with the narrative
No questions form   no one's taken aback
        almost as though *someone* would have ended up
                hanging with the mannekins
Someone sure of being   deep down   a dummy
        but a dummy who would *matter*

His course was elective
No grade   no teacher
        it was just his getting along with learning

Beyond a story
        her words accessed a World War's derangements
                when art is a law laid down
                that says, "To die is to live!"

Some fulfullment   branching such
        it will be thought an exquisite root
                a hangman's longing

Not since '96 had I heard anything as morbid
        when a morning FM micro-station blared
It was radio hate-speech
        an odd intrusion of intense animosity
        brought to the bedroom
                or anywhere evil could go to mate

It had nothing to do with not being right
        being a study in emptiness
                like mannekins caught in a mutual embrace
        clacking
                    dumbfounded   by love

He awoke with a rope secured

to what follows imagination
a grim melding with gravity's stopwatch

2003 is stuck
the century to cease and desist right there
A girl has said
who unlocked the zero his act acquired
and it was a dictionary of wants unrequited

Was he so uncomfortable
the final knot was troublesome?
Did he talk all alone?
Or did the mannekins listen with understanding?

Perhaps his recitation was harsh   with rebukes
Was he a Russian still in mourning for the Imperial Court?

His was a nihilism
with fashion ticking down the hours
preferring to create them
no matter how much trouble

What to wear when you die
or in striptease conclude
to be silent as flesh tones
and a lightweight body   unhydrated
A good impersonation
where the person's blank appearance's sake

And passersby declared
it was a subtle ensemble of the anatomical
and no matter how much they talked tough
the 'models' didn't mind
Were past caring   none fallen down desperate
Only a *Theory* of failure

While we don't have a full understanding of 2003
It is still her account that *matters*
her outline
the beauty of one sketch
the first drawing
submitted to the Artery

and Crimson Rose
responding   a nexus

Life and then death
        the secret proposal left out of the plan
        as *he* was left out altogether
                his hanging like an afterthought
                that's both portal and reset

88. TEMPLE, STAIRS AND SLINKY PEOPLE

It's just so easy to make bad choices
Around *here*, even
        there's only a week
        and you haven't been to the Temple yet
                                        so *now*
                                now would be good

Just install yourself among the memories there
Join the others sitting quietly
                embracing
                writing
                        someone, perhaps with a handmade flute

Get religion   just when it's forming
        when there are not yet any followers
                or scrolls to puzzle over
A religion of sunlight through slats and cracks
Warming   ambient
        so that the Temple's interior is teacher
        a physical *and* a spiritual shelter

This is easy also, isn't it?
Be closed-mouth and go   yes
                and now *would* be good

Later return to the stairs of Panorama

where the Slinky People practice
from the forty-fourth step
        practice flipping the rainbowed coil
        and trying   trying   for all-the-way-down

There are no birds above the playa
Sing your own flight over
        your own self as distance
            a long way empty
            yet with voices calling
                    that need no punctuation
Being artefacts aloft in search of museum space

The world is very real
        good friends   good choices

Black Rock City is a radial awareness
Its layout tending to vectors
        lines of sight from a single source
            the hub settled on
            one day of planning   over red wine perhaps

There is fixity   the map is year-to-year
You will not be lost
        you will not be forgotten

On the desert
        a sextet of cupcakes is spinning
            their chocolate machines just a color
Look out, they're fast!   and their batteries are fresh

The Temple is near
The sextet has whirled away
            no obstacles   Ganapati has removed them
Ganesha took care of it
        he protected
        there would be no collision

I wonder who's wandered by the Cuddle Puddle
Oh! but that's a dandy wayside
            and zoo of compatibles
            you believe and belong to the animals

There's only a week   and it *is* a test
The longer it seems
        the better you did
The only place where something can truly take forever
            and you'd still want more after that

I'm a roving art project
My artist set me loose
Said once I was created   and released
                the piece was anybody's guess

The artist is done
        and done for
            the work free to be restless
            as now   with voices indistinct
All is holographic and relationships are over

A Russian machine of the Great Patriotic War appears
It clanks in the dried mud of the lakebed
Intent on destruction, it's never stopped its advance
        though the Warm War *and* the Cold had ended

Now, as rogue armor
        its barrel trained on nothing in particular
            it fires blanks at the Temple   at random
            why?
Because I accidentally conjured it
Attempting to stay serious
To make the artist who made me wonder what's up
        question the art
                now on its own   on the move
                and possibly immoral

Is what was released a *worthy* construction?
        or a Frankenstein's body
                with no use for the Shelleys
                Percy or Mary

Was the couple glad to have been stranded?
Inconvenienced by the cold snap?

Switzerland it was that detained
        and they wrote and wrote and wrote with Byron

I'm going to stay soviet
At least until the crowd gathers
        and there in the Temple I'll forget offensives
            forget botched brain transplants

I'll know the peace
        not only of grandmothers and grandfathers
                fondly remembered
            but the myriad *other* loved ones
Cats and dogs in countless photographs
        framed
            each image personal for anyone who sees it

Not only those remembrances
But next lives   the other side
The so unseen it outsmarts genius
        but is kind to the dumb

Educates with stairs   stairs up to a top step
        where the Aten pours its sun-self
            on Slinkys
            ready to rainbow down
                    in short bright arcs of spooky plummet
Like a clever principle trying to explain itself
                        once-and-for-all

Will Anya be there next time?
Observing   helping   proud of the stairclimber
        who's climbing in the midst of all that competition?
        (there were always eight Slinkys going)

See a religion forming always
        but one that's not enough faith
                                to cause a ruckus

And   as if to annotate
The tank and all my artistic ascriptions
        have disappeared into a quasi-soviet daydream

No toll taken
　　　but a few inches of precious time and timeout
　　　　　the past and other times
T.S. Eliot refuses to speak to me
We're not, repeat, *not* on speaking terms
But we *are* exchanging ice cream cones
　　　from — wait for it — time to time

Goodbye for now to the Temple
Goodbye to the stairs　　*and*
　　　　　　the brave and powerful Slinky guys

89. THE BURNING BAND

There were quite a few of them
Many more than ever before

Just as the week now counts seventy thousand
　　　the Band has also added to itself
There were drums and trumpets
Everything a band is supposed to have
　　　　　　　　including a tuba

Some were playing less than others
Some had uniforms　　some did not
　　　　　　but the sound was freedom

Such a Band!　　Burning Band!
　　which stopped
　　　　all by itself
　　　　　　a totalitarian takeover
Since a band having that much fun
　　　　would never have allowed any otherwise

The cacophany was proof
　　their serenade successful
　　　　and Big Brother charmed

Don't know why or when or how
        but there can be no doubt
                the saxophone alone has been sufficient

And   you know   it was amazing
How hearing the Band
                had turned a tentative daydream
                        into actual snoozing
                                so restful, too, in spite of the racket

I'm snoring in Center Camp and feeling looked-after
                                                safe even

90, GLAM-COCKS, BIKES AND A GIANT CAR

Memory is tested

Memory's unhappy and wants back what's remembered
Having no way to *do* that
                the mind is making up its mind
                        and amending

That's all right   let it stray!
It won't get far and possesses no weapons

The subject is Glam-Cocks
        and how nothing is known about them
                how nothing may be recalled

Oh, it would be so easy
So easy to click and drag and search
Ten seconds   then
                whatever the Glam-Cocks were would be known

But that's no fun   that's not going to happen
Reason insists imagination's preferred

If they could not make any impression at the time
        and ended up as just a jotting-down
        "Glam-Cocks"   and nothing more...
Great!   we'll go from there
The notice never taken

Maybe and perhaps
        whoever they were   or are
        it's all about glamor
            glamorous cocks   and costumed
            cocks civilized yet undisciplined

There were probably bicycles
Many bicycles   there always are
        and they were probably riding them
        turning circles in the sand

There could have been a gathering of Glam-Cocks
Maybe they all piled into that giant car
There was a giant car   seen running around
                that is certain
                at least one
The sheer size of it
            letting adults drive to first grade again

"Glam-Cocks"   I kind of get it
        without a recollection
And so brazen a concept
            you want to strut just saying it
Don't you think   ideally
        you'd want to be a Glam-Cock though
                    for five minutes of your stay?

With so many other possible personas to be
        it's better without a memory   easier, simpler
            less time spent
Let's piece a version together
And say   right off
        that a Glam-Cock's soul should be sincerely "glam"
            all that's required

Let's have them letting it all hang out
On those bicycles maybe
        a gang of them
        going places all at once   to enthrall

Make them Canadian!
That red leaf worn
        Canadians are well-liked
        and I wanted the Glam-Cocks to be admired
            as much as possible

Can they be another species, too?
Sure they can!
        they will board the giant car with their dates

It's likely curiosity will have its way
Make the online inquiry   spoil everything
But a little longer wonder
                it's better
                it's preferred   a cock tease
        we'll wait and see

Burning Man was always an idea mostly
                                what meant the most
                                a concept first
And if there ever *was* a second discriptor, well...
Search for it somewhere your first year   HELCO

First *best*   for myself   1996
Touching down east of the Calico Range
        as if on a faraway planet
        whose place names are like our own
            and the *places* like our own places
Neither Left nor Right
A political ground zero

I think the Glam-Cocks will time-travel there
And exclaim, "My! how life has changed! we'll stay!"
In the double city that was that HELCO year
        they might ping-pong
                between the parachutes of Center Camp
                and the rave collective's separate stage

235

The giant car could be sent back too
A controlled experiment   a thought experiment
It's sunset over the Calicos
        with neon beginning to glow
        the Glam-Cocks themselves lit like 2016
                wearing fiber optics
                wearing all the lights of this future
                                in a very specific past

The giant car drawing quite a crowd
        before it's driven back to our year
                and blares a soundtrack of HELCO's drama
                    its Glam-Cock passengers exulting
                    and more devilish than before

They carry news of a downsized event
A city barely laid out   and vehicles in the night
        with fatal collisions possible
                and you do not leave alive unless you pray

This is why the many bicycles roam
In the brand new millennium a very old invention
        despite no more history
        millennium of glamor   we're glamorous!
                just cocks and what they can do until tired

On the other hand!
It's a great time to be alive and not a slave to libido!
Though proof is needed, proof will be found
Examples of what's important!
                global warming is real!
                you just don't notice, really   really!
The adverb paramount
The terraforming of other worlds
                        waiting on the fixing of this one

The computer is ready
I'm looking   and the first discovery?
        there is no hyphen   sorry about that, guys
        it's "GlamCocks" and so much more
                beautiful   gay   and empowered!

91. THE FAERIE GWENDOLYN AND SYNCHRONICITY CONCERNING A MOZART *RONDO*

The Faerie Gwendolyn conferred
            with a new-found friend

It was a synchronicity that had joined us
A *Rondo* in common that Mozart had written
        or "copied"   that's how the genius described it
        the process   the composition done
                        by the time a pen is found

The Faerie was delighted!
This synchronicity had astonished us both
And I wanted to hear *her* version soon
        how *she* played the sprightly *Rondo*
        the one that conjures the Turkish Janissaries
        the one that is so very familiar
A minor *and* A Major

Back in the day   make that 1683   September 12th
                Vienna had been in danger
                with Islam at the gates
And then it wasn't   and the city was made safe
                for a later Mozart
            an intelligence community

There's a level of interest now
Since the Faerie has appeared
        she and I are friends in five seconds
                our discussion touching on the long-lost
                like the Austria-Hungary Empire
Never revived till Gwendolyn

Gwendolyn the teacher, too
        her students certainly keen to study

So far our language is English
English will be the tongue of a restored Dual Monarchy
        a tongue stuck out and making fun of the Turks
            with a slight chance of residual danger!

237

92. A MISSING SPOTLIGHT

If it's lost, it's the *principle*
    no light is secondary

Ask the FBI   ask around
    though the asking makes it worse

Since it's gone, *more* must disappear
Peace   peace of mind
    and the actual pieces of the mind
    that fret too much
        and are deterred from pursuing happiness

And oddly, even *found*
    the spotlight's too late to stop the sadness
        that which is still arriving
        as well as the sadness *waiting* to arrive
That principle, again!
What is it?   oh, yeah
    could be a damned pencil lost!
    it was not paying attention that bothers
    that not *caring*
        so that before finding and after's the same
        the retrieval moot recovery

Think the spotlight is out there or nearby?
The uncertainty's a torture
If it's missing for a *minute*   only *that* long
    it's gone forever or might as well be!

We can talk, right?   *fortasse?*   perhaps?
Talk Latin
    talk the sense of that language
        to calm down   say and think differently

So bright was the light!
So helpful   like a wife
    bright enough to startle the day
        so that it reaches a conclusion ahead of time

The FBI is missing too
So much is missing
      there must be *something* found soon
       else entropy must overtake   close in
And be all around
         lost keys
         lost minds
            don't even start!

Where can it be?

Buying another is best
Buying another is simple math
      being out the price only
      being content to retrieve a thing *that* way
Then the spotlight's back
As if it's a magic act you're good at
                   with applause
If there's a lesson, it's merely retail

An even better trick is stealing Death
      and hiding *it* away where no one can find it
I'd take no credit
       though spotlights
       nay, *searchlights*   searched for me
                        to reward

There was a heft to the spot
A grip satisfactory
     and   heavy   you held it
       aware of the weight
         wishing for more
         so that   *shining* it
         you took gravity to task
And made it make the light solid *streaming*

Oh, missing spotlight!
Your reassuring batteries tucked
      inserted like ammo
         and your screwcap twisted 'round
Be blinding!   Again!

Oh, brilliant accessory!
If Fry's Electronics only sold this
        then the chain goes to heaven
                and all its employees   waving

Where *is* the damned thing, though?!
Come on!
You'll be happy again, but not today
        just drink from the Starbucks bottle
                drink the frappuccino
                        think!   *listen,* too!
                        that *helps* you think!
                                and   think of all you can

Go find it   or find something else in the dark
It was your light that lit the little fox
        that night of scrambling on Old Razorback's spine
        nearly descended, there it was
                sleek and curious   circling the spotlight
                        the spotlight following, remember?

A trance state accomplished
Brought to light
        how the delicate creature stared!
        russet   pastel-tawny   faintest orange
                who could say what shades exactly?

I'm repeating
It feels good to recount what the spotlight did
In the soft crater of its photons
        a fox came closer than it ever would have
                otherwise and when

Better than a camera   than video
For who would want the fox any other way?
        live in relation to another, different species
        the fox was simply   plainly enraptured

The missing spotlight could have undertaken more!
Come *on!*
        where the hell *is* it?!
                would you just sit down and think about this?

240

where last it was seen
              well, of course
              it had to have been left for the fox
A subconscious offering   the likely explanation

One possible place   naturally
Those minutes of confusion when they came for us:
The Earth Guardians   returning
        for the camper-outers
              and I'd been too quick to board
                  spacing badly
                  it was haste

And I was tired   excuses   the overnight gig
The Trego ditch had dulled the attention
                  its medicinal soak a disorientation

But I am now a prime minister of all sorts of doubts
        wanting the air to be conditioned
        with short-term memory
What's wrong I'm lapsing?

Be quiet!
Let Chopin be heard instead
Let him qualify this aggravation
                    though I have to play it myself
The lost light has nagged like an endless NPR show

Guess I'll take action
      beg to go along
            when the Earth Guardians return
            bringing *others* to the hot springs, yes
A chance to look in all directions
The place at the base of Razorback, Sahra's Mountain

First thing that came to mind
        as if thought itself sought the light
              the way the body craves healthy living
And there'd be no crowd to distract
Just a few volunteers   a shift change

Wish it could make news: "Spotlight Found by Fox!"

But it will not be a famous flashlight, not really
For its brilliance belonged to solitude
        to reveries of justice
            default wisdom
                what the years add up to

My whole life *has* flashed before my eyes
            but I didn't die   rather
            it was like a series of instructions
A show!   a production!
No credits and the script anonymous, AA stories
        that *start* with sobriety
        and conclude   recklessly   with PCP

Where was the light then before it was lost?
Playing Chopin, I sadly asked

93. ON THE FIRST DAY OF *THIS* SEPTEMBER

The spot is still gone
But Sherryl and Jim were here
        and Sherryl was singing
                    The Bird is the Word

She was a journalist
        and an amateur astronomer
She talked up The Great Red Spot
That Jupiter storm that just won't go away
There were jokes about *other* spots
She had a theory how a storm could last so long
        four hundred *years!*
        that *is* a long time for a single cyclone!

While she theorized
            Sherryl served us chicken and mozzarella
            there was applause

242

Someone began reciting Shakespeare
He sounded like Laurence Olivier
        a true thespian   (the word with a lisp)

There followed a discussion
The topic being our hearts' desires
        each of us kind of on-the-spot it seemed
            and having one too many desires myself
            I thought I might have hogged the conversation

It felt like we were getting somewhere
But it had to do with the excellent chicken
        I was prepared to believe in UFOs at last
            if it meant a second helping

Music started again
There was a ukulele played   but not the small one
This was the *baritone* version
        wonderful lower notes!
            and there was plenty of poetry in the lyrics

Jim it was who strummed, "Uncle" Jim
And he said his goal was good government through song

Sherryl danced
        said she had some moonshine
        that would change your life   "if you *let* it"

It was two o'clock ante meridiem
We rode out on the playa
        towards the walk-in camping
            a company of dreams pedalling together
We'd done everything the Muses had asked of us
And they'd asked a lot

There was now a lull
        perhaps they were *sleeping?*
We heard distant explosions
And the strangely soothing drums
            that   from far off
            were underlying early morning
                        the desert in a chill

Planes were landing that first day of September
A World War had started once
            on *another* first day of September

Globalism...
        what if they'd won?
            keep pedalling
What's left of the night will hide away the answer

We were eager to talk despite exhaustion
It was almost a collective breakthrough we achieved
And the journalist did her job
        and   a search was made for Jupiter, too

Awareness itself was trying to intensify
        but somehow I was ill-prepared for enlightenment

Next time   next Burning Man
I can be a monk gourmet
            specializing in the uses of mozzarella
And I'll have a dozen spotlights to see what I'm doing!

The Bird is the Word   her version my own

94. ALL ONE HUNDRED-AND-TEN

Did *all* one hundred and ten floors
The more-or-less height of the former Towers
        World Trade stairs

Did them right there on the steps of Panorama
                    while Slinkies flipped down
                    springy, multi-colored
Rainbowed versions that bounced amidst children
        a two-year-old boy made joyful and giggling
        a little girl with transparent wings   *serious*

her Slinky keeping up
keeping time with the guys *topmost*
with their incense and tiny drums

It was some ritual in progress
And their mumblings took awhile to say
the incantation long enough
for the fifty-fifth floor to be reached
though the deed was up-and-down done
on a flight of just forty-five stairs

So exercise happened at Panorama
What's always needed
the heart of the matter   *el corazón*

Life in the desert's enhanced with its beating
tattoos of motivation
what one does to return
to a two-year-old's concerns

It felt wonderful to make the effort there
The floors achieved while the Slinkies raced
Delightful to see the toys make it all the way down
though stop-and-start had a charm
and taught persistence

The chant above it all continued   the incense burned
the scent of it contagious
whatever the *words* of that chanting
the *tone* was what had mattered most

No eleven whistles blown could have interrupted
and might have even ended up coopting *the* spell
Such was the concentration up there
the drums had a cardiovascular intent

The Slinkies were a little too large
The smaller width of each stair caused tumbles
Uncontrolled descents
and so   inevitably
luck was a part of this
and the Slinkies *veered*   left and right

                    some plunging
                    entering free-fall

It was impossible to be expert   a "professional"
Panorama's staircase was solid, though
            and railinged
                    you'd have to be crazy to fall

It was a drama school of freeform
I felt courageous taking a part
            no rehearsal allowed
            no counting, either
                    each floor accomplished other ways
                    keeping track
                            with an "abacus" of objects placed

Found altitude in a place that was flat
Wanted all of Franz Liszt's *Evening Harmonies*
But please, little girl!
            don't get distracted!
And *parents!*
            pay attention!   watch the edges!
                    though it's probably safe
                                    it's not quite a dream
                                            not yet

The sound of the Slinkies thumping
            their "singing" coils
                    the squeals of achievement!

Binding arbitration
Where the law has gone out of the words
            and floats
                    a disembodied jurisprudence

A celebrity's performance
            whose merits are: it's really amateur
                    all one hundred-and-ten flights of it

El corazón!
Nevada *was* Mexico once

Uh-oh!
The incense had slipped out of somebody's hand
        and fallen to an awning   a canvass unknown
            still burning, too!

Whatever broke the fall broke the spell
                        for just a moment
                        for the incense
                            the incense, sensibly
                            was retrieved
                and once again was wafting

95. THE GIRL IN WHITE WHO SEEMED TO BE SUZETTE

What culture?
What talk?

She is why gravity was made
    what shows her grace
        in a white dress   cotton
        her side of the story of Life's lost art
                            science, too

If I were Alan Alda I'd know what to say

She is extraordinary   edge of the world
    though the Basin is planar   edge *another* way
    the precipice dimensional

Suzette, the culture of one spirit directing
Her language easy
        she journeys in the sound
            Suzette *returned*
            a gossamer being returned
                a heroine attempting to follow the future

There is reason to believe her high IQ is for real
        a coronal result
                her intelligence catching
                so that one starts to intuit
Loss   gravity   cotton   reunion

The girl in white remembers black
Remembers songs sung and lovely rain in parched oases

She says there is a European bird
A robin, the ruddock   *erithacus rubecula*
        and she has drawn it
                an expert likeness
                she wants to give to me
Wishes I should take it   the culture of gifts narrowed
                to avian offerings

She speaks polarity   as if to encompass extremes
And her bird begs for an opposite

She will soon be lost to the crowd on the Esplanade
        and not knowing more turns to urgent wishing
                in seconds she is gone
                her double   Suzette's replicate persona
                redirected
                to more of Out There

Alan taking notes
        and taking time
                with his *own* recognitions

96. TAKE THE SHUTTLE AND BE DONE

Take the shuttle   the *Star Trek* shuttle craft
        and be done
                not that it's actually *going* anywhere

Take that shuttle
Make it Antares to which it goes
        a shuttle released from the *Enterprise*
            and given directions
We'll get as close to the giant star as possible
Explore its sunspots   (Antares spots!)
            look for any planets there may be

It's only shone for a few million years, though
        and planets take time
                    there might not *be* a solar system

You take notes   I'll steer
The science officer will explain the mighty star
            make us glad it's not our own!

Playa shuttle   *play* shuttle!

The ways we envision reality...
"Bubbles!"
        who said that?
            some theory
            reality as a bunch of bubbles, right?

Well, the shuttle craft is one
"Get in!"
"I *heard* you!"   yes, I *will* get in
            though I *do* have some fundamental questions
            like "What am I getting in*to*?!"

Oh, it's much *roomier* than I thought it would be!
But do we have enough fuel to make it all the way?
        I mean, to Antares?
Okay   it's a *thought* experiment!   I forgot
More than enough propulsion in that case!

Not enough answers   that's why we're going
Hey, it's *sleek*, too
        by the way, what were those *Star Trek* numbers?
        yeah, those numbers on the hull?
            1701, maybe   the Trekkies would know
Wasn't *Forbidden Planet* referenced?   with letters, too?

Too bad sci-fi had to modernize
I liked the rockets just fine with fins
        and the ships Flash Gordon flew around in
                it just would have been nice
                if they'd flown a little longer

Yikes! hope the shuttle's shielded!
Don't want the cosmic rays to enter in

In a town like this one
        our beloved Black Rock
                there is no time table
                        no spaceports
                                no worries at all
We've thrown a government together
                                but we're rife with rebellion

There's mining in the hills
Rutile has been found
        I'm told it's tetragonal
                a crystal system full of titanium
                        the metal so useful for spaceships

The inhabitants are high on conservative principles
But only long enough
                to enjoy the slide into sheer hedonism!

The playa's our special *two*-dimensional Spacetime
All we need to get around
        and all the red giant lights of Black Rock City
                like multiple Antares stars
                        wait upon our interstellar outreach

It looks like we'll get there
        funny how the little runabout NCC was so lovable
                and could get around the galaxy
                no kidding!   it's uncanny, *uncanny* I tell you!
Amazing how many places it's gone!
The big black hole in the center
        the very center of the Milky Way, even
                yet it wasn't considered that big a deal

We'll be done and call it a day
        as soon as we visit those globular clusters
        and find out stuff
What is the meaning of their being in orbit about the galaxy?
The next big story...

Hope you're taking notes on this journey
I get too excited and scribble illegibly
        where's the mind recorder promised?

Our top speed of one trillion miles-a-second!
What a great galaxy!
        good thing there's hardly any traffic
            turned out we're alone after *all*
                I'm *glad*   no aliens   it's better

Just the ones the studios portray
CGI   all you need   I'll settle for that
        our presidents are aliens, however
        Larry Harvey *definitely*
            he and presidents people the City
                extraterrestrials for *sure*

Wait a minute!
Come to think of it, *all* of us
            we're all the aliens in the universe
            and I'm not going to change   I *like* it!

Meanwhile, in our NCC 1701, there's confusion
We've been driving in circles
        and no news from the *Enterprise*, either
            but we *have* normalized relations
            with a bunch of virtual Klingons
Now was the time for the estrangement was substantial

Aliens   others
Who *are* the "others," anyway?
        why, they're us as well!
            and just now, this "other/alien" wants to be bad!
                take over the shuttle
                    then the starship *itself!*

251

One more futuristic thing, if you don't mind:
We need a Five Million Years Plan!
Let's face it
      not a five   not a ten   not a hundred or a *thousand*
         but a Five Million — count 'em! — Years Plan

I've asked Scott Boggs to help *make* it
      and *sensei* Mel C. Thompson has said he'd join us
We'll make sure no asteroids strike
We'll find a way to survive flood basalts
We'll have a giant lead sphere constructed underground
      make sure there's always some people inside
          in case of a gamma-ray burst
We'll move the Earth away from the Sun
      so that when it bloats and turns red
         we'll just have magnificent *sunsets*
        instead of incineration
And we'll make a concerted effort not to evolve too much
      because there should always be a Raquel Welch

I don't think it unreasonable
         to want Lichtenstein around
         forever, if possible
But five million years at least

Oh, but I digress!
How much food's aboard the shuttlecraft?
Is there any more peanut butter left?
    who's hungry?
        what's in the Space cupboard?

Nice to be able to be Everywhere, isn't it?
Who would have thought
      our own Black Rock Milky Way
        could be so utterly colorful
          it's better all fiery and festive like that

Let us abolish politics
And get down with pulling the strings
      for a new *Theory* of Everything
        now that we *have* everything everywhere

I was worried for awhile
        a certain megalomania
                wrong reasoning, certainly
                        but I feel fine, now   really!
                        the anti-tyrant serum is working

Engage!   whatever!   we're done!

97. THE GALLOPING MONSTROSITY

Those who've found their way to the top of it
        seem so very happy up there

The see-through sculpture
                heavy enough to sink in the silt!

You yourself will never climb it
        a huge wild boar rushing in metal stop-motion
Is it Leonardo da Vinci who's devised the monster?
                would certainly like to know

The animal would go bye-bye and all   if it could
If sculpting would allow it and just let go
        release its grip
                then the thing must be bounding
                                lickety away
                perhaps to a lair in the Selenites

But its flight is arrested
It can't get over itself
        and pauses   mid-stride
                in synch with stillness

They said to write what you know
It was a telepathic urgency
                and what I know is: this boar frightens!

253

so that you catch your breath in witness

Let's all go crazy!
The artist *wants* that!   crazy holds the attention!
        the way the creature's held there
                then there are the *hand*holds and *foot*holds
                maddeningly obvious
I will trust in the fantastical
In terrible ground-trembling truth
                        too new to be rusty!

In the perforated shadow
        think it's at least a Colt-45's installation
                and accruing bicycles
                        the unmoving attracting the mobile

It's a hollow thing
As though zoology were through-and-through
I wish all ideas were like it
        all species of thought left open
        not that the solid parts are tame
                rather   iron ironically controls the rest
                a creature so vast there's been only one
So *far*, but thanks to the metal
        it's more-or-less immortal

Hell, let me be its offspring   strong!
        and taking *after* the beast
        roaring,
                "Extinctions never last in the Land of Memory!"

A time mobius is twisting somewhere
Stranded DNA in Dali's brain assembled
                commended
                the past on pause and ready to run

Big art menacing carbon capture
Says, "I am here for *you!*"
        and those aboard do not recall the climb
                they pose on the spine
                slightly hypnotized
                        their friendly fire suppressed for now

there was no one willing to be disarmed

It's clear the monster wants to mingle
Though it's a cryptic company that went aloft
        and gone are all the reasons why
                yet a play is in progress
                multi-level
They've done enough and should dismount

Too dangerous!
Come down!
I'm keen to conquer *too*
        but how many times?
        how many ways?

How well-rounded and sleek is this statue
Its several component parts like irresistible sinew
If there were a Pulitzer for the wild boar
        would the artist accept
        or say "No!" to a prize
                just to be different
                as his creation is different?

No prize could serve the principle   "for the sake of..."
There is only big bucks   big sculpture
        cry when it's done

The artist has started talks with paleo spirits
And the work is charged
        reckless   evolutionary power
        mayhem cocked and ready
                as the beast itself must be
                full speed announcing momentum
                        with thudding *virtual* rhythm

The hominids safely dismounted
And the day being quite hot of course
        they seek the shade allowed
                the perfect interlude
                as long as the animal stays in place

All that furious energy and hair-trigger posture!

255

As the week goes on
      its spring is wound   tight as history
          and *before* any history
            to the even more dangerous triggers
                   of random mutation

It's a show-stopper, too
      the ribs   the snout   the broom tail
Something one is not prepared for
That   and the nearby Sunrise Cafe
Not ready for beauty
         but gain some weight
            make it all memorial

I want *them* to remember
Those who danced and waved from up there
Perhaps a shared recollection's a better account
             than this solitary assessment

It is the best art so far
It would teach us to gallop
      a *good* monstrosity and kind

You want to stay and let the sun go down
See if it moves
         as you suspect it *may* after all
         race its decidedly heavy metal
           to those pagan hills
           and the wilds of the Selenites
              mountains lonely for the megatheres
Again given the night to roam!

98. THE "WHAT'S-IT?" AFTER DARK

The "What's-It?" veers
      an omnidirectional design
         pedestaled   posted

A composite weather vane of cloth

Well, that's *perhaps*
        for it flaps and responds to the currents
        a *lovely* tan
And somehow
        you know full well
                it's the future that blows
                        and billows these sails

Though *maybe* "What's-It?" is a doctored theme
Unfunded
        the thought of a single afternoon
                uplifted   and held tenderly

The many installations are islands moored
They are come upon slowly
            even with bicycles
            even with art cars
                the best way is walking
Less equipment is walking

Nothing to lose or keep your eye on
No attention divided

There's a lot to like about the canvass
It's minimal   modest as suggestion
                and   it's just said to wait awhile

Seeing the "What's-It?" could be key to seeing the rest
The noisy and vast undertakings
            at the ten o'clock and two o'clock domes
            those extravaganzas on the edges
                where the streets of the City end
                and Black Rock's map is empty
And has nothing else to say

After this simplicity seen
        the great geodesics can have cursory inspections
                and still be understood   completely

So get the "What's-It?" right

all the music of the nineteenth century
        hovering in Chopin's miniatures
          his *Preludes*   and *Mazurkas*
Comprehend the canvass and it's like that hearing

And the artwork here in the twilight
        is dancing a slight waltz of airiness
              always is the wind seeming to blow in Black Rock
              like an expectation travelling all over
So that even when it's still
                        there is a current felt
                                        albeit philosophic
                                        that flow

I wouldn't say the art is unique, totally
But the force of gravity doesn't seem to be operating here
          in proximity

I'm writing notes quickly
The way you would first thing on waking
        in a brand-new house
              having dreamt of the *old* house
Oh, if there were someone to sit down with now
Someone to talk to about this   I'd feel much better

The vane   like the start of a corkscrew
      almond the color
            pale   neutral
            suitable for a country of one citizen praying

The stairsteps lead to a pedestal
        and a simple platform
              perhaps the parliament
                    where you talk to yourself
Or a House and Senate combined
        where you may boast
              of your small nation's accomplishments

Out of the swirl surrounding Black Rock
      Tom Stolmar will appear out of a sense of loyalty
And we'll reminisce about the Temple of Rudra
When it burned at 3a.m.

the going and coming uncertain

Tom *could* show up
As unexpectedly as before
        amidst the general carousing
                and both of us lost in a dust storm
Does anyone know what year anymore?

It is stage 1 existential
Turn away from previous Fellini films
There's so much I want to say
        like Proust in the *Remembrance*
        in French
                though *my* account can't get started
                        sextains?
                        out of the question
And the adverb "secundum" so beautiful, so unusable!
Unless...unless...

Where is the IQ required?!
Where's the machine that will improve it?
Smarten me up!
Let me live in a house
        with a building permit
                to add an extra house to the house

It's hour three since my father gave advice from the void
        and it was the same good talk
        as the time he said to study more than just music.

There was no punch line
He didn't know where I was
        but his voice *has* sounded in the City
                his voice being liberal
                in search of a safe harbor for his son
A final push, perhaps
        to make up for neglect

He may succeed
But it was never neglect   not really
        for who would set out to do it?
                I mean *deliberately* abandon a child?

I'll be abandoned by choice
A refugee from wooded hills
          who's arrived the open playa
               to gaze at this "What's-It?"
               specially constructed
                    to ensure mental health

There are five imaginary children playing
/ will protect *them*
The wind is stronger
          and they might get lost in the dust
The forecast's unknown
                    the clouds there are seem centuries
                    like a mist ·
               to match *adagio's* maximum sustenance

If this were a rescue at sea
          there'd be a life raft
               ·or a breeches buoy
And we'd be careful not to rock the boat too much

But *here*   another saving is possible
Another drowning averted
          the mind given everything
               the soul identified
                    the *body* improved
                    given new springiness
So that you say,"I feel better these days!"

Omnidirectional, the vane continues to veer
One is energized
          as though in the presence of an electrical grid
               whose positrons are personal subatomics

No frustrations   ,   no nagging beliefs
          international gods will not be arriving

Step up, briefly   and be a part of "What's-It?"
          flapping in tandem
               short stories to tell
You know full well it *is* the future   easing

Less ideological   the real world finessed by a breeze
It is lovely   tan
        or perhaps vanilla
        a color doctored by gentleness
                and available fantasias

You don't have to *say* anything right now
But you *do* have to *do* something right now
Explore with me those islands
        art islands
                those varicolored dots
                pins stuck on the Artery's map
                        precise coordinates
                        Crimson Rose assisting

What will burn and when
The thoughts of a single afternoon

The canvass remembers   and asks for more
        wants keys to jangle after this simplicity

All the music of Black Rock will start
The nineteenth century hoping to be heard *also*
Expectation travelling
        a slight waltz in the twilight

But it may not be as late as you say
Philosophy is possible
        that which would make *this* island ours
                so that all over's comprehended
                        gravity   the other forces
                        how many, dear?

Dream of the Old with resistance
        insisting it forward itself to the New
                houses   trains
The art world's pieces of eight
And yes, Infinity's there
        refusing to count past its very own number

Let the currents stir the corkscrewy fabric
        completing the work already done

A cursory inspection, then
One citizen praying for his very own *planet*
        after sunset
                or perhaps before   lovingly awake

Tom, you can join us   as you have previously
The most grown up of children
                who seeks no less than Parliament to scold
                and will not be denied!

And you, my treasure, have also said
                        to study more than music
                        study *everything*, and I will
Though lost in the dust of a blue day's finale
In our beliefs
        with building permits pre-appoved by remembrance

Does *anyone* know what year anymore?
And can it some how qualify as stage 1 fright?
                        getting over it, I mean?

99. WALKING THROUGH THE WORKSHOPS

Da Vinci belongs!
And the Guilds have come to town!
How many will be comprehensible
        and which will acquire apprentices?

Darkness soon   it may put an end to the smelter
        the Dragon Smelter
        what a word that is!   "smelter"
                take away the second syllable, it's a fish
But *oh*, that smelter!
They're fusing the ore
How far did they get?   what came of it?
        let's see   milling with the others

Guy's operating a red lever up and down
                    there's smoke
                    it's serious
                    it's crowded
        and the costumes are many

Only the dilettante can see it all
Visiting the Guilds this evening *also*
        the Yellow Jacket people
                their multiple stings in check

We've gone Italianate
The effort made has been substantial
        for it was determined our Renaissance should rock
            and be as detailed as possible
            as much as the sun would permit
                prior to utter exhaustion

Then there's "The Man"   short for "The Burning Man"
One is uncomfortable without the present participle
"The Man"   not enough by itself
        to say what the wooden statue is
                    the prime mover of all this

"The Man" sounding the word for law enforcement
        police implied
                in a place of radical self-expression
He's standing there   who was supposed to revolve
Perform Leonardo's cartwheels
        but it was not to be
            the mechanism to make him spin
            was too clever   too much
                            and poorly understood

Still   the attempt was a good one
The would-be machine *aesthetic*
        the gears to make it go
                easy to see what was intended
                the famous drawing to come to life

Let's explore some more
The Guild's are busy!

263

And we'll cruise the gallery, too
                    under orange clouds
                    for a sunset further east

Are you with me thus far?
Somebody's sunburned
                    a fleeting bare arm

Yellow-and-black!
Yikes!   a jittery dualism
                    light-and-dark done
                    for pollination's sake

The first sculpture's a minotaur
        restrained by sprites
                    it may have been captured outright
                    a masterpiece   a plinth   and a text
A little "narrative story art"

From one to another go
Seeing figures   exquisite
        well-made
                    without caution
                        stand-alone beautiful
Be under the spell of their storytelling forms
A dignified gray dimming down

Each platform's embossed   rectangled
Shining with an odd reflectivity   somehow golden

The *purpose* of the stories is unknown
But each statue is kindred
            we know and trust this
                    and are rendered uniquely thematic ourselves

Arrive the gallery when the space is uncrowded
Alight like a Martian   to consider the gallery's merits
Behold   with artist sensibilities
                    the highest definition

Yes!   right now is best   like a promise kept
The arches in early evening are dimly exceptional

Who are the patrons?
      who in history raised up such creativity?
        who might have gone to war over much less?

And just as Burning Man may fund and encourage
So princes of the Mediterranean
      might bless their artisans with riches
This swirl   and that earlier vortex   equally profound
The sketchy workshops no less vital
    for all their improv and haste
      when original conceptions
      and even *blueprints* perhaps
        are subsumed by what's practical
            what's doable

Sit beneath a gossamer evening cloud
      to inspect
While meticulous drums manage a serenade
Marvelling at wheels   and *more* wheels
    in complex arrangements
      sixteen spokes   little barrels revolving
      with prongs and pegs
        the worlds within their woodwork
      secret   authentic

These crafts were caught up with *late* in the week
    after initial interest had lapsed into workaday
Excitement's died down   like the day
And what is seen is seen subdued
    interaction that must be subpoenaed

Now, the eight smaller arches are vacant
Or seem to be
    until   moving closer
      a rhinoceros is observed
      spanning three-at-a-time   *filling* them
        the creature's inner workings revealed

There were charcoal sketches of winged beings
There were chariots and cypress trees

Each workshop's enclosed by little walls

Here is one devoted to modification
        The Last Supper painted without the Twelve
            just empty chairs
            the disciples have left
                Christ has left

Linnea is here!
I don't believe it!
Here and blowing glass!
                but calm down
                she may be an illusion

How she loved the furnace, though!
So much, perhaps, she's managed to manifest here

She'd always have Haydn or something rococo playing
Though a Renaissance flute will suffice this day!

100. *MORE* WORKSHOP REVERIES

That's still a very orange cloud up there
It surpasseth understanding
            like pre-Islamic Arabia
            the place *before* just one god was allowed
You wonder what it might have been

There's a lot of lumber thrown together
        elsewhere wood
                nothing grown hereabouts
Wait for the morning edition of the workshops
Pretending the cloud is a.m.'s moisture
                            happening ahead of time

Good the playground's outgrown the kid for once
        and now includes the Quinn River's boggy finish
                near to the namesake stone
                the Black Rock itself

I'm the know-nothing child
        just *starting* to get a sense of things
                Leonardo da Vinci
                    osmosis
The drawings, the sculpture
                    the entire Renaissance

It is believed the catalyst was China
Those big boats the emperor sent
                    looking to reconnoiter, perhaps
When they arrived
        so did amazement
        and commerce
                and intricate artwork was everywhere seen

Let's think so
And think a giant junk
        could have sailed the ice age expanse of a lake
                could have navigated Lake Lahontan, too
                calling at all its ports
                        and cities of the mastodons

This is a kind of twilight breakthrough
Sudden health after decades of flu
If we meet again, you and I   I'll tell you the rest

It will be a little like *Prairie Home Companion*
        though without the prairie grass
                I'll be your own personal journalist
                                if   you'll let me

"Go deeper!"   the command made
                    by a helmeted horseman
                    he in his armor
                            astride a charcoal horse

The orange lingers above

101. GOING DEEPER INTO THE WORKSHOPS

"Immediate experience is
        in many ways
                the most important touchstone of value
                        in our culture..."

Quotha!

The infants agree   and, naked, wrestle in the crib
In a phone booth may you talk to God
        despite the queue
        and all of its dimes   waiting

An alien lies in a mesh of suspension
                his protest unsure and dependent

What chiseled wood is this?
What panel
        that seems a parade of well-cut craftsmen
                joined hands to shoulders
                        and greeting someone
                        a person of great importance?

Or   they pose
Cocksure and proud   with tools
        well-dressed
        as befits their station

Another scene:
                a man gestures to his handiwork
He looks underfed?   no, he's wiry and eager to work!

A movie should tell it   one by Buñuel
For though I see everything
        I am without direction overall
                so that my love letter falters
                needs underpinning
No reason to *leave*, exactly   still...

The Japanese are also needed

Their most gifted   talented
        to encompass all description
            know all degrees of chance genius
                                and insight

Do not wish to escape this region
Not yet   no evacuation
The chaos is ordered
        there is fire safety   spiritual guides
            genetically modified scrapple to snack on
                gay marriages to be a part of

In some of the sheds of the workshop enclave
        no one is home
            no one is left
How convincing were they?
How tired afterwards?

It's all extrajudicial   no judges or juries
There's no place to hide
                but absolutely no reason *to* hide
There are only mistakes   the *best* situation

Almost everyone *is* asleep in some sense
The drones and the robots do better that way

Look!   the guy with the pale green cap
                                and white feelers!
His hands are black-gloved
        and he seems to be considering what's next
            his project involves some bottles
                candy-colored bottles
He demonstrates and remonstrates
                        assistants leaning
                        the workspace swarmed

Suddenly, a child sprints past a bulbous corral
Sure of his speed
        some youthful distraction started
            ah!   with the western Granites silhouetting
            or nearly

Dusk has allowed some purple texture

Continue   let the Guilds be your way of walking
        delighted
                no mantra in particular
                    a contrary gait without shame
                    a map of the mind unfolded

I treasure the yellow flags of da Vinci's factories
Dispossessed are all belongings
Those who labored here have absented themselves
        to fully engage their respective muses
                some of them carefully crafting, *indeed!*

Explain all this   a keen violence in abeyance
Understand the message of inclusion
                        falsity stripped of its power

Will I go any further now?
        Know family relationships again?
                Conjure Loie on the playa
                only to find she's here *already*
                    and had a ticket all along?

Deeper into backup and backdrop
Stanford medicine standing by
This is perhaps part two of part one
        the sudden child is part three
                a third condition
                his blue body a blur
His explosive beeline
            like a competition of one athlete *only*

Where he goes is where *I'll* go
His exit the example
            even here, the Supreme Court of Youth
                            and its rulings
My walk is investigation *after* the fact
        after the Renaissance was assembled   set up
            with heat stroke always possible

I'll bring you a program back   fondness back

Leonardo could speak
            speak to Larry Harvey one-on-one
            maybe he has already

Burning Man—"The Man"— is seen from the side
Edge-on
      the mechanism plain
            that would have powered his spinning
            undoubtedly to cheers
Vitruvian Man!

Would the cheers be the same as political cheers?
Can you even tell what a crowd wants, really?
Is it the terror you hear tell of?
      and is a crowd a terrorist *singular* or *plural?*

Maybe it's the Donner party in bright sunshine
         fully rescued and no need for cannibalism
            maybe there's menace
            maybe nothing of the kind

Think!   think like the Scarecrow!
Set the history tapes aside
      or play them
Slow, so the narrative's deep and low-registered strangely
Or *fast, fast, fast* like a screechy bird's cartoon protest

Here is school the way it was taught in Firenze
         to be followed by a Finnish sauna somewhere
            the partial address 3:30
            so it's 3:30 and... and...
And always incomplete hearing
                           of a time
                           a place
                           an event
         hearing other words than what were said

A guru school!
Yes   Jan Luc has made it so
         and there are hands
            hands painted on a wall
The class still and well-behaved

Preparing to learn   waiting on instruction
Though to tell the truth
        that hour spent would be Eternity's talk
            so full of lecture
                is even the slightest of pauses

And the beast that hugely poses in its galloping stride
        is here reproduced
        severely downsized in the Guilds
                winged this time
                    but there's no mistaking
                    the anatomy's a match
That see-through frame and top-heavy musculature!

This version of the monstrosity is mounted
            like the other sculpture that's schematic
                the artist out of apologies   over modest

No one will ever win these arguments
                and art left alone is art understood

There's light purple seen in the classroom
Level students   a blessing
            in addition to instruction
                    trickle-down intelligence
                    voyeur scholarship
Those smartphones abandoned   one by one
An important step

Someone's telling lies
There's no doubt whatsoever
        "Leonardo was composite..."
                but wait for how and why
His genius narrowed down to better explode
The soul's purpose allowed after background checks

Let go   like the gears
        in the artful frieze
        built into the beast's high chair
Gears with arrows
            gears with a conscience

gears gone to bed
before the last light is done

102, "LA BOTTEGA" THE STUDIO OR WORKSHOP OF A MAJOR ARTIST

Learn to spell: *battega* is incorrect
You can't spell what you can't see
        and there's another sign:
            "Piazza Info"
                    but   no questions
                    the connectedness is obvious
Previous lives lived the last minute of *this* one

There is a woman in blue gloves
        pointing and explaining
                "What is this thing?
                this is a z-axis gantry system
                                Renaissance-style!"

However, note the laser cutter
        the neat wood complete amid lavender drapes

There is much to admire
Those rows of stars in the wraparound windbreak
The late sun's lanes on the workshop's rug
                        where the tent was incomplete

Next   the Amalgamated Debris Assemblage
ADA
        they're busy, all right
        makes you want to get busy your *own* self!
It's like the day after Christmas in there
All the presents put in a pile
                and those that are willing
                    in love with rearrangement

On one of the post supports
luminous plates are nailed
a dozen or so
in a lilting enhancement
of the roughhoused Amalgamation
irrational
irresistible

Roll the tape to see the chaos
It's a *surge* of handiwork
Unlike the rest of La Bottega
not going so far   and so long
there's overlap in the assembling
Your hands are others'
And what is combined is as easily divided
there's just no telling
the aggregate uncertain

Just to assemble's the idea
No matter the parts serve other purposes than your own

Like a marketplace
where the goods are never quite sold
one's extremities are multitasking
in tandem with the limbs of others
Being witness to what happens
When togetherness strays into mental monkey bars

And "This ain't over!" is *going* to be over   and soon
The combustible shacks dismantled and loaded
no vote taken

There'll only be that da Vinci Man
Vitruvian Man   unspinning still
future spending come to the playa
after the frugal early Nineties

Before "spell-check" took the fun out of guessing
Spell *La Bottega*
spell *colonnade*   if you can
what about *pharaoh?*   can you?
bellwether?

inoculate?

Wait a minute!
I'm not anonymous enough to blend in
          but I'll ask
If it means I'm a kid again...
And some *are* kids who amalgamate
          so very busy with debris   I could join

I'll spell *everything!*
Like a spelling bee
          when the word you spell is said before you spell it
               and *repeated* after
The reward, if you're correct, is
               you can stay eight years old

You never see grandmas and grandpas competing

Rest here   the essence of the Theme played out
          nearly
               the overhead of orange clouds
                    dispersing   fading

Can a Guildsman also simply *onlook?*
Would Leonardo not have been cool with that
                         and lost patience?
How often before the spectator's forced to leave?

Spell *grok*   the verb
Do that and get close enough for the jazz of a journal
Include everyone tasking still
               and include the sparse gallery
               open air
                    open-hearted-minded

Please, sun, stay down this time!
          all the hiding places hard to find
               and *deep* because we *did* go deeper

All the costumes
          bells and drums
               whistles and lutes

All of this was needed deep down
And painters' *and* sculptors' eyes of course!

103, THE MODEL SOLAR SYSTEM

I don't know where the inner planets are
But *yes*   *maybe* they're here
        a part of the model   yes   probably
            how could they *not* be spinning
                and orbiting with the others

Let's see...
Jupiter   there's Saturn   all the giants
A beautiful Neptune
        Uranus   *oh!*
        is that one on its side like it should be
                        and rolling around its orbit?

It's okay if it's not
It would make more sense
        if Uranus *wasn't* so inclined   so tilted
What the hell happened out there in the dark of Space?

And its moons!
They're wrong, *too!*
Columbo, please come back
            and be astronomer
            planetologist
            cosmologist!
Whatever you *have* to be to sort this out

You know those so-called "rocky worlds" like our own?
Mercury?   Venus?   Mars?
They could have well resembled the gas giants once
        before a "T Tauri wind" arose
        that crucial day
            when the sun blew away the atmospheres

and the close-in planets went naked
ever afterward

Maybe there's an Earth in the middle of the mighty one
Jupiter
and all his nasty radiation
waiting to kill any crew foolish enough to visit!

Maybe that Earth is there
Down deep   so beat up by hydrogen, helium
it's a hot and molten home world   compressed

Stay calm   relax
Let the model of the Solar System
say other things
than what might have been

The installation's ingenious-metallic
It has swiveling
the armature's substantial
the planets motorized   in sych
with the years spent
going round and round
How natural it seems   how bulbous the gearbox
Central   celestial   mechanical

You kind of wish Copernicus had erred
had been wrong about the sun
Just to see how the artist would have managed
those epicycles adding up to complexity

There could have been asteroids and comets, too
If there were a sponsor willing   *and*
the grant generous
And a nearest star   at *this* scale, maybe Sparks
Proxima Centauri a brilliant chandelier in Harrahs
a big one   and blinding!

What's scary is the math
To think it's actually possible to know
that *both* Mercury and Venus will transit the Sun

will transit the Sun at the same time
on July 26th, 69,163 CE

Oh, they *know!*
 those smarty-pants
 those suave and cool-headed ones
  the exact time and the exact *paths*
   across sunface!

Stop right there!
Let those same brains solve social ills
 make everyone happy! get *on* it!
  though they probably can't
   not exact enough a science
   there are no equations possible...

Fine! the whirligig again
Style over substance but in a good way
I'm a *different* kind of visitor to these worlds
 having wished to go for forever
 ached to space travel
And "terraform" if I might
Find the bottom of the gas giants' clouds and survive

The model's all that's needed
That and a Summer of Love for all things alien
 you can hear the cheering at liftoff
  for Jupiter Saturn Uranus Neptune
We will attend their universities

We're laser-focused on this future of ours
  whose first novel could be the last

Steal away (what spirituals apply?)
Swing low
 yes! and swing around
 like these planets
Grab one if you have the reach

Too bad so much is known
 yet you just can't get there from here
  unless you play with this strange helicopter

104. IT'S LONG AND OBLONG AND WAY OVER *THERE*

It's long and oblong and way over *there*
Long and white
          oblong and able to be both green and blue
It's like a 50s saucer hugging the ground
          and doing its best to perform for the paranoid
          who see lights in the night and day and go crazy   ,

"What *are* they?"
"*Who* are they!?"
"Where do they *come* from!?"

Distance works in the object's favor
          and lends credibility   secrecy and mystery
          no charge
                    and people could evacuate if hysteria starts

Just look at that thing!
Is it really possible?
It is a cause for wonder
          an earthbound UFO   its hyperdrive relaxed

I came to be as far away as the saucer seems
                    white and remote
                    though still this side
                         of the orange perimeter's plastic

Good that the playa stretches
          and joins the expanding universe of Faraway

Could catch a ride myself
Find out more   with ten-power binoculars held
On the open road
          wide as Nevada
                    a rendezvous's assured
                                        vector *in!*

It's possible *Loie's* aboard and heading for a party
There'd been no plan   though we'd tried for one

by the time she'd had her tenth massage
        I'd gone to the desert with a wandering mind

There is no middle distance
        just the Earth's curvature told in dust
There's migration going on
The non-stop night chill
        is part of its unseen *pavane*

She will seek a soft seat in the bustle of transit
        blue-going-green
        with oblong dimensions
Possible it is   with Loie able and determined to ride
Keeping her attendance secret
        searching the playa with new-found friends

Perhaps she's brought a thumping-good read
        from the Palo Alto Library
                and she's staying at First Camp
                        a guest of Crimson Rose, even!
Far and near vision like enchanted glasses worn

The long white saucer
        that's also green-and-blue
                this can be her transport   professorial
                her mystery of day-for-night imaginings

Everywhere's a likelihood
Time may explain itself
        say it's not what it seems
                write a letter to the living
                        that says not to worry
The Universe is making progress on What Comes Next
Outcomes that might surprise the prophets

Let's find a way to find Loie!
Enough guesswork's been accomplished
Let *certainty* ensue
        reunion "bustin' out all over"   like the musical

The desert is not so dry if your voice is heard
And it would carry across the alkaline immensity

I don't know what you're planning   *but*
        the broken glass of churches needs attention
        as *I* do
And being delusional
        I've put away the bootstraps
                and wait upon your better judgment
                        to get started again
                        and be sensible
Even here in the heart of Fellini's empire
                                that beats overwhelmingly

I will stay flexible until you show
        chaparoned by E.T. types in their limo saucer
        or walking silkily   the warm summer adorning
A way of understanding the night winds' appeal

I came to be distant as Freedom advised
        yet knew your intimate touch with every draft
                turning this way and that
Chaos has never felt so right!

Loie, *listen!*
Listen to the music intermittent
        from the palace of *Don Giovanni*
                where, reformed
                the skirt chaser sings "Viva, la libertà!"
                        with a reinterpreted license

I'll do everything I can to find you
My *own* voice level as this plain
                for I cannot abide your absence

The *pavane* has begun
        and   faster than light is the journey
        the dance illumined blue-green
        with white a magic angel's light
                                maybe thousands'

"What are they?"
"Who are they?"

Remote is the machine
        the ignition having crunched the numbers
            those supplied by artificial intelligence
            hoping to learn from Loie
                            the letters of a better love
                    bonobo-style

Early September will make any city safer
You'll see!

105. THE TRIANGULAR HEART

Climbing the triangular heart

They were pick-up sticks
And stacked such there was room to climb
There'd even been the possibility of an idol suspended
        a geometric heart   triangular
            reflecting the last light from the west

A pyramidal mirror
Maybe cool   closed to pity
        until, clambering, someone embraces
        and is brilliantly connected
The fallen-down desperate gather

Be acrobats for Eros
See into Russia   its oligarchs' holdings retired
        except for these straightened monkey bars
                        their austere assemblage

I face charges facing the heart
It's like a crackdown conducted by jealousy
        an agility enhanced with homelessness

"Don't leave me!   don't leave!
        it's a long way back..."

282

Shine, four-sided temptation!
No economy comes calling
        you are priceless pendant
                in the center you're at home
                        the rigging   the angles
                        arbitrary context

The triangle as oracular-schematic
what's important has dimensions   stays ideal
        a cluttered parking lot of aspiration
        many-limbed attempts to caress
                the courtship stylized   unauthorized

The climbers are a small community of suitors
They scramble for favors   their prospects uncertain
        rest   and they are lost to others' commotion

It's like an open-air lair
        the heart on fire with reflections
                blue in the midst
I would fall for you   in transit of your tepee sticks
Hands-on acrobatting their pick-up lean-to poles

Speak to me!
        there's time for further palpitations
                tell us of the quarks
                        in your indestructible pyramid!

Whom to credit?   was it some rogue spirit?
The stack without the hay will not supply the needle
        and its robot mind may not be reduced
                                to a meaningful simplicity

In the season of affection that is Burning Man's weather
        cry out loud for the crimes of neglect
        abandonment
                cry out for silence
                the better to hear the electricity
Trapt and wanting credit
For passion that outlasts a lifetime
        and partners with eternity

all planets deconstructed
and the suns that had warmed them

Right now three climbers test the bars
those same that hold the heart in place
And their scramble's like a frantic reconnaissance
for love withheld
its Cupid a stingy archer
whose arrows veer and splinter
before a matrimony's done

A *paradoxical* heart
whose hardness ensures longevity
Half a diamond only
bewitching all ages of infatuation
so that a best guess is made
in place of wisdom
filling in the blanks with assumptions

There is no security
and the trio is a three-part loneliness
They drop out of courtship one-by-one
find their bicycles again
and pedal away
to a more reciprocal object

For a week
its sparse architecture has tricked with gleaming
and postponed fulfillment
letting the collective heart of the city perform
and instigate rescue

Black Rock's drumbeats
to better summarize arterial longings
the aspirations of lions
and elephants' *infants*, even
In the all-or-nothing future
wide-angled   all-consuming

The installation   *whatever* it's called
calls out *itself* for rescue
from a too-sure compaction

All sentiments compressed   sourced
          as if a singularity ruled inside the pyramid
                  and Egypt's left dangling   priestless
No sacrifice sufficient to undo the stroke

Still does it radiate!
Desires tied to a periodic table
          hoping   in a chemical way
                  to somehow enhance the universe
                                    with scientific love

One that may be metal let loose
          and dating others of its kind
                  getting away with going through the motions
                          even offspring may be possible!

106, ORNATELY CONCEIVED

When David Best brought his wood to town
The first time   the year 2000 sawn to perfection
Pieces, scraps, a cut baroque precision achieved

And right here
Right now   before us
          something of the same
                  additional persuasion accomplished
And it's extra filigree   a tidy, perforated ply
Symmetric   mesmeric

The design like a script prepared for the literate
          whose trust *alone* was required

And   somehow part of the idea
          a dragon's silhouetted by a suddenly cold sky!
                  the wood still tan   just *barely*

The façade's black-bordered
The few square feet of the interior   hidden
          a single lamp seems *introductory* light
          a preludium to understanding
It is oddly, redly tinged
                    as if one step ahead of comprehension

107, BEST PIECE

It needs elaboration
          but just these words for now
                    this briefest introduction

Suffice to say
          the isolate vision
                    was every delight that might connect
A delicate beatitude
A ladder in the road   and lifting you
                    where directions would divide

So beautiful!   your path is petals!
Yet no matter the compass
          you rise to no ordinary heaven

Discovered men in the middle
          making better their miraculous achievement
                    exquisitely pale
                    its rhetoric softly realized

It would be difficult to turn away
          I'll learn the dictionary well enough
                    and capture the perfect vanilla
                              the tone   the shade

Those who labor and tend to the petals
          are striving to improve   to connect
                    and otherwise complete what's proximal

close-in

It is   quite simply   the best Burning Man art so far!
        keeping questions to itself
                being sure of being beautiful

And the sight of the men at work is no distraction
        but an added   *interactive*   necessity
They are movement
                even ballet
                with their tools and adjustments

At twilight's optimal moment
        they busy themselves
                behind a skein of holes drilled
                        in diaphanous laminae positioned
The xyloid enclosure a see-through domesticity
        painstakingly illumined

What colors they are needs another spectrum
Virtual perhaps
        the middle green and nearest blue
                not ready to blossom in the real world
                but exist *deleterious* even
                        in a realm of chromatic flirtations
                                probability   overrun with living

Capture then the certainty
        that what you are seeing
                is all twenty-one Burning Man years
                        made manifest mistique

108, GIANT LETTERS SPELLING "HOME"

Block letters
        blank verse
                Earth is Home

Home is Earth
the equal sign between

All of it *sheer*
At the limit of "unaided"
if you wanted to be topside   be careful

Though some letters are harder than others to climb
all the moves would be tricky
and the ablest and fittest struggle
grasping   searching
a leg over
and a hand feeling for what's next to do

Then there is tall standing
The letter of your being formed under
and the question of how to get down postponed
with shaking and doubt
the *nagging* kind

For if getting down may not be done
then a qualified success was the getting on *up* there
subtly   and publicly   at that

109, THE GIRL WITH THE TASSLED PARASOL

There'd been only three seconds of seeing
but it was you, all right
resplendent   in your white dress
the one promised
And you held a tassled umbrella.   the *"little* shadow"

Umbra   the larger
Like the shadow that will come to Oregon
the day the moon hides the sun   next year

But *you* are *this* year

                petite   solo
                    in the perfect place for sudden fashion
And all else withheld
            still I would be happy
                        to watch you twirl your tassles
                                while standing almost still

I always knew you'd find your way to Burning Man
            all the drama to behold
                    remaining *quietoso* yourself
                    part of a calm court

And those three seconds
            seem like quick modelling done
                    for the sake of a pattern
Doctor Hal doesn't know it yet
But you are the winner before the show even starts
            being a fashion show of just yourself
                        unconcerned there's any pageant

Debussy has taken notice
                        and doodles at the keyboard
He's like the rest of them   waiting on a vision

In *your* case, however   the *vision* waits
On a word   an impressionist piano piece
            poses for a video of three seconds' duration
You are apolitical and care not for parties
                        unless the parties have a DJ

The background's a bleached land
                    bright as your white
                    and it contrasts only a little
Context a sympathetic coloration
Distant haze an ambience found out
            a trudgen accomplished
                        in the middle of a *very* dry lake

You really *care*   as if you're brand-new
I think to myself and you hear
            ask every question back
                    that takes a "yes" answer

Russia's Anastasia!
Can I go steady with you?
It could be said the Romanovs are done
        that it's treason you've committed somehow
            yet here you are   wanting to play
            play all day in a skirt
Reliving the teen years of the twentieth century
Having knowledge of *The Invisible City of Kitezh*
                    and   *Kamennoi-Ostrow*
                        shimmering!

Here have you come
        with a certain mischief
            a coquette on a limited budget
                Orthodox   Old Russia for a week

What percentage of good will brought you?
What sun has deferred to your source illumination?

That which you wear is childhood's dress
And when it touches the playa
        its pleats are elongate   spread out
            a wedding
            the bride positioned
                    to hear vows to *no* one
                                not yet
Matrimony's fashion awaiting a groom's messenger
One to say a husband's too soon
        or too *late*
            for vows altogether

A virgin keep   if only *for keeps* is sought
                            the idea still pending

Three seconds umbrella...
The little shadow   like the briefest sadness

And the longer-lasting "path of totality"
        that will be the Moon's mission on Earth
        an umbra to confound!

Yet even this shadow must travel
Though believed in such you prolong its duration
   fearless of a blackened sun
      for eclipse is longing
      and longing has no ending

Even later   *after*   the after of science
    only the beauty of alignment lasts
      so that one keeps seeing coincidence
        and how it is almost supernatural
              like your image

Would that German could start!
Those words set to music by Schumann
    slowly   though the song is all passion
   the moods of eastern Oregon

What law could not be broken now
         if you are a promise to appear
         if you are so desired
             the umbrella is lifted?

You are almost still
As artists' skies when the twilight's slowed the brush
    those tassles of yours
      like a minimalist spacing
      of temptations   dounced   trembled

Are you so self-assured no sustenance is needed?
No hors d'oeuvre of St. Petersburg?
You require *nothing*?
Would you refuse even *absinthe*?
Are you the reason the Russians were endangered?

No   no, you would never misuse your powers!
Forgive!
    the economy of Love has changed
      less is best
      when your merest *Mona Lisa*
        could make unstable the heavens
        and hundreds of years
           of three seconds!

110. THE HOURGLASS BEACON

We're going to want to know all about it
But for now   let its varicolored facets gleam
          like a Seventh Wonder   *Pharos!*
               downsized to model lighthouse proportions

It is a lighthouse imagined as Time
          in a two-part arrangement of panes
               the hours to be tipped
               according to the colors

The inversion that's *reversal*
Forwards   backwards
          a time of one's choosing   can go either way
                    or stay motionless
                    safe in safety from the clockworks

We're going to have a closer look
          its components to discover
               that we might tinker with our *own* selves
               analog timepieces
Minority machines inclined to jumble chronologies
Mix it all together   for convenience

The fourth dimension *privatized*
          custom-made to be lived in dangerously
               over and over again
               one of the Wonders, surely!

That a dream at age nine
          may be a next door neighbor of this very morning
               and seemingly adrift
                    in a semblance of Truth
                    the way Truth is an emotion
The only hands are hands without numbers
The only face
          your *reflection,* my dearest!

You have come to rewind the hours
                    that comprise the glass

And most gracefully adjust the colors of the years
                    to match intentions
                        longings
            the sands running weightless
                replenished with kisses

An autonomy lit from within
        it is a lanterned apprenticeship
                high school revised
                high you are the way you wanted all along
To be elevated
Told the girl you had your eye on
        has agreed to go to the prom
                    though you hadn't even asked

And the Latin
        that seemed a tangle of endings
                and impossible plurals
                    became a tongue you spoke
                    as valedictorian
                            effortless as expiration

T. S. Eliot, you were *wrong!*
You got all those times entwined
                        when they needed discretion
Then you dared to suggest
            that they were all "perhaps" contained
            in just *one* of those tenses!
Nice going, you manic depressive, you!

And while we're at it:
When you rolled up those trousers
        you might have also done a little jogging
Then the mermaids
            you claimed were singing "each to each"
                might have sung to you *after* all!

Oh, I'm sorry!   this is so disrespectful!
Go ahead and murder me if you want, Thomas
            can it be in a cathedral?

Don't answer   but forgive me   I'm not myself

It's this hourglass so beautiful
        bewitching those who look upon its lighthouse panes.
            one "Quartet" of colors at a time!

It needs only resolve to be complete
Like a sabbatical
        perfect research abroad
            that featured good weather even in the Alps

It needs only shine
Like a Christmas once in Tehachapi
        with voices singing, "Shine, shine, shine!"
            a *yin* and *yang* flaring of the Yule.
            though it's mostly August and September
                        spinning the planet

We're going back to the shores of Egypt
        where the hourglass of Pharos glistened
            think of it also thin-waisted as this one
            upper and lower halves squeezed
                for a technicolor witch
                    demanding ruby slippers
                    the red sand beginning to fall

Gods in between will be compressed
                with no one to hear their prayers

Can I find my way home from here
        and here's footlights?   sidelights?   backlights?
Garish supplement
            to the nacent modesty
            of the main attraction

Strangely balanced
        in spite of a queasy solar plexus
            and suffering
            not at a time of one's choosing

Though the blues are repeated with fresh anxiety
        the beacon is escape beheld
                    however tentative

Listen!
They are singing!
The words are only "Shine!" in every language
                                    even the discourse of Oz

III. THE LOST TEA PARTY

The five teapots traveled
        tangential to the Temple

And they *may* have been lost
        but they certainly were *large*
                carried aloft on curved metal supports
                                        amidst many torches

There was something Russian about the procession
Were they not unlike those samovars?

I could have misheard
        and heard *"Last* Tea Party" wrongly
                but the party appeared to be a blast
                                        in *either* case

It was truly wonderful   passing lugubriously
"Lost" or "Last"
        the Temple's three storeys   well
                they seemed *especially* winged in response

Perhaps tea will really be served
                abundantly
                the crowd beginning to remember

It is the stirrings of memorial
        augmented by immensity's buckets
                brimming
                        pouring tremendously!

112. DIAMOND OR SQUARE?

In the Temple's timber
      symmetrical   fractal
          like the start of a kalaidoscope's day
Tier on tier converge on a zenith
And that central pendant nearly touching the ground
As if   though the design was meticulous
      a delightful haphazardness obtained
         something built into it
         a soul conceived
And asked what could be done in a heartbeat's span

The entirety asks back
        "Am I diamond or square?"

The difference   a lovely moment of geometry
     rotating the figure
        reacting to the attic's reach
           gazing at the work of Pythagoras
         quiet as open air discovered
             in a monastery's inner sanctum

 It is *all* previous temples
            since the first
              hurriedly raised
              with little attention paid
Though it *too* was elegant, beautiful

This one's a grand slam compound
It sets you counting   like beads
    the ornaments and beams of the rafters

This one is like growing up
You can make yourself a goral
    goat and antelope together
        made possible by architecture
          that's light as animals of the plains

Experience you wish to tell in telling dimensions
Excited by the math   yet calm in other ways

comforted   enclosed by space

That and more
The idea this entire construct   2016's Temple
        is also Nature
                as much as the fox on the mountain

And the sky
        still azure beyond the entryway
                is a *measured* twilight
                an equation
                        whose complexity deepens
                                                with nightfall
And every possible chance for enlightenment is taken

Later will astronomy start
        the naked eye enough
In the Temple talking softly
                one's perspective is revised
                                with each upward glance

The ceiling seems to recede
Like one of those telescoping Hitchcock effects
        everything elongating strangely
                                but invitingly
                        coming closer and fleeing away
                an artificial intelligence to it
Or news from another dimension

Imagine the Rhode Island School of Design's involved
The expertise of its entire faculty
        striving in tandem
Refuge as immensity
                balanced just barely
                and *toppling* should doubt ever enter in
                        and be unhallowed

The colors are easy
        the form   more difficult
                teetering
                        depending on a faith
                        in what these miles around can support

And the commencement of Kalaidoscopic inside-out
      is correcting and adjusting those timbers
            balcony on balcony built
            in a heartbeat's moment

Government of the diamond
Village of the square

The Temple's guarded
Ray Bradbury's here
      though his Fahrenheit's for later
            when a formless *expert* orange
                  burns past a careful conclusion

Memory gone homeless again

113. THE PEACOCK CAR

To put an end to meaningless hellos and goodbyes
      she boarded the splendid peacocky artcar
            its fantail spread with display and exhibition

This is one car that will *never ever* crash
      going so slowly with the crowd surrounding

To be a part of the peacock's court
      she jumped on   illumined
            by electric feathers splayed
                  and teamed up

It was a mobile *justice* system of light
But mobile just barely
      and the center of attention
                        receives another center

She went from meaningless to glitter-fickle

Put an end to wondering Why
        and tricky gearshifts' hello and goodbye

114. THE BIG MOUTH CREATURE WITH PLENTY OF ROOM INSIDE

"I don't think they'd mind, do you?"
"Darling, it's dark enough, let's just hop on!
        they've stopped for the moment
                but you can tell they're going places!"

"Yes, let's!   I /ove the glowy light
There's an underneath
        blue, like my nephew's show Chevy"
"That's a nice touch   and look!
Someone's added violet rope to accent
        such fine *ornate* beads   and bright!"

"There are stairs in the back, c'mon!
We're part of the party   a non-*political* party
                partygoers!
                and we're goin'!"

"Honey, I think they've paused to see the Temple
        so we could be here awhile..."
"That's all right
        here, there's a seat all yours on the second deck
            get cozy
            you see?   we've been accepted
                the ticket to ride was your smile!"

"What do we call this thing?"
"How about 'Big Mouth'
        same as beer I once drank?"
"Sure!"
"I mean, it's a creature, right?"
"*Decidedly!* and it certainly *does* have a very big mouth!"

299

"With plenty of room"
"Oh, yeah!"

At this point in the conversation
        a passenger who'd overheard said,
"Hi! I'm 'Belinda', 'Belinda', 'Belinda', 'Belinda'"
"Uh, you just said your name four times..."
"If you say your name four times, people remember"

"We see   well, at least I do   do you, sweetie?"
"I think so, yes, that's reasonable   I'm willing
        my name's 'Missy', 'Missy', 'Missy', Missy"
"And I'm 'Davy', 'Davy', 'Davy', 'Davy'"

Belinda was pleased
"Very good!   let us now consider our playa names!
This will be a little harder, but same principle"

She offered her hand
"I'm 'Robot Suicide', 'Robot Suicide', 'Robot Suicide',
        and one more: 'Robot Suicide'   there ya' go!"

They stared, amazed
Finally Missy said,
"I've not yet acquired a playa identity
We're waiting
        until I do something I can be named for
        you know, the way Native Americans handle it
            'She Who Chases the Fox'
                something along those lines"

Robot Suicide smiled
"I like it!   good plan
        but Davy, what about you?"
Davy was a little shy and unwilling
Then he said "wildcat2"   he said it, yes, four times

"Wonderful!   what happened to the first wildcat?"
"Taken"
"Oh, you mean like an email address?"
"Well, I saw a wildcat one time   close up
        came upon it exploring a mesa

300

surprised that wildcat
and the wildcat surprised *me*
Made me into a second wildcat in that moment!"
"Cool!" said Robot Suicide

Others were returning to Big Mouth
and   the driver turned the ignition
"We're off!" said Missy
"We're also *very* interactive!" added Robot Suicide
"Are you a robot that's come back from the dead?"
this from wildcat2
"Oh, no!   nothing like that
As a robot, I can't really die
It's like an impossible goal
that the robot aspires to
And *because* of this it becomes very artistic
Romantic, even
yearning for a beautiful death that's unattainable
you see?"

"Makes sense," said Missy, having considered all this
and carefully, too
"Yes, there's something   something profound..."
Wildcat2 was also impressed

"I feel like a *commuter* on this thing!"
Missy could have been going to work
"It's the bus-body," said wildcat2
"It may *look* like a monster with a very big mouth
but we're not fooled, *are* we, darling?"

Missy shook her head
"Not at all!   by the way   I was just thinking
how we're kind of like People of Earth
you know, what the *aliens* call us
when they show up and make announcements
'To the People of Earth...'"

Wildcat2 said, "Think of *ourselves* as the aliens!"
Missy brightened
and Robot Suicide liked the idea
"That's *right!*   to the saucer guys *we're* the ones

We're the extraterrestrials
                  that's not even a stretch!"

"We're moving"
Wildcat2 and, for the moment, Missy
        had made a new friend
              and although she was a robot bent on suicide
              they were confident
                    she'd be around for some time
And not even depressed
        because *circuitry*, they all agreed
              was immune to mood swings

Not to mention the titanium
                    she insisted she was made of
Albeit a kind of *soft* titanium
        that was apparent when they had a group hug

"I think you should be on the cover of a magazine!"
Missy suggested this   then asked, "Which one, though?"
The robot was sure
        "AI   'Artificial Intelligence'"
"Oh, no! you're not *artificial* at *all!*"
Wildcat2 also protested and at the same time reassured
"Definitely real   the intelligence part for *sure* real!"

The double-decker Big Mouth lurched
        an artifact of unearthly engineering
They were all now creatures of the Creature
And sightseeing the art near to Sunday's Temple
        they trusted the gears to get them around
              and while they jabbered
              they realized they had big mouths *also!*

But it was   curiously   all good

115. A CLOSER LOOK AT THE PEACOCK

To see it close by was to see Aztec plumage
      perhaps something akin to Quetzalcoatl
      lit for all the Empire to marvel at
              not a peacock at all, not really

Each outsized feather firmly arranged
      so that twelve of them were equally spaced
And they were glowing strangely, altering their hues

There were perforated globes embedded
      orbs in the midst of things
         each like spherical decisions made
         in Mexico's prehistory
Schematic   a plan of conquest
One that doesn't count on Cortés
      his arrival from the eastern horizon
         to make a parking lot of Tenochtitlán

Purple comes and goes   and green   and blue
And the display was such an *orderly* sequence
      one could not imagine disassembly

So let the artcar persist
      and the fourteenth century recur
              subtly
Or flashing money of the jungle even in the desert

116. BIG BEAR IN THE NIGHT

You know anything about the neighborhood
         you know a bear's out there!

Oh, he's *easy* to see in the baby spot
And he's rendered soft and teddy

despite his height above us
Darned near to *maximum* bear   biggest *ever!*
          call him *arctotherium augustidens*
          the experts did

The bear is restorative
A truly benevolent presence
The neighborhood's improved
          he's like news that matters

It was in South America it stood
          the largest bear of all time
               on his hind legs eleven feet
                         two million years ago

But here he is   representing thousands of his kind
You know anything about bears
          you know it's years of consensus
               that they're downright disconcerting at times

And *arctotherium augustidens*
          he would have had you trembling
               and reciting variations on that "Oh, my!" of Oz
For this bear was magnificent!
With a raised paw he appears to be training *us*
               teacher bear!

But wait, there's more
As if perspective entered in
          the animal was cautionary   he had a context
The contaminated future
               has dragged him back from South America
                    to remonstrate
                    and warn us of the perils
It is not just whimsical incongruity

More like he's the Other
That "somebody else"   the *outsider*
Outside time and circumstance
          saying   or rather, *asking*
          "What happened?"
If a bear could write a book there'd be admonishments

Connecting the dots
Speaking to a time when the Truth has gone extinct
        and Nature become unbalanced

You Know anything *about* that
        you'll want to do well
                be that six-year-old
                whose teddy is triumphant
And, the neighborhood safe
No religious crusade undertaken
Nothing "in the name of"
        new government arrives
                that resembles a child's clear complexion

The bear's an expert   all things ursine he knows
And he imparts this wisdom
        a new job taken
                teaching in the night
                    lessons on coming of age

He reads something
        though it's telepathy he uses
                you Know what the bear Knows
                        in a neighborhood *crowded*

He's a Farewell Bear   a lovely light-colored bear
Whose brown's a perfect match for what's left of the day
        a rather electric blue beyond the Granite Range!

And the bear's attended, too
        has visitations
        hands-on   pressure applied
"Tell *more!*"

Feeling animate   it is so good to be here!
        where it's spacious
                all visions elided
It might be important   meaning so very many things
And unforeseen   our codes scrambled

Oh, night bear!
Early evening bear!

your paws belonging to a nocturnal zoolatry
height and depth in the open playa
Distant bicycles swarming
            in the to-and-fro of the desert's diameter
            with its streaming LEDs
As though some console somewhere
                  had been switched on
                  and touch applied
The many fingers providing ignition
                        with the consent of all the ages

And Psyche
      for whom I once constructed a home
      an octagonal gazebo in the wasteland
The desert to which she'd been banished
This same Psyche approaches Big Bear in the Night
                  to lend the light of obsession
                  to tell of her wanderings
                        her continuing love for Eros
                                    her devoted search

The night bear will let you concentrate
Yes, on Psyche
      she who was afflicted   punished
            for looking at Eros
            couldn't take her eyes away
It was the gods' court order she be banished

Though a shelter was built to make her comfortable
A sympathetic carpenter
      and the bear   before and after her visit
            governs
            surveys
All the colonnades of the night   decades at a glance

He is her power animal now
      who brings understanding to bewilderment
In the subways of Olympus he will hibernate
Until the gods are forgiving for the long term
            granting Psyche immortality

All of which she may have foreseen

through the gifting windows
of her outpost gazebo

Big Bear seems willing to risk   a second extinction
risk a return to fossils   the state of bones
gamble everything to know she is safe

The myths   revised   reenacted each
All the furry premonitions
in all the neighborhoods of Black Rock
roaming freely as all bears have done
the *biggest* bear ever
being a version of the "short-faced"
a name that stuck
though the face itself   well,
it's thought it wasn't really short

Psyche will not need the Latin to summon him
Her protector will know
She has only to *think* it and it's done
being psychic herself

You know anything about the creature
This bear has *not* a predilection for deserts
The desert's not his habitat

All the more mysterious, his presence
like a revelation

117. THE TORCH

"It was a murder he didn't mean to commit"

This overheard
said wearily   while deeply troubled
And all the while a torch flared
With waves of color coming

twisting upwards
the object like a tulip   or bud arising
        as though a shoot had progressed
        seed to plant entire
                with assurance   instantaneous!

An *apotheosis* of plant
                all glowy
It was a rapture directed
                guided
                stabilized
                        endless
                        and the murder was subsumed

He who had committed was a prayer in the light
        blushing every hue in the flame
                in a continuous reality
Underlined with basic blue
Like an overture to what's above
                where crisis seems to sublimate

The night air is painted by a family of lasers
        whose dysfunctions ceased
                when their beams turned productive

It is the last day of August
And this torch is like a summary
        a month sequestered in the glow
                        of pulsating angels

How like a flower is this hazardous torch!
An *expensive* botany   bursting with creation!

Could one say it was a version of American Express?
One that does not involve credit
        but flames with barter and the best of Disney
                being animated lighting
                the colors slow-walking the stalk
                        to chimney into the nighttime?

BC oracle!   miracle of Rome!
It is a significant find!

with a significant torque to it
            indeed, a *commonwealth* of brilliance!
And so very consequential
For those lucky enough to be connoisseurs of its light
As if they'd grown up
            in the benevolent corral that is its spell cast

I, too, am a tourist of the torch
The psychedelic enhancement
        of Liberty's Staten Island arm raised
            marigold tulip   rose
            all interchangeable
                the wellspring inexhaustible
                                    unsparing
The spectacle that would detain in the Land of Rights
If only to garner appreciation

Nothing in the night may extinguish this
The government of Truth   which
        though we are mostly unprepared to understand
        yet there is lingering there
                and being alight and optimistic
Like new employees in a bath of miles

Each color   a new idea for betterment
With tyranny overturned in such a way
        it shines with opposition
                to what was   saying,
"It was murder I never meant to commit!"

118. THE SEGMENTED UNICORN

It was a unicorn   segmented   armored
The several plates in tandem
        as if it were the *armadillo* we saw
                in a dream of zoos
                those moveable parts bright white

You said "unicorn" because of the horn
        but it is certainly a silly horn
                kind of a candy cane thing   and striped
So that later   the unicorn out of sight
You'll *also* say, "I know what I saw!"
                and *I'll* say, "Sure, sure..."

It was a "unique-corn"
        its flanks
        all those armadillo look-alike plates
                        flexing
                        with some hidden purpose

I'm proprosing we ride it
        pretending a rodeo in Space
                where no one can hear your "yee-hah!"
                and the trophies disappear in the dark

Assuming the segments comprise a one-of-a-kind creature
We will certainly need to protect it
                        from animal kingdom come
The time not yet arrived
        when a unicorn's *skull* is all that keeps company
                        with virginity

After this, may all mammals be as loosely bound
        though immune to any pull-apart impulses

The unicorn's gait is a leisure
Wherever it's going has made no demands it hasten
You know, this is a strange unicorn *indeed*
        with a penchant
                for resembling others *not* of its kind
                an albino *rhino* even
        if you let the spectacle have its way with perception

The only girl to walk the floors on Altair 4
        could have tamed all the animals it's trying to be
                could have calmed each one of them
As Doctor Ostrow proposed
                on that same Forbidden Planet

his commander almost convinced of this
and adding
"Oh, you're quite the heart specialist, Doc!"
in the deleted scene

The segmented unicorn goes
The Earth very much a planet in its own right
A place where demise is ongoing
        and Nature's struggles deter the optimist's revery
            is there anything *not* another's prey?

But let's hold it right there before our brains are full
Leave room for some answers to form
        and their urgency appraised with caution

I wanted great nieces and great nephews to see this
Said their names softly
        Kindred spirits
            Savanna   Tanner   Porter   Suzie

Zookeepers of vision!
Tracking animals of time and remembrance
        constructing robot hippos
            for unspecified menageries

What's mythic is transferred to the children
That their mythology may gel more spectacularly
        and they will dream better plans than the movies
            night shows
            and day shows
With bands to play those circus tunes

Less than thirty seconds I'm ready to join them
        the bright white one to waddle in

"I know what I saw   and *you* saw it too!"
In the traffic jam of critters
                the most miraculous of all
The infinite Serengeti awaits its pawfalls
                        (okay, *footfalls!*)
There will be plentiful grazing and room to roam

They used to say, "Talk story"
                    and we do *now*   without drugs
                    simple speech
               that belongs to a playground
          vast
          full of square miles and counties

I wondered if the segmented unicorn was insured
If it comes when called
Is subject to tantrums
          with a longevity depending on kindness shown

Make a pretty park of the playa
               the "beach" full of reckless beauties
There's evidence of shapeshifting
Bachelor and spinster lives led
          to keep the herd a minimal concern
                                   inconsequential

The animals are saying goodbye to evolution
They like what they *are*
          what they've already become
               especially the segmented unicorn
               replete with those plates
                    that somehow dangle   loosely
                         as it travels
                         no law enforcement required

Oh, but *do* give it gender!
Call the creature a "he"
          and say he makes it easy to love him
               supply all the care that's needed
                    to keep him going the best he can
                    without violence

Because he's *parts*   he's more explainable
And the mystery of the *whole* can be delayed
               more-or-less
The clear water of Reason drunk
          things adding up
          and you never finish counting

Would that / might be articulate, too!
My *own* segments assuring piecemeal survival
        in the wild world to flourish
                penning approximations sufficient
                to tell the time at least that death prefers

Is there a music to parcel these changes?

The unicorn's a lesson learned
Now we both can see
        though you see better
                the barbershop snout
                candy minus the cane

There is evidence the myth is not killed off
But roams the playa
        modern   gone to pieces bright white
                and wishing still
                to rest its head in the lap of innocence

119. BLACK POLAR BIPOLAR EXPRESS

Did they   whoever they were
Did they say it was a "Black Polar Express"
        or a "Bipolar Express"?

Whichever   it had a catcher
        perhaps to keep "normal" out of the way
A cowcatcher up front
Its grate backlit with a blue enlightenment

It was a cross-town train
        running on psychic principles
                the tops of each hour
                announced like a protest

Should "White Polar" be its name?

And is the train expressly a psychological choo-choo?
        when "going mental" is going by rail
            to unspecified anxieties
                    shunting the extremes?

Maybe a malady's both a dark *and* a light condition
Able to travel that way   in contradiction
                tracking opposites

Listen!
The mournful blasts disguise an onboard levity
        and the whistle *is* a comprehensive "toot!"

Hot-and-cold running all over
It is a locomotive murdering the miles around
                    on no medication
Proud of the issues raised
        by the anguish and euphoria *both*
                that coexist in a black-and-white boiler

It's a night train with absolutely no schedule exactly
The engineer gone, gone missing
                        his consciousness derailed

Let steam tell the story that therapy suppressed
        say "yes!" to express
                and obey the executive orders
                of pajama-clad patients
Who reenact *One Flew Over*
        using a train instead of a boat to slip the bonds

There's no *guesswork* to Black Polar   Bipolar
Random is Meaning
Unstable sanity consults its watch
        and works backwards to beforehand
        to intentions deferred

It is open-carry of the mind's misconduct
        a false narrative tamed
                and told the truth *about* the truth
                rubber banded
                    like fiction's never-ending elasticity

The mumbo and the jumbo have boarded
        with tickets printed by Shakespeare
                and King Lear at the throttle
                    exploding!
Having a great day and night of madness
        on invisible rails
                    riding their dastardly parallels

Come *on!*   come aboard!
Perhaps it's *Colonna's Trolley* of your youth
The one that crashes over and over
            and there's still enough life left
                to make a record of its screeches
                    for children to play
                        until its vinyl grooves are worn

The train is beyond the jurisdiction of medicine
There's a wonderful *weightiness*
        the locomotive's desire to express itself in steel
        black and bipolar
A roisterous libido clearing all in its path!

"How old are you?" it asks
"How old do you *wish* to be?
Let me take you there
        before *Les Miserables* happens
                            backlit by terror"

Get to know the town
        on your way around Everywhere
                Black Rock Depot the starting point
Set out in the unseeing dark
        running on impulse pistons
                    drugs and alcohol unknown
Your ultimate destination is desert left alone till now

·The realm of pure protest find
In the grown-up night
        where a constable
        a Javert   Law's mental case
            waits

Wishing to jail that which runs free
                    and dusty anxiety is raised
                    pushing back

The better-off among us
        clamor to mingle with the passengers
            want a house to be born in
                    this polar noir careening
Barely controlled   in motion   in love
The nature of daffy
        intricate as its engine's plumbing
            connections   innate legends

Feel so much *better*
Bipolar, Black Polar
                the options implied by the words
                the beauty of two states
The *freedom* of that!
And doing nothing wrong stoking the boiler

Go ahead, never-ending Extremes!
I embrace your outposts!
        both light and dark
            attest to "woo-woo!" and daring
The playa warped and yielding
        where the train pursues interwar
            running Dada
                on a schedule drawn up in 1925

Shunting, yes
Turning aside the *other* years   each of them
And whistling other dates and next days
            before their arrival

A mournful gaiety
        the two classical masks together
            tragedy and comedy
Contradiction laughs
All the way to Escalon, Sulphur and Gerlach
                    our intentions wisely deferred

The engineer's a *concept* basking in the nighttime

Colonna's Trolley enjoying a happy crash
Unstable sanity to blame
        if there is to *be* any blame

The Express is *euphoria's* therapy
        the cure a part of the illness

Listen and remember:
They are affordable pajamas!
        by God!   Bipolar midnight's married light
            made a new schedule
            and is getting up steam
                for all stops
                    in the Land of Dastardly

120, THE COLORS OF THE HOUR

Purple was trending
Blue   was *also* a color   trending
                bestseller light in the night

It was 7:30's "key"
One of the City's plazas
        clogged with bicycles
The biggest party in the world
        and nowhere to park

A certain obscenity
        like a sheriff's stuttering proscription
        a nail in the tire of Now
The mostest dog in America denied a bone

It's a purplish-blue   running wild and weird
The concept training henceforth
                in the art galaxy's corner

Trending sand   and revelry's *almost* satori

121, RED PUZZLE

It was live
It was assembly
    those giant pieces

Was there a picture?
Was the puzzle anything at *all* in the dust?

A blank accident   jigsawn large
You walk around it
        through it
           hauling plywood   live
A present participle dangling with "Where do I go?"

Red puzzle piece missing its place
    and others   scattered   curvy
      unsolved
      abandoned

Is it late in the week?
Is it interest lost in the "rockets' red glare"?

And the dim puzzle's imperfect
    unfit together
      by a president of ruddy incompletion

122. PANORAMA DESERTED

The Slinkies leap unseen   down
    their rainbows' rings are dulled by the dark

The stairs are alive
As I will be in exercising *on* them
Now   tomorrow   or after that
    the heart's bottom line:

an EKG's healthful oscillations

They call it "PANORAMA"
And the view from the top was terrific
    those forty-two steps leading to overview
        I'd save them past their deconstruction
      and while Burning Man lasts
           look forward   each day
                    to their lumber

Save the mornings too
      those early appointments made
      climbing begun with daylight's start

Deserted are the streets and alleys
Those sweet homes emptied
      a slight claustrophobia exchanged
        for the better phobia of *out there*
           riding the waves of the playa ocean
The Purple Palace crowded
      but in good working condition

Here might be directed a sparse play
Panorama part of it
      some entrance or departure
        being on the way to heaven
           past the arcing Slinkies

So much depends on this stage
The conscience cools somewhat
      and grace seeps into celeste
        to quieten nerves
First cultures found in the silence
So that Indian carnival is parallel light and dark
      light and dark carnival too
        a libertine holiday redeemed

We're stalled   albeit thoughtfully
Licensed dreamers
I'm Genghis Khan's love child   dozing
      campaigning from a crib
        money no object   nor subject, either

The next generation's at sea   but in a *good* way
          floating   their artcars gentle
                    unsinkable Mollys

Even the judges are here
                    their gavels keeping time

You may not ever know why the City so attracts
And   stretching desertion to distraction
          the future will explain itself
                    and Nothingness will dwell
                              in the biblical streets

The Lord God taking an assumed name
A playa name
And dancing alone
          just pocket change left over from Creation

Panorama   Panoramic
Noun or adective?
          its forgotten which
                    suffice it was there   inviting
                    the Big Picture
Just climb while counting
As if each stair were a lottery's payout
                    and beautiful plans are made!

The world's smallest baby steps
          the easy way   green-slicing aridity
                    and keeping in place beginnings
                              that *simplicity* might stay a reference
                    and reason be ascendant

Forty-two is a number
A summit of wood
Let the stairs last as long as / do
          still constructed
                    the construction a consciousness
                    retroactive exercise
                              an act of intense resistance
                                        with jazz happening

There will be no cloudbursts started
Just lumber's thought-for-thought
                    the demons stay away

Internalize the Panorama
        giving money to Within
        so the heart may explain itself to giants

The stairs are indeed alive
Their wood grain dusted after all that's gone before
Making a friend has never been easier
        with a Slinky's descent
        continuous
            in the vicinity of Home Sweet Somewhere

Imagination's oscillations
        the number forty-two
                counted to deserted
                the *party* striving in the open playa
                    non-political
                    aboriginal, even
The Purple Palace picking up
                    and dropping off
                        Glinda's drunks

Lottery of companionship
Of neon grace   a personal culture
The next thing we know
        as the next generation knows   pensive
            a panoramic quota

Each day the height of the former World Trade Center
        its one hundred tenth floor gained
        as memorial   only in America
            where a gavel is strong suggestion made

Find a way to have the City *empty* at times
Then empathy
        and entropy's beatific plans for nothing at all
Or the Lord God finding something to say
            something that will help for once

321

                    prayers answered
                              whether fervor was involved or not

Internalize!
Or make it such a command
                    it will use only one syllable

Be constructed as these stairs are   from within
While the solitude should last
The world's smallest baby steps taken
                              that uplift
                                    to a comprensive heaven

123, SPHERE

Sphere fire paused and waiting
A hollowed globe like a miniature planet
                              carved   and going places

A schematic Earth as hearth
                              whose heat may travel
                    it is all aperture
              and learning
              done in desperation
The mind accelerated for a time

It is too late
        for this portable furnace
                    to speak of a suicide in 2003
Mannikins suspended
The artist having hung himself among them

Why does this sphere   this artcar
        why does it summon his art of death?
                              when its heat is so undoubted?

The world is renounced and burning

is confined in a porous consumption
a flaming sculpture
wanting a careful immolation

124. THE PLAYA DIVIDED

A whole desert to see!
no two square feet the same

It is the Black Rock Range that divides
that separates
so that there's a west
and an east
to the playa
And what's between is a story of rocks killed off
and buried whole

The layers   the gulleys
aching for oblivion
All of it burning brown and tan and chalky-white
until their shades of meaning
need : a desert's signature

How do you figure those camels?
Camels once lived here!
got their start in barren North America
and crossed the land bridge to Asia, yes!

The Black Rock Range is a huge art gallery
Serious, too   and wanting a reception
no roquefort morsels set out
no wine or mineral water
and no opinions divided
on the merits of the work

It's sure there are no artists' statements
and   nothing as yet has been sold

Far to the south is *another* afternoon than this
In a dusty place
        the event from which you traveled
        though just arrived
Having cleared the Gate at last
            and being free to roam the City
                still you fled
                    to be properly out of doors

There are no celebrities here in the playground
And the little playas at the pass make us wonder
When was it *they* filled
        and knew a pluvial awareness

With painter's eyes
        prepare the scene for pastels
            let it be a commissioned show
                notes taken
                that become unintended critiques

I want to see that lake again!   Lake Lahontan!
I want a wetter time
        so that *water's* what's divided
            and the Black Rock Range
                is then a long penninsula

Lake Lahontan is *inferred*
Something one may do ten minutes at a time
        the former shorelines discerned
        and *seeing* those shelves left
            is obsession   is
                almost unhealthy in a way
For Nevada's inland sea stays fictive

As the water is invisible
Its previous edges are a tension   a tease

How is it
        that the imperceptible
            may perform such a theft of attention?
With what soundless music does it feast

on what is seen!
Strongly insisting on conception
Forcing reflection
        a total confidence come   honorable vision

What would *you* do here?
Oh! look upon!   include the others
        holding vigils
            a little at a time   in old clothes
Noting the sun's position
The smaller deserts of what divides

There was no obligation to go
        yet the entirety was asking so nicely
                                    for a visit
                    and so you clamber
            over a paint-by-numbers land
One that has a superior knowledge
            of its own erosion

Left and right side
Absolved of any preference
                down low
        or up high
            overlooking the end of the world
                            as soft a preview
                            as faith in air
Mountains intruded by fragments of themselves

If I can't have the Lake
        perhaps the rain at least
            perhaps *all* time will visit *this* time
                and attempt touch and feeling

There is no falling down.   desperate
Only learning
        the same that filled kindergarten's aisles
                        days two weeks long

Still a little kid   but much bigger
        there is no time of day
            that's divorced from military time

                    its oh-so-very thorough clock
For this looking is an operation done   sort of

Getting here was a drive home
A game of gears played
               pulling into the divided desert
               and warming to its intentions

And your presence on the ridge
          is an overture played
                    that will never conclude
The extra steps taken to enclasp the light
          make it official:
               the mountains of the Black Rock Range
                    are eliciting superhero behavior

This exploration   a love
Something to be good at in the sun
A real mission!

The saddhu is welcome
Turns it any way he wants
The dark and light-colored rocks
          exactly inspired
               right there
                    the inside outside
The sacred planet's sunlit half is teaching

One's footing is therefore assured on the stony top
A sport of posture
          a not-to-worry feeling
Like being in the View-Master's ancient stereo
Even this dilettante is allowed a complete picture
               no job
               no family
                    no fault

Friends picking you up and holding you close

This is what it looks like
The country of cracks and grooves
                    and feverish wandering!

Why *do* these long deserts converse and conspire
        encourage and train the mind
            to abandon comfort
                and empty *other* places?
Why would they care that much
                being desolation's example?

The playa's divided
Separated by a range
                    occult
                    lonely
                        and irresistible

125. WHAT *ELSE* DID YOU SEE?

What *else* did you see?

The same   though magnified
                    to include mirage and mines
                    the slightest remains
                            of pioneer thought

The same made shaky with blowup
An *apprehensive* review
A greater enlargement
        than was ever thought possible

I am here for *you*, desert!
                as if for a loved one
        and the crisp stone alleges harm done
                        and *danger*, too

What else
        was the close-up of drainage
            turned tan, white
            all the ways *water* refines

The hills with creases fit for augury

We were asked to watch the hot springs
The source and upwelling of interior absolution
Asked to keep a vigil there
        that no use be made of the waters
            unless *locals* showed up
                they, we were told,
                were to be left alone...

It was not enough just watching the pool
We'd look at *more* than that
            study the backdrop
No phone calls or texting
And the only music   a comprehensive fermata
        that most restful of musical instructions
            silence
                mid-sonata
            symphony
                and aria

What else but the same
        the way geology insists on extended stay
            and improvement
                though what gets better is eyesight alone

We will tolerate knowing
        the time left talks down to survival
Our sneakers are footwear's repeat performance
It happened that notes were taken
        for we were not trusting the ascent alone
            to be specific enough

The sun (what else?)   *stubborn!*
Some Egypt up there
        staring down and drooling
            from a celestial hospice
                        on the taxpayer's dime
Or is this supposition the gist
            of a low-grade sunstoke?

I'm sold out of meaningful

and hallucinate high school
A former classmate attempting to relearn geometry
                    and dead reckoning
        a student barely graduating
        barely in touch
And one who will not succeed
                    despite remedial genius

I'll be suited for this, however
Climbing the sides of the Black Rock Range
            and surveiling

What else did you see?
Rough Arabia   Pakistan, maybe
            and Iran
Fahrenheit's lands belonging to hardship
All these square miles of bare subsistence
        voices lost to the unamplified wastes

And looking beyond even this treeless safety
        to imaginary miles more
            in the dry washes and scorched crevices
                the pioneers pretend
                say it's a comfort
As *you*, dilettante,
        seek one afternoon's namesake discomfort
                        totalizing

There's the Black Rock itself
Indifferent   a geologic summary of Why and When
        whose summit and summit plaque
            were a swirl of busy flies

But I'm still here for you, forlorn war zone
Where the *conflict's*
        a struggle to trade a thirst for *power*
        for a thirst for Gatorade

It's science fiction
        a planet barely reached
            before the fuel ran out
                (it was a rocket with *fins* by the way)

329

And   the careful survey made
        no one is saying there's life as we know it
        and there are some that are *glad* about that

Did I say there'd been apprehension?
Yes, but getting used to it's going to be fun

Burning Man is miles away
You can tell it's there
        just look in the direction of dust
It's better to be *here*
        a way of attending
                that keeps you a virgin
                a pristine witness

Upon descent from the ridge
                find the pool   and purity
        letting disbelief soak for awhile
Odd   how ancient dangers
        though they seem remote and old-fashioned
                and we're *grateful* for that
                still I'm wanting them back
Wanting old peril
Preferring basic scarcity to atomic abundance

If only uranium would decide it won't work anymore
                and not be split for anyone
Then the test site before us reverts
And no blinding fission erupts
        and what else might be seen
                does not include a crater

See as a kaleidoscope
See the colors *better,* then
The fractals informing more exactly
        yet fanning incomprehension
                the slightest remains of recognition
                and then the sonata's instructions!

We will tolerate this unknowing bliss
        while the sunstar permits
                        and even insists

Choosing relief from sorrow
    lest some angry angel seek opportunities
        to rearrange
            the rocks   your mind
                    all else

126. DO NOT LEAVE IT EVER

"How long ago did you leave Love behind?"

Never mind!
Saw the beginning and the end of this
    and *you* were there   instructing
       making understandable
         the ruined landscape
         playa-scape   sage-scape

All sides of the namesake stone
Not as black as black can be
           but foreboding even so
      as though something archaic lived inside
      prepared to shape our destiny

There's enough grandstanding possible
    to fill all of the stadium that is Nevada
      slipping and sliding
        to every podium outcrop
All parts of the satellite hills that surround us
    and promise easy climbing in the sunlight

It's all oils and acrylics
The palette comprised of delicate earth tones
        sepia   burnt umber
Not only those colors but an impossible violet
    and ochre's pigment, strange and deathly yellow
      all vie for inclusion

Somehow the millions of years
        must hitch themselves like pioneer wagons
                to the briefest reconnaissance
Or "Do not leave it ever" is recited
                and made a command
                no *return*

The sun will down   it will not matter
But wait!
        the visitor log
                the sign-in   of course!
A chance to write the words that will detain others

Write, you will   earn a degree
                on a schedule of free time
                the curriculum that of Beauty
Which, though arrested and held
        is soon freed through the expert help
                        of the gods and goddesses

Talk about that   and more
It's a planet all right
And it wanders   just as the Greeks had asserted
        long ago
                the Earth in the company of Jupiter
                of Saturn, Mars, Venus and Mercury

What you might have heard on ancient talk radio
That same radio *now*   that's always silent
        but that is what you *listen* for   out here

I truly love this land
                but you love it more
And that is why I will see it *with* you
        and restlessly
                so that the trails   *all* of them
                        are taken

The kind of magic where thinking makes it so
The pool of the Black Rock Springs waits
Almost too hot

bubbles   a mushy, oozy bottom
          with reeds crowding
               and zephyrs stirring
The little dock for dipping extremities
Glorious!
The mirage close-up   and soothing

The absence of crime
          like the twin gulfs of the divided playa
And laws that might be changed
               are mostly forgotten
                    moot enforcement the winds abide

A cologne derived
          from the sophisticated cities
                              of nothing at all

I'm with you
          until the basins of Nevada refill
               with Ice Age love come to lower elevations
And Lake Lahontan's a fierce blue
               in a future peace, finally!

I'm guessing you know when this will happen
You'll be discreet, I hope
          so it stays our ecological secret
Time's *backwards* finding *forwards*
          by accident
               by design
However your affections trend

When they said "Welcome home!" at the Gate
          they meant this Mars
               when it's possible to know
                    your home has no boundary   no end

First Peoples at new-found freedom
And you do not leave it ever
The entirety, a planet
          a wanderer *we* wander on
               as far as the voices say
                    till silence says the rest

and yields to entropy

127. DUSTFISH LONGINGS

The stage at Dustfish had filled with longing
Call it a quintet taught by a pinkish ambience
    the ensemble "sweet"
    the way that word is now a yearning
      and commonplace benevolence
        sweet...

Say it in time to the music
The Fish is gulping playa dust
The Fish is a forensic quest
    pink in the dark
      the hopes and fears
        of our millennial selves

The desert's stolen the show again
    for the desert is channeled
        a stage possessed   acutely

I was growing fond of their act
I wanted to take them home to Berkeley
    where they might enthal the Freight and Salvage

They've made the Dustfish happy
A Cinderella band going on and going over
    like a good ad that wants you to dance
      space out like an astronaut
      absorbing that lightness
         and weightless pink

The outside world attends
    color coming to its severe film noir
Perhaps it's given up pretending to enlighten
        through fright

Is it possible for me to elaborate?
Would you mind, terribly?
Will you hear the music in the words?
    "Slow *down!*"
        "Take it easy!"
All the names you've known, and what's *in* a name
        brought to the Dustfish to swim as entertainment

They're *good* enough
        the audience will say, "That's all for today"

Let us have some coffee to continue
Dustfish has been here since 1999
        what someone said
            what someone meant
                recounting

Hey, wait!   there are *seven* up there!
A septet!
        the drummer and the dreaming sax were hiding

The only lyrics were "out of the house" heard
        and the lead singer means it
            jumping and striding
            as though dance had come to her
                            unannounced
                        and lent persona
                    lent meringue

A god of clear complexions spoken for
Blue words for a violet marquee
        an *underneath* language allowed translation

One may never undo
Let a// that's happened instruct
Thanks be!   for guitars' forget-me-not notes!
        for how music may acquaint the listener
            with every nuance
                of the Cosmic Sounding Line

A pink stage powered by improv

The musical miles-an-hour of its sharps and flats
They're nuts for blue notes
          as is the foreground silhouette
               lurching   invisible

A strange voice in the night:
          "Give up, now!   you've done enough!"

Uh-oh!
The thought an AA "sponsor" said he most dreaded!

Let the little band be continuation
I'm sorry I went there, to the place of worry
          I'll need to hitch to return
               the music's counterclockwise
Time for a ride back to Rock 'n' Roll caves
          to be safe in safety from the clockwork inevitable

Performance as a plan carried out
          and carried away to sweet distance
               almost automatically

Say this in time to Dustfish longings
               and go for a waterless swim yourself!
                    concept is all
                         concept is a liar raised on the Truth
All it takes to imagine the rest
Lake Lahontan can refill
          if you simply say it's the Ice Age still

Being fond enough of the septet
               to wish their gig were indefinite
My own millennial self
          is immersed in Freight and Salvage right here
Cinderella singing solo for her sisters and step mom
Who are actually nice people it turns out
          and who knew that until the dust arose?

And the dust having brought forth its dusty sealife
          it will outlive us all
               having given up pretending
                    "time being" is worth our scrutiny

Dustfish   like a steady job taken
        when all you wanted was casual labor
                and just being called now and then

Pink has a destiny that wants to include you
And   luminous within   are letters blue
        the sign that's invitation
                bicycles bunched in response

It is another beckoning
        as much as any other show on the Esplanade
                and you want to be that Newbie yourself
                        not settle for vicarious   but
                go   place to place
Living initiation all over   all week

The guardrail's gone and the Fish is hungry
Listen to the band
        singing "out of the house"   but that is all
        the *only* lyrics for now

Approximate meaning
                maybe the Fish is meaning something, too?
                some revamped Christianity
                        a mummified faith
                                finding   new life
                                        in empty lands

128. THE GIANT VOLKSWAGEN

The giant car traveled
Lit   and bluely   it rolling went
        like a family tradition
                running around and running on empty
Or a leading lady who's enlarged with purpose

You could say it was a Volkswagen, too
        albeit *not* from the factory
A busybody car going everywhere *it could* go
            before repair is impossible
                going on errands unknown
Somebody's version of the People's transportation
The fascist machine having shed the stigma
                the totalitarian paint job

The showroom's on the move
        with one-of-a-kind German engineering
            the "kraut" gone out of its pistons
            to be simply Deutsch at large
                and *written* large
A reality TV's World War of what-if

"The Bug" is become a benevolent tank in the street
And with well-roundedness
        attempts to edit aggression
            and cease the selling of *Lebensraum*
                to whomever will listen

At Burning Man the public's private
                the difference sleek blue
                another "look"
One that takes a populace apart
        and makes daydreams common knowledge
            of *Quo Vadis?*
Of a spectacle with Victor Mature behind the wheel
A strong automotive storm
        and ultimate high point of
            a continental fantasy

Now it conquers the dark in a sunny century
May the car contradict a nagging unease
        and disreputation
            that something good
                may come of something bad
                and pass the finish line of war

A Kars4Kids thing
        in the sense it was built bigger

to resemble ordinary machinery
ridden by adult toddlers

For they remember the age
when chairs were outsized
and tables and steps
And kindergarten road rage alternates with naps

This Volkswagen was the *roomy* edition
whose warranty exceeds the needs of children
now "playing chicken" in the dust clouds

Perhaps "memorial" is the word that best describes it
The familiar lines in a right-of-way of dirt
A peaceful blue   blue-*electric*, even
the better to be seen
and be a drivetrain *extraordinaire!*

The giant differential
was a bulbous hub of Kaiser gears
long after the abdication
way past the demise of the *pickelhaube*
The knowledge of good and evil   is
a knowledge of suspension and wheelbase

The U-turns of U-boats confronted by destroyers
The metaphor of Stockholm and its Syndrome
when acceptance hovers
between affordable transportation
and unwillingness to dismiss a symbol

Despite the Volkswagen's substantial prodding
It's possible to deduct oneself from history
When the real thing intrudes
it could be a sign
but a sign of no significance
Every decision taken for a ride on relevance

And   strangely
the scene seems a barren Missouri
Truman's wheels ready to roll
with "Little Boy" and "Fat Man"

Fear tells me to get in the way of that thing
And end it all before a last   and *sixth*
                          extinction
The doctor says to do the same

"You're restless
              only hit-and-run for you..."
Be brave as only eight years old can make you
      acting out demise so often
                    nothing can keep you alive!

Before 9/11   death was *so* romantic
                    so *easy*
It will take running *after* it, now
              and catching *up*
              to a King-sized demolition derby
                          of one Volkswagen

Do you hijack?

I'll sing "I'll be Blue for You"
              since you're so blue for me
And it is certainly Country hereabouts
The streets as wide as the Lake that was
          well, the dust of 7:30's street, anyway
                    and the distance
                          towards which your fenders fly

It is no fault of your own
          that a bloated engineering
                    should prowl without a permit
Made to advertise the sky
                    in the middle of the night
                    with a clutch for all occasions

Getting there is over
          and coming back cannot be done

Say it's a giant car that will be *lost*
                          in spite of its size
As in a dream   "Where?"
And you just *can't* remember where it's parked!

what avenue of Black Rock...

Please! it isn't fair!
Walking for hours and finding it gone
        but finding it later full of beer bottle glass
    oh, whoever you are!
    don't destroy it that way!
It's still an automatic automotive vision
            fat tires for traction

Everything's done but the driving
And there's one last chance to qualify as chauffeur
        hope the shocks are good

Don't crash!
Watch the turns 'cause I'm watching *you!*
            true blue
            in the dark   with revelers
The dark with *slim* blue lines
        outlining   outliving 1945
            by seventy-one years   so far

Let's call it something else, therefore
Let it rhyme with "photo-op"
We're well inland now
        and allowed the freedom
            to name what's blue and may be *green*
            as it flashes ambiguity

The pulsing of a higher purpose
More than spiffy
And so slow   it seems on *hold*
                waiting for giants to board!

129. CENTER CAMP BAND

The were explaining   onstage

There was no music
        no snare
        no sax
        nor clarinet
                sounded

Was it they'd not yet submitted to performance?
No   the band just couldn't quite quit the stage
There was instead a talk in progress
        the roadways of thought traveled
                and all those sharps and flats stayed put

It was a Wednesday night they stood there
Stalled   while the guy with the mic was pacing
"On the *other* hand..." was all I could hear him say
        the only phrase that was undoubted

It was like an audible epigraph for the new century
Will the secular enter stagnation?
Continue, even?
Will enervation define this Third Millennium?

Band Gang, that's right!
And I thought,

"No music make while I get a good look at you
                mid-week
                you look entitled in a *good* way
Shakespeare could have used you
And however sparingly, you would have loved it!
The ultimate talker making use
        the band playing fanfares for royalty
                their arrivals   and departures
                and subsequent scheming!

"Thanks so much for your cacophony to date
And   this being *Wednesday*
        there's more to come, right?
                express conflict while you're at it"

The performance was posture
The performance was *over*

And I surveilled the denouement
        the aftermath
                and the nonetheless encore of spoken word

Whatever tunes were taught
        now was the report card of sharing
                "on the other hand"
                        guess they couldn't stop as planned
                                as programmed

I say they're the best band of all *time*
Though they stand in the problem spotlight
        of apparent *doubt* that this is so

There were enough musicians on the stage
                        to ignite a musical if they'd wanted
One that would have had a successful run
But abeyance was all
        in the limbo of chatter

130. "YOU CAN TALK TO ME!"

He's white-nosed   the lotion slathered
Her nose is naked for now
He's with a slouch hat
She's letting her black hair take the heat
He's tank-topped grey
Her gear is a red two-piece

They are entirely sunglassed
        but I *think* I see
                think I know them
                        how we got to this century together
                        our many years collected
                                connected

And something made me say,"You can talk to me!"

"We *can?*
"Yeah, I'm not taking *pictures*, I'm making a *movie!*"
"Ah, but wait!
        remember way back
        when a Clark Gable
        or some other handsome actor
                would tell his love interest,
                        "You oughtta' be in pictures!'"?
"I get it! Of course!
'Pictures'   that's what they called the movies then
        so will you both be in that bygone
                and talk some more to me?
                make a moving picture
                        of just one minute...?"

The girl began charmingly
As if it were an audition
        as if she were certain of a role
                and forthcoming fame
And her boyfriend postured
Assumed an action hero's minimalist stance
        when   the less said, the more *manly*
                                somehow

"Are you happy to be here?"

Not a trick question
It was asked as if I were asking myself
It may not have comprised a question at *all*
        in this environment
        in this geology overlapped by Pop
                happiness was *always* possible
Customer satisfaction
                when "out there" is right here
                        an intimate distance come home

His beard   a 21st century's *pioneer* shag
                in concert with smooth-shaven science

We are treating each other to digital rapture

244

"Could be here all *year!*"

All three of us enjoyed the absurdity
A week was all we could handle
       because those seven days
              seemed to have extra hours
                     enough to add up to a permanent stay
Huge stress that was balanced with exaltation

Our movie was quintessential Burning Man
How instant affection seeps into chance encounters
It's never been easier to say,"Hello!"
The secular reconciled with every superstition

Ecstasy is not required
       a dream has overtaken the day
              "Stay here all year?"
There was laughter and a kind of armistice
A change of key made in Texas and heard in Iowa
       all *over*

"We don't have to leave yet..."

For some reason this was very funny
And it felt as though
       when we *did* leave
              all the changes
                     would be a takeaway such
                     the whole year happens at once

Started a conversation   *Sixties*- style
       as if we built to an insight
              laughing to some conclusion
              when we'd tell some important story
                                          together
                                   lives
                            extended

A belief seeming stronger
                     for having that consensus

Even saying "Black Rock"

was meaning Papua New Guinea at heart
And all its jungles converged   enveloping
A green aggression
        despite undoubted dryness
                summer's awesome dessication

"You can talk to me..."
"...and contradict these surroundings"

She had finished the sentence I'd started
                capriciously
And they both proffered gifts
Lotion and lemonade
        I *did* accept
                being careless my *own* self of that sun
                forgetting to hydrate, too

And I still think I knew them
        the moment their movie
                their *picture*
                        our picture
                                was completed

Our years collected and saved for later
Years as many as the new century holds
Betty Grable   Clark Gable   on location
        colored red and colored grey

Answers on tips of their tongues
        the spoken word is remotely imagined

131. INDECISION AT ELEVEN O'CLOCK WITH A HAMMOCK AND BREAKFAST WAFFLES

It was a matter of going or staying
And *when* in both cases

The waffles were promised
But a van would be leaving I needed to board

So   a breakfast   a hammock
The pleasure of a multi-colored tent in the sun
Or the urgency of taking a ride to Sahra's Peak
          to find something lost
                    not being sure of what was missing, even

It was a matter of queueing
                    for the gift of "Good morning!"
                         served regimental yet delicious
               and getting somewhere else entirely

When a ranger makes long-distance rounds
Of Double Hot Springs
          Black Rock Springs
                    and of course, Trego
                         shift changes in progress

I'd go along
Look where last I'd volunteered
                    hoping to best absent-mindedness
                         recover equipment
                              whatever it was
                              that got loose

Tentative   I'd entered into waffle-love
There was a hammock, too
The walls of the tent: triangular decisions

Immediate   fundamental
Transparencies saying things in primary shades
          When breakfast is a spectator sport
                    that's been underway
                         since eleven ante meridian
                         amazing conversations taking place
The discourse enhanced by master chefs
                                   brought to life for a day

It was a matter of sure nourishment
                    or dubious searching

347

132. I DO NOT SEE THE FAERIE GWENDOLYN...

Had to make ends meet
Had to meet ends at the Furniture Camp
     where the cars are sofas
        and the hot rods are chairs

We're democratic!
We vote!   we rally!
     in a happy hospital
     getting better than ever
        amidst soft transmissions!

Where's *Gwendolyn*, though?!
She'll miss the fashion show she'd advertised

Just to be clear, she hadn't *promised* to appear
Maybe it's the end instead of the beginning?
     but surely we would meet again
        signalling at a distance, enthusiastically!

Everyone's ill with a good car sense!
Everyone's sick with exponential contagion
The ramp is ready   is a red-carpeted pathway
     and it covers the ground
     its ends not meeting
        though the separated cloth
           is committed to reunion
           to fantastic innovation!

The lost spotlight was found   in the *van* found
The spot that had found the *fox*
After all that riding around
     it wasn't lying in the dirt somewhere
        it had stayed in the transportion itself

Happiness *then* finding happiness *now*
Remembering the ranger, Sasquatch, who drove
     how he knew all the ruts of the playa roads
     and how to veer and vector in

He'd have enjoyed this show of furniture
    rallying with the rest of us
        going from symptoms to recovery
        finding ways to undress
            that place a spotlight on style

It hasn't started
    but the signs all point to "Yes, it will, and soon"
      no spectator turned away
        from brushes
        and paddles' *spanking* good time
The checkered flag to swish for those various fannies

4:40 and counting...
Never mind   the company's delightful!
There are recliners and drinks
And, while always grateful for shade,
    still, nurses will be summoned
        to make it better yet
Fevers to "brake" like the furniture

There's a *baby* getting better, too
A tricycle tot
   and look at 'im go!
     at liberty   at easy
     his quiet revolutions
        competing with chance adults

I'm liking the decor
    white curtains and tent ceiling white
      the structure dispersing the heat of the day
      whose criminal sun insists on misery
A good-natured star with a mean streak
      faraway
      yet all-consuming

Gwendolyn!
Oh, Faerie of the Piano Keys!
Your longings carried another along
    to a meeting's beginning   or end, perhaps
      progressive and conservative
      combining their percentages

Only your absence
        governs the afternoon's increasingly level light
            soul of the Esplanade
                a global curve to it
The fashion is backgrounded by middle distance
                            bright with bicycles

Furniture Car Camp has a view of radio heaven
What you see is what you hear
        the FM a fabulous wheezing and static
That remonstrates and demonstrates
The worst thing in the world
                tuned in and turned off   or not

Here is a racing career that's *certain* comfort
Everything is planned
        is nothing but last moments
            ends unmet
                    acquaintanceships deferred
                        while the social media parade

All our mothering and fathering
        and then   put wheels on the furniture
                allow the RPMs to lull

Though feeling safe is no longer required
        feeling wonderful *is*
            and is related to fashion
I'll say it and be judged a creature of poppycock
Here, it is the look that matters
And for how long depends on the mood
                            perhaps a toddler's

Gwendolyn!   *dahlink!*
Wit's end!
        meet me here in good faith
            your flair supposing   surpassing
Gwendolyn, who practices Chopin slowly and carefully!

What's right in the light
        and deserving of affection!

133. THE CONTESTANTS, SLIGHTLY DUSTY

Ready or not   they come forward
    two-legged and more
        each performing a sashay variant of strolling

Let the record show the show was a sure thing
            suffered by the "homely"
If you're a contestant, you win!   that's *it!*   that's *all!*

Rite of passage
The path is Beauty's ramp   slightly dusty
Afternoon accepts the unfurled checkered flag
       commencement

It matters   every move
    the crowd in a huddle to learn how it's done
        let 'em *go!*
        make news, twirling!

The bar is serving   *burgers* are waiting
And the judges register unanimous approval

Just visible: the bright portico
    through which
        the ructious winds pour their mischiefs
                overable
                incisive
                argumentative

Exercise the black-and-white-and-red.
Runway's on a first name basis with everyone
    Its forename is fresh
        and the furniture's positioned for camp
                  for rally

The contestants are dancing
With shawls   with hats   and corotating dust
    a pageant of two-at-a-time
There's an Isadora Duncan
        ghosting   kind of supervisory

            her choreography a whisper
                    the opposite of hate speech

The show an amendment to fashion
        and oddly formal
        the only *slightly* jazzed version
                of a czar's procession to Kamennoi Ostrow
Godsent royalty revised to suit carefree

Life is shifting its parameters
And the House of Phantoms is refilled with frolicking
                even dusty entropy is revived

No signature was required
Our dreams are forever
        nothing heavy   gravity relents
                lightness loves the contestants

There's one in green   a leprechaun, surely
        and it's an Irish moment
                a negotiation with agility
And taking apart the long trip made from Ireland

Seeming to say   even in peace   what war is
Its extenuating circumstances
                dancing to a ceasefire

A green cessation
        each day of the week, month
                and *year* of reprieve
We've all made a trip
At the very least, walked some distance
                                towards the mountains
Each dusty performer to know
        a sense of the process of Becoming

I said all this and then came:
"Uh-oh! you watch out! no zen babble!"
"Yeah, it's only a party! here, have a beer!"

They were right, of course
        though I *did* continue

a teetotaler reporter
        back to being young
        as Furniture Car Camp itself!

134. THE PURPLE UMBRELLA AND MORE

In the beginning was the purple umbrella
And what followed
        sprang from the spell of its purple weave
            as if wanded
            as if conjured by *Les Enfants du Paradis*
A twirl to please Garance

It was incipient color in the service of flourish
        broadcasting a checkered past
            nights around a wartime radio
I could want that   and call it cozy, too

It's royal right now
                with that umbrella spinning violet
                    an intro to ultra
Aiming to protect from a terrorist sun!

We will also be talking to the spirits of NASCAR
        that inhabit household recliners and loveseats
        now subject to servicing
            oh, yes   checkups and changes of oil

The rally's underway
        and running smoothly on no inhibitions
            and it's so very all right
                        high-stepping and strutting

The Land of Nod has never known itself till now
And carouses   broad daylight
        unwitting yet profound
            the way a cloud may enlighten

shapechanging its cumulus
        to proposition the imagination

And what the purple umbrella ushers in
        is what we saw beyond the back door
        beyond the playground

It's been years since a drink   a *long* time!
Long preparation for this very day
        when sobriety's laws are knockout connection
Every part of the body involved
I don't think I dance
        yet I dance with *them*
                let them tell me where I'm going
                        on the magic crimson carpet!

Let camp eyesight say   and never mind
                                        that's all

There's a harmonica somewhere
An evocation   well-spoken
It's an afternoon of do the same, for once
                all you have
                all at the same time
                        pledged to this cavalcade!

Wonder what kind of stairs
        have birthed such Dyonesian persuasions
In front of the company
        dignity and pride have emptied the briefcase

I will document the cult
Try to resist its invitation to oblivion
        when succumbing ultimately
                would be all the more delicious!

Do you remember all of this?
        seeing all of purple's procession?
                do you think back at all?
                        to you and your sister entertaining?
                                putting on shows for the family?

Oh, yes!
With each performer at the rally
    a remembrance
    of our "Night-Night" Theater of Everything
Like ultimate science in a childhood home
        long before Gwendolyn
            her invitation to *flamboyance*

But when I'm *here*, I *live* here
And Time's rolled out like the red mat of runway
            down which no mistakes will follow
                such excellent fooling around!

Judgeless purple hears applause!
Inserts priceless into ordinary
Glamour happens
    and precision makes its way
                    effortless
                    umbrellaed
        the white noise of the Esplanade
        running at the mouth

A moneyed celebrity vanishes
Each embrace like a slow motion marriage
    an early film with hand-tinted frames
        the plot left open for extras
        more purple to go with the red
                color enhanced for the pairing

Such a good AWOL is this
        that's going to be the source of dreams!

The "little shadow" shades the strategies
Those of pleasures in public and feeling secure
There will be the consequence of more of the same
    an ambition to just sit down
                and   admire the millennials
            for awhile
            for Gwendolyn

I have already decided to join them
Comply with the rally's parentheses

Make this month the only
        going purple   going royal
                              with elite hallucinations

Not theirs but my own documents of love
Unassisted by ecstasy
            unless it is the kind that resides in nirvana
            when even home invasions are welcome
                background by clouds

No one's leaving
No one's tired
Furniture Car Rally Fashion
        as mentor review
            like an investigation
                concurrent with any and all crimes
                though no offense was taken

On and on is what we imagine   what we believe
The triple threat of sun, youth and westerlies!

The umbrella has a voice
        a progeny   so many delights!
            the fingers and toes of the hominid
            so delicate-artistic
                nothing may be done
                    that is not called greatness!

The acrobats' thoughts are my own
And long-lasting into other shaded summers
There's poetry in the foreground
        going on and going to the end
We have come from the cities to sort our lives
            like hoarder storage spread out
            examined one last time!

A "possession"   no problem   it's left
Goes on forever
            discarded
                and these dance steps taken
                    are disorder's disassembly
                    a purple deconstruction

I'm next!
I'll find a cape and checkered shorts
                    and partner with a vixen
                    everything in her power shared
The better to be acquainted with umbrellas' lands

All laws illegal
The better to start all *over*
        and be in the power of strange beginnings

135. PLIANCY

It was a disc problem transcended   a feat
Something incredible to puzzle the specialists
        the chiropractor at a loss
                no hands of Jesus applied

Her *pliancy*
        was a plan she conceived as autodidact
                going to school with her entire skeleton
        to find the perfect way to bend and flex

She could just as well have been a rubber pretzel
        her constituent parts revised such
                        double-jointed's even possible

I remember *well* what she said: "Watch this!"
And her orange hair helicoptered
                as she acted upon a posture
                an army of one solitary trickster

The victim transcends her body
Makes loving demands of its structure
She's even a threat to "seeing is believing"

The days of summer deserve no less than her expertise

357

arrived at by thought alone
                    proving "do it yourself"
                              is   just a limber state of mind
And she is a quick reminder
            without authority
            the imagination may prosper

She flops   she rocks   she spins and leaps
Her good form derived from the forms of Plato
If she's known assistance, it's Greek
            and she amazes the moron bodies
                    with their lawyerly blaming

She's cordless
            eschews *hauteur*
                    continues to aspire
                    star of the red runway
                              trained to do as she pleases

A holistic blur
As though her stunts
            were the several languages needed
                    to set the sun behind the hills

The spine is safe
            and all the bones that *keep* it safe
She'll be taking calls from the *Cirque du Soleil*
                    proving somebody gives a damn!

Thinking lithesome
            enroll in consequence
                    father proud   and mother, too
                              though their parenting's past
                              that ever led to commencement

Here is her exercise depth charged
            with a counterintuitive levity
How many organizations might she foster and sustain
                              with agility!

Joining them right now is suggested
She's a court case settled

before any arguments are heard

I think, "Get through mortality soon!"

For this preview of its opposite
    must follow us around and exit Black Rock
        to keep us yearning for ballet
        for the beauty of fashion
                underpinned by the miraculous

Her spine is aligned
    and spinning orange dreams in the daylight
        a checkered *health*
                insisted upon like a stingray awareness
Pliancy's state-of-the-art completion!

136, FURNITURE FLAG

They had a flag   or *did* they?

First, let's look around
        and really *see* this camp
            called Furniture Car Rally
For there's more to say for sure

Music is heard   like an afterwards, faintly
A music almost intuited
And the rest of the camp as well
    and oh, that awning draped with white linen!

It's 6 o'clock and overcast   that's *good!*
One tries to make it stay that way with wishing
And we've all gone International now
        the bar resounding with accents
            as if to celebrate xenophobia's finale
                        go-carts crashing
The shores of ancient Lake Lahontan

are peopled with hunter-gatherer ghosts
who gaze in native amazement
at this high-powered future we've managed

Got the checkered flag and floored it
The accelerator stuck!
"What on earth?" is what's in Space and spreading
expanding   like dust to fill the playa

A red carpet left in place to impersonate the Oscars
that glitzy lull in the Battle of All the Sexes
And the fine particles
that dim the day
and decolor the camp
They spend their grains   in drifting
over abandoned bikes
and artcars

There's a ladybug wagon   waiting   riderless
And there's a flag
what nation, though?
maybe it's the camp's?
Is it Tajikistan's banner that blesses the company?
And for how long has it waved?

The colors are close enough to plant in the steppe
But if it's something else entirely
those stripes and yellow stars
And signifies more than a region of central Asia...

Let the answers flutter and make the right sense
Ending the questions   their idle, synaptic detour

There's drumming now in the bar's serenade
percussion to go with the cashews and pickles
life is intermission
while one's standing's ascertained

If the deities are angry I'll try and rest
do nothing to further annoy their omnipotence
fixate on the available transport
That Radio Flyer

which has nothing to do with going or coming
and knows the bliss of the ladybug
That incredible go-cart stuffed
with furry pink and furry white
Mobile as all Art is
Enough of us agreeing
the avenues of Black Rock are drivable ruts

To-and-fro companions as loveable strangers
you want to wrap it up but the socializing's great!

Should be a podcast   maybe it *can* be
One that repeats
like a favorite sitcom
sky-high with irony
that such a watering hole
may fill with mirage
"Should I stay or should I go?"

Even the Fifties and Sixties can exist here
with fruits and veggies
a sensible course and balance of nature
part of the Gaia hypothesis
that suffuses the collective
When that same term means the sanctity of the solo voice

The Good Samaritan Camp with an infinite vocabulary
Took *me* in   and I *needed* that taking!
the open air slightly closed
barely turbulent
but enough to dance upon the surfaces
and dustily

It's a friendly country   unknown till now
There's more to say needing music to say it
At 6 o'clock and later into further
the overcast having gone international

I'll try out the rest of wistful and wishful
Ride the couch and the go-cart
Master the sofa
the mobile chair powered by ghosts

and the will of hunter-gatherers
                                    wearing white linen

I'll try to guess the stripes
        red, white and black   or is it *blue?*
                just three colors
                        white, the middle, with three gold stars
Like an extra well done assignment's certificate

I'd be willing to wave it, regardless
Defend it   follow it   themed
        in tandem with other citizens of Furniture Land
The a.m. and the p.m. both approving
                        of our parvenue patriotism

And just putting this out there, I think it's helping
The way Rachmaninoff's Eighteenth Variation does that
        the famous theme brought to D Flat Major
                        from its homeland of A Minor
Jeez! it's the Russians again!"

Can the Rally continue?
Life stories told?   tonight at midnight?

Prepared to explore, I'll ask Gwendolyn to go for a ride
See if the Faerie is free to travel in Space
        the Space that is expanding
                that has the great taste of a vacuum, *pristine!*
                        and is "What on Earth?!" explained

The ladybug's flown   it was an easy getaway
But a snow leopard's *arrived*
        even *here!*
        proving improbability loves the playa
            has a flag
                    a top speed of five miles-an-hour

Let answers happily arrange their detours
To drumming mixed with piano and orchestra
To probable cause and placing a flag in the overcast
        soloing Rachmaninoff's *Dies Irae*
                all the way to "Well done! have a drink!"

362

More music to say the last word
        amidst our socializing ancestors
                three stars for life stories
                        that take an Ice Age to tell

137. UNSHADOWED

No shadows
        like Schlemil in *Tales of Hoffmann*

No shadows!
A project of the shrouded sun
                        trying to save money
The stars on strike
        and sent in gray to cancel its autocracy

Those colors of the rain that *sunless* speak
                may more truly say what shade should be

This sky will only last a *short* while
        the temperature changing
                                like a side effect of mercy
So the party picks *up*, unplanned, unshadowed
The City put back together
                with the shade of reprieve

It plans to keep running rehab and recovery
        while an enemy sun relents   *and*
                before it blasts once again out of the zenith
Black Rock now is a meanwhile place
        slightly incorporeal

And the overcast says to be gentle as its clouds
        spilling from shelters
                like dust bunnies peaceful yet exuberant

The playa *survivable*
The daytime art truly appreciated
    art unqualified by yellow scandal
        the solar floodlight deferred   paused
The extravagant lady is better seen
Lengthened   inflated
A wondrous balloon being that reclines for the moment
    as if   awaiting the courtship of Macy's

Like C3PO closing in on nothing in particular
    its artcar windows a see-through sci-fi
        another life volunteers its beginning
            unshadowed
            non-specific

Says it wants you to be okay at 3 o'clock and G
Do more listening than talking
Take measured steps   each *unshadowed*
    health-conscious with sunstroke downplayed

Perhaps the cracks in the lakebed will reappear
    and everything revert to *undisturbed* unshadowed
All distance   undermined
        vastness become an intimate dimension

"Follow *me!*"   this from C3PO
"Get used to the future!"
And the sky is streaky with preview
What you learn is indirect
    and hidden from an otherwise fierce afternoon

And this afternoon's unshadowed p.m. will repeat
For having once happened   it *always* is happening
    having once existed, magic *always* exists
        a cleaner and more well-kept desert, too!

Strangely, high school's relived
    without shadows this time
        without social pressure
            and your best friend, well
He's found to be a *helpful* adversary...

An unprepossessing gray
A version of "Not so fast! be friends with *everyone,*
                                        it's better!"
                                the grown-up
                        in tandem
                with teenage dreaming
        clouds
        like these elitist cirrus
    teaching every subject and elective

The Tales of Hoffmann commences
Peter Schlemil dotes on Giulietta in vain
There's no appreciable warming
        and he blends into the unshadowed day

No casualties   no shadows
        no Furniture *consulate*, even
            a safe country and breezy

The median age is unknown
We were having a conversation
        the sun disappeared
                and a white light spread
With stripes and elephant ears flapping wisdom
And making immortal a late afternoon

138. ANIMAL CONTROL IS LEAVING

Animal Control is leaving

Apparently they've controlled all the animals here
        and they're leaving to find more elsewhere
It's a bandwagon *red*   with peacock pomp
With a double platform for captured critters
Could'nt control 'em *all*, however
                for some are completely invisible
                a million years of evolution

has made them elusive

The prow of the thing is a duck   most visible
And it's a ducky duck, truly!
Above the waterless pond it floats
          flying south with its roundup

A company called away to further catch and control
          albeit lovingly and briefly

139. THE CRIMSON COLLECTIVE

Yet another summit meeting
A convocation of red-clad   mingling

Are they Red Rovers on a stopover
          preparing for a group bike ride?
Is it a socialist pep rally?
Valentines Incorporated?

The heart has a costume
The rose is drest
          and seeing red is seeing brightly
               a favorite number made of red licorice
                    the color of success an old story shared
                    that warms everyone up
Warms those *cochleae cordis*

If only two people agree
          it's an occasion for crimson's obvious cheer
And even Darwin's happy then
          the struggle for existence relaxed a little

Yes, it must be a summit of some kind
The red-minded are red-handed assembled
                                   and we'll know what's up
They are truly lovely and *pink* plays a part!

plus the *other* shades close to just plain red

The rose is reported   scentful
Aspiring to greatness in response to a wavelength
        they nobly pursue the late Thirties
                both their own ages
                and the age of Art Deco
                        not minding that both are unobtainable

There are so many bicycles it's Beijing not so *long* ago
Or an iteration of the Wright brothers
        blood brothers masterminding an outbreak of biplanes

An autonomous *province* of roses!
Oh! if only the crimson party might last!
                like a job
                a good wife
                        that we might know red entirely!
                        with updates automatic

Seeing red has never been so easy
Disturbing in a *good* way
The rose is recalled   red spread around
        it's possible to become a customer
                        check into its warm hotel
                        spend money taken from its bank

The Red Rovers have come over and hover in tandem
        the game broken down
                broken up and having small talk
                the exact amount   and
                        nothing sarcastic
Their conversation a mutual tip they give themselves

Or something settled out of their crimson court
Just enough to be a social dessert in the desert
        thank-you notes spoken with rouge on their cheeks

If I say "crimson" again
        it is not to prolong a tableau, exactly
                more to say the color for its own sake
                notice how it tints

even *stains* the letters it needs

Today, I think Dad is here
        and excusing his son's many distractions
            understanding how all is recess
                and occasion for Red Rover
                    time away from triple "r"
                    readin'   writin'   'rithmetic

And then, "Keep Away"

I'm critically ill   without built-in escape sense
But just
        just let it happen   socialist thought
In the *beginning* before it explodes
Those first glimmerings like radiant wishing
        untutored by cadres
                and unbuilt are the barracks
                    no "direct action" taken as yet

Pink, the modest red, is *still* trying to take over
Lightest shade of crimson's pallet
                crimson that lectures:
                    "Blood is the oldest color..."
Calm down and let the deepest hue explore versatility
        a version of itself that's innocent-sanguine

The takeaway paint-by-numbers moment
An economy of color
                the right path beaten to the rainbow
        crimson come before us now
Wishing to fill in the rest of the arc
                            with this primary red alone
                            unhurried heart

Dad, I know you're watching
Even all of Massachussetts sees the sundown people
        far to the west
                inclining to purple in the end
                    kermes
                    carmine
                    cochineal

alizarin add
But leave well-enough well-read, *please!*

140. CLOSE-UP CRIMSON

Get closer   love people   stop complaining!
There's a fence, gray-slatted
      the camera's magnification dulling the reds
        and making pale the promises of scarlet

The detail! getting this close and staring
Almost myopic   and the scene is a flashback
The recollection of a dream that was somewhat erotic
      less than perfect birthday sex in broad' daylight
        or did I just *imagine* I dreamt?

Being teenaged, we've slipped back
        to an outdoors high school
          truly public education
          masquerading as a blow-out bash
The fence like wooden modesty's afterthought

Need to find the ambition to succeed at crashing this thing
But it shouldn't be *too* hard to go and join in
      maybe as a *gradual* participant

Ordinary riches!   red is still the color
Crimson that's spread
      though the lens has artistically lessened its intensity
        sent it halfway to black-and-white
We know a wellness inhabiting the hidden mind

Say "Sangre de Cristo"   the blood of Christ...
The words that make a mountain range
      in far-off Colorado
        and what's dangerous is beautiful
        a "Fourteener's" crags

The crimson party's the Savior's peril
But there's no timetable to the intended sacrifice
        just scrutiny
                and deconstructions sweet
                        in the realm of magenta
Random ceremonies which unfold like articles of clothing
Creases of a crimson robe
                a vision to take you through the unshadowed afternoon

The fence is more a prop
A metaphor by Robert Frost
        left standing in the aftermath of poetry
                one is invited to join the reading
                        invisible to all but the most perceptive

I accept the zero   tolerance involved
        when it comes to mere spectating and judgment
The point of entry to the party is fresh air's path

In the Land of Deadlines
        a sudden clearing of the calendar
                and   allowed to take part
                take time
                        get close-up
                                pretending to be a new parent
                                beneath the Doomsday clock
And feeling nostalgic for Cold War happenings
                                        did I lose you?

Perfect wisdom's wearing red
Picks up where stupidity left off
And, although red is an illusion
        yet its crimson is a lovely deception
                with the fence snaking through it
Right through all the bicycles like a territorial innovation
        demarking flashback from flash-today

A dream has parked itself here
                quoting Jung and others
Take another picture   telephoto
                from nearby's vantage

a tourist trying to make it stop
but still clicking away
As if the scene were fusible revelry
                          within a previous meltdown

Beyond the close-up   the unshadowed *mountains*
Diplopia
        the hills having brains and crania
                for maximum comprehension

The babies being born demand *more*
                more than mass production!
Perhaps this is why there's a gathering
        and revolutionary parenting will see to it
                make sure the children have a playground
                are not *too* perplexed

Perhaps they are discussing the object of Red Rover
The true *meaning* of the game
No matter
        'tis the same meaning taught by the year 1996
                that Burning Man
                        that certainty and showcase learning

And these subsequent summers
        spent wandering the playa blissfully
                adding other chapters to the first
Spelling other words than what the *Gazette* asserts
        and *Piss Clear* was wont to promote
                their usage prescribed   *de rigueur*
                        these summers
                        are also a crimson
                                close-up

First chapter   first time   1996...
Before the new millennium
        the New York towers
                our "new civil war"
                was the fantasy of HELCO realized
                was Stephen Heck's *Piano Bell*

And these ruby-red celebrants join

The paler crimson discerned
        enters history   chattering   gregarious
            1996 accreting
1996 getting better and better
Playing games in the overcast of a nameless sky
        marvelling no other afternoon but *this* one will do!

I entered the close-up
        the telephoto
                the scene beyond the lens
                        careful of splinters
                        for the fence goes on and on

The tattoos were better in person
        the several reds restored to their original luster
                the roses selected   scentful, crimson
Full-flowered attendance!
The flamboyant bicycles jammed or leaning
                                conceding no space

Royalty's a shade of meaning
                    of coloration
                        a menace of crayon wax

The roof is white that the sky has built
Its slight chalk a cosmetic applied   diffuse
I am close enough to the jazz of crimson
        to want its color to flood my very own arteries
                        with a deeper hematic

141. A THURSDAY'S HORIZON

With headlights starting to appear
With granite's outline west   and
With stillness like a pause before parades to come
    let my absent wife make a speech
        tell me all she knows of Nijinsky

what *really* happened
between him and the impressario Diaghilev
so early in that century

Let her talk to me as she would a crowd
And be compelling   as usual
Be charismatic in the dim day's finale
          cracked open for one final sky
               that says,"Keep looking!   listening!"
               though its white light is miles away
                    amidst the clouds' obfuscations
                              persisting like tenure

With cranes striving before it's too dark   too late
With a strange haze enveloping the Esplanade
          and seeming to engulf the camps near to vanishing
With emptiness expanding to include all the art cars
               let a far-off voice be heard
                         to go with this distance

Let her presentation be performance
          an effortless entreaty
I'll coauthor   go along   no opinion but love

And let her wear the same dress
The one she wore in Frenchglen
               the day we set out for Steens Mountain
               the first day that was clear in a season of fires

When this is over
          I'm taking her to the Magic Castle down south
She'll appreciate the dress code
Just because such codes are rare
          and knowing everything there is to know
                    of card tricks
                    and other illusions
                              she'll be rewarded!

Right now she's still beyond Thursday's horizon
          and sky paint a magic trick of the sun
               roughhousing with the atmospherics

But she's really *Coast to Coast*   like the show
A nocturnal being allowed the light
          all the light of the ages
And her learning's ongoing
               one of the mind's miracles

When this all has ended
And the playa has regained its delicate fissures
I'm bringing her to Cedarville
               and thence to Lakeview and 395

We will once more come to Paisley and the Paisley Caves
And that way drive to the waters of Summer Lake
          and the cat named Fred
               curled up on the nightstand

And if my wife desires it   we'll see the Crater
          Oregon's only National Park
And I will invest in her genius
               see to it she gets to class for the first plié
               and adds extra positions
          to the seven so far assigned ballet

Perhaps she will explain Serge Lifar
          and how he lasted so long
               in spite of having collaborated with the Germans

With more and more headlights
With granite's profile failing
          like final thoughts on entropy
               right before it happens
With the nearby installations glowing scientifically
          having traveled hither from thither
               let her start in Kansas
                    be beginning once more   incorruptible
               gifted as certain angels are
                    in hovering

Let "alacrity" describe her nature
A readiness to conjure

And let all her books be read

by the children of Prometheus
who's here to light the night on fire
what Jim Morrison tried to do
at least he *said* he tried

And lastly, with panoramas turning theoretical
And vistas finding homes in our heads
With unfinished camps and lookouts leaning
their builders succumbing to mid-week exhaustion
three days short of apotheosis...
With Black Rock City's map refolded for good
and serendipity made the queen of discoveries
let my wife be absent no longer
and brought to Burning Man as sufficient finding

And let me tell her this in Thursday's last gleaming
someone for whom an anthem might be written

142. THE MAYANS

Slept better than ever
after the Mayans' deep healing
drum-powered

Like seeing a different kind of doctor
out of BCE come to alleviate anxiety
slept as well
as when Massachussetts summers lulled
and dispelled all danger

And yes, there were Mayans this far north
Far north of their temples   their jungles
still dancing
still feathered and with a perfect symmetry

Old culture dusted off just in time to prevent entropy
Like a movie on pause   modern music, too

so that drumming is all
and it follows the Universe
to *whatever* ending it has planned

The Mayans are immediate action!
Their significant questions rehearsed
so that their answers are a trend in the dusk
and amenable twilight

It's hard to believe it's made in America
Vespucci's indicted   high *time*, too!
Oh, sleep well, all within hearing!
the Mayans are softening the outlines
blurring the borders of European overreach

How strongly did dreams then appear!
Like analog endings
imagining cut stone upon stone
to be a platform's observatory for Venus
her five paths found in the sky

I may escape these warriors   quit the pyramid
Or perhaps be a willing sacrifice
the transition seamless
the Mayans adorned in such a fashion
there's no safe distance
and one's archaeology's undone

They have come from the Land of Questions
to answer in the dust with twirling and whirling
their feathers making huge and weighty
what flies

They dance me to a dream of slow-motion culture
Taking years to catch the gods in the act
invading slumber like a village
to assimulate, acquire, to convince to belong
While the sun and moon play month-long tag

They must show others
the dream will spread
and make surer the steps

There may be more on the way
                    the way north

The questions will accompany:
Why Mexico and not Nevada?
Why did the pyramids stay in Yucatan?

Slept better because the Mayans seemed nocturnal
        and they will help us to overcome
                    the way the Sixties overcame
And *having* overcome
            we'll start a new Mayan calendar
            and strange things will be known

It will all be a legacy
This twilight dancing and drumming
        prelude and preview to Mayans everywhere

Well past bedtime
        the tempo of their drums a Burning Man lullaby
            blending with the ambient dissonance
A constancy worthy of inscrutable traditions begins

But the Mayans have brought understanding even so
A first step   then a second
                        a last stair climbing exercise
When I will have an unobstructed view
                of the jungle surrounding

This is sleep that is sacrifice
A Seroquel superior to the Kaiser's German remedy
        war becoming peace with every tribe of oneself

143. THE MAYANS, THE OLMECS

Do the Mayans remember?
Did the *Olmecs* remember?

Transition there was
Those heads   those giant stone heads?
          they were discontinued
                    everyone tired of pulling all that weight around
                    when they wanted to travel light

Still watching the dancers
          but from an *afterlife's* perspective
                    it's a beautiful beat!
                              a thumping skin
                              staying steady as guesswork's connections
The long list of percussive options reviewed

The ending was a "nothing to lose"
Everything now is numbers
          surprising numbers   a mathematical land
The Mayans are right there helping
                    feathered geniuses
               do they know
               in their eternal summer
                              that this is wisdom?

The Olmecs...   what was it all about, anyway?
Know anything?
          it matters
                    remembering the Olmecs makes you truly modern
                    makes you *recent*, oh Mayans!
Later than you think
And Olmec absurdity so off the rim, off the grid
          even the priests are befuddled
                    and fiddle with their baubles

How good a detective *are* you?
The Olmecs' absence is the Mayans' presence
          cover the *story*, ya' gotta' know where to *look*

Footwork   sandals
Yearly, the desert for a week   then the Yucatan
               nothing in the night is anymore ordinary!

They are blowing horns

390

Their feathers are black
Without a good guess
        I lapse into a Mesoamerican oldtime harshness
            that is tinged with newborn fuzz and koochy koo

144, SHOUTS AND CHANTS

There were shouts and chants in the deserted Mother Ship
        what we'll call the glowy interior
                    of a mostly empty Center Camp

The counters were clear
And the flag flaps of the queue lanes were moot crowd control
        no scheduled entertainment happened
            and the body sculpture
                was a minimal aerobics

While the space was cavernous
        yet the entirety was warmed by lamp yellow
            keeping promises of *other* shades as well
            sharply outlined or diffuse
                            a civil rights of the rainbow

Red-and-purple was the hoop of skylight's circle
Open   the saucer's escape hatch

And there were shouts and chants by the few
        those who'd boarded the starship
        with whoops and rhythmic words
                and waited   upon a massive liftoff

There was one barista working
"Mocha for wildcat2!" she cried
And I answered "Here! present!" as if it were school
        she was good
                they *all* were!   all *week!*
It was easy the way they prepared the drinks

Or *rather* they made it *look* easy
	you learn to love watching them

There's a deadline:
Sunday, you don't need to be an expert
	they'll volunteer to leave
		have trouble with recall
That is why these shouts and chants
And every color of the parlor counts right now

The designer Hippies inhabit a Holodeck
					beautiful
					transcendant
		science gone to fiction's bed
	a GDP's theory of everything spatial

145. HANGING WITH NUMBER EIGHT

He sang about eight		number eight
The eighth girlfriend he'd known
From the tempo of the tune
		it sounded like they got along just fine
		and there might not have been need for a ninth

In the purple haze of the music stage
	that is so beautifully managed always
		the eighth came alive
And the man who loved her let us love her too

He'd stopped at eight
	for he'd met Infinity's daughter
		and she took him to the moon	and beyond
Their conversations now are mostly telepathic

He sang a song in the key of Look No Further
And he carried that tune like a bride
		across a threshold named Resolve

to an exculpatory ecstasy

The music stage is bright imaginings
The eighth in eighth notes   all of them free

I'd like a transcript
          the arrangement for piano
                    the better to keep his eighth love
His last and last hope answers all my questions for free

It is a fascinating violet tinged with blue
          that cocoons his lyrics
                    each measure a prompt, saying
"See to it the eighth woman in your life
                    has all she needs to be happy!"

Even the technician's nodding in time
          in his Center Camp music booth
                    the canopy schooling heart-red
                    in the ways of virgin love

146. THE ASTRONAUT

She has returned   like Apollo 13 to the Earth
She is Christa, safe
          Christa McAuliffe
                    come back to teach me
Her spacesuit is high fashion, beflagged
          Space having forgiven NASA
                    and never-minded their faulty o-ring

She's returned
The way a prayer that goes out
                    is supposed to produce results
          and all the time
                    if God is truly paying attention
                                        knowing it all

If *superstition* functions
        and just the right hunch gets the job done

She says she has her Earth legs again
Well, *almost*   she's been careful
        since she landed in time for Burning Man
She's wearing dark glasses and seems a little shy
                perhaps it's disbelief she's safe
                and getting coffee with the rest of us

Is she going to fly again?
Will I return to Bruneau Dunes
        my *own* space flight to reprise?

There'd been a lecture that time
        NASA   pure chance
            the state park hosting the heavens
Another woman from Space   she'd taken questions
            what year had she orbited?
            for how long?

There were children
They pretended the dunes were Mars
The observatory was opened
                    the telescope searched
                and a bloated Jupiter appeared

Word up!   don't go there like you'd go to the Moon!
        there's *radiation* at Jupiter
                lots of it!
What a shame the biggest planet's off limits

The other astronaut was loquacious   assertive
You could tell she lectured often
        I can almost remember the gist of her talk
And *also* remember the blurry book
                with a blurry Jupiter from 1951
        nothing known but mass and volume

There were hundreds gathered at the dunes in Idaho
        those RVs and campers all over the place

I think a helicopter came
            and whup-whupped in a field nearby
        a medevac?

Start of a school year
Whole classes   the latest science
    what it would take over and make a home
            that *observatory*
                    with its 25" Newtonian reflector telescope
Must be quite cozy in there

The astronaut lady *that* time was the *opposite* of shy
In Idaho's dunes she recounted her flight
        the Space Shuttle
                its successful mission
                        mostly nothing beyond routine

But gravity quits when you're up there, right?
It's floating   imprinted
Sure as hell the rockets flew
        there was always funding the vacuum
                and no mistakes!
                        God's empty mind
                        the health of that brain confirmed

"She'll be safe   entertained by the Cosmos"
She'll cross the Starbridge with a net loss of Earthly cares

What matters is solid fuel
        Space is a lavish lifestyle
                though the suit seems ill-fitting
So much to bring to Bruneau and its dunes
And so much to gift in Black Rock

There, she's different
Christa's demure in contrast to Idaho's festive jam
It's what she's trying to say so quietly
        and I want her to repeat the words slowly
                I want to summon others
                        until I realize
                        "No   keep it one-on-one for now"

Her modest opening segment
                    will   stay a privileged recital
She'll teach without haste
        being sympathetic to the living
She'll wait for her student to be serious
            not doubting she came from the skies
            a knowable alien
                new to our summer
                    yet undoubtedly pleased with it
Finding everything out as a student her *own* self

Her workplace   her *classroom*
        is wherever she lands   a live event
            right now
            my education's complete
Just don't make any sudden moves
                    she's getting used to being back!

Arthur C. Clarke is here to help
He heard all about it
He knows her survival is more than a story
                            and will stay unwritten

Christa, who's transcended science, science *fiction*...
            she's almost a hologram
                and so much more than corporeal
Had I intercepted a ghost?

It was an *exclusive* interview
        there would be no pressure

She is innocent
As only someone who's been Beyond can be
        but, you know, it's a pretty good start
She wants a drink and we oblige
            and Arthur says he'll provide her
                            with a lemon tart

She's still demure
        and shies away from the fuss we're making
            as if   undecided
Was she somehow Indra's daughter?

Was she Agnes
        darling daughter who descended
                        with Strindberg's assistance?

So endearing...
I want to say her life is now vacation
                but I lack the authority to insist
Christa, it's 2016   thirty years after
And I'm so glad to see you here in Center Camp!

May I remember?
Can you say just a little?
        was it morning?
                this is morning
                        your own special sunrise!
                        though it's dark as Space in the lounge

If only your modesty might travel everywhere!
If only it could be our general demeanor
        and "nothing doing" an acceptable hiatus
                until such time as *your* time is understood
                like the final notes of a Mozart symphony, *any*

Think I'll catch what she has
Settle for a sense of returning
        tentative   but in a *good* way
                the way she seems most thoughtful

Be part of something completely unknown strange
        join African converts
                to a Christianity brought by a true believer
                in the possibility of a longer life
                                than biology proposes
The jungle just green and kindly ever afterwards

Pure chance!
        please teach the art of weightlessness!

147. SOMEONE'S BROUGHT THE BRIDGE!

The *Bridge* is here!
    the Golden *Gate* Bridge
        and though gold *is* involved
        it's *really orange*   well, orange-*red* maybe

Of course, the playa version's downsized somewhat
That's for *speed*
    the original couldn't have moved an inch
      let alone match the speed limit of five miles-an-hour
        the whole bridge would be *welcome*, though!

The bridge is an *also* artcar
Being slightly tourist in nature
A tourist *site* in search of visitation

It may be a first
    thing is, there's only *dust* to cross
      and the gate is wide, wide open
        for a limited time
          it roves with the rest of us

Funny, but seeing the bridge
    makes me wish I were safe in Colorado
      Colorado that had been forsaken
      abandoned for the Bay of Bridges
Exchanged for rusting iron and perpetual paint jobs

And now it's a little like pursuit
    with that thing running around
I hear its motor straining
It wants to fit in
It's looking for a gap to fill   with rivets flying

The desert bridge is not as "mutant," maybe
    still, the DMV   Black Rock's version
      the Department of Mutant Vehicles
They approved   no problem
Perhaps the brand was too iconic?   too famous?
Yeah, might as well be a mobile Eiffel Tower

as if clichés just will not stay in place
                                    let those pyramids roll!

Say "golden" long enough, the color's a disconnect
        a spectral dislexia
                hell it's gold!
                        make it orange-red and trust your eyes
Belief suspended like the span

Infrastructure's on the move ·
Bridge design has designs on Nevada
            miraculous construction   detachable
                with traffic   ping-ponging
                among girders gone to town
Gone to Black Rock
                to play a card game based on its name

Brought 1936 along
The year of "At last it is possible to cross!"
The *Depression* tried to hitch a ride
            but the Golden Gate
                that is really orange-red
                    Kept going and finished it's motion

In the middle of August we heard a great bell
It was a summons
        a principle, really
        cheerful despite the tolling
                    a period placed on secular despair
And *more* rescue when a faith was found

Not so much a major religion
        but one reinvented
                as a color paraded in slow motion
                where we stood together in rain squalls
Never content until the waves were seen
The edge of the bridge abandoned

And we resolved to steal what was already stolen
Our history has an artcar
A bridge that was lonely and followed along
        forsaking suicides for a new unknown, glittery

```
             the speed of light
             made a human number
                    almost      like walking distance
```

148. HOTEL UTAH SINGS

What is her name?!

Please! you *know* her!
She plays the accordion   she'd come to the Hotel
The Hotel Utah in San Francisco
        not *often*, but she would

And now she's wrapping
        it's the end of her hour
              and I've come too late
                    having just arrived I wish she'd do more

So charismatic is she!
Keeps a crowd engaged   *always!*
              focused
                    though the ambient sounds of Burning Man
                          are noises plentiful
                                like uncertain scholars
                                in search of a theory

She can always get an audience to sing
It's that wonderful staccato attack
        her accordion notes
              no microphone required
                    a morning, noon and night show

But what is her name?!
Perhaps if I were to study her photograph
        meditate upon it
              just think awhile
              see what comes to mind

A CEO would know   would remember
They've trained themselves to do that
          a matter of business success
                    the names!
                    the *names* of potential buyers and sellers

Wait a sec! Nadine?
Hers *is* a name beginning with "N"
"N"   and *then?*
          it is just not known
                    uncertain   guesswork

What *is* certain, though
She has entertained a most difficult audience
          a stray path of listening
                    and it would have been wonderful
                    wonderful   to have heard her whole set

Oh! that distant Hotel Utah and its magic open mic!
For so many years   so many acts
          the skills of emcees Bob-o-Magic and J.J. Schultz
                    hosts extraordinaire!
                    the show a love fest

We called it "Burning Man Away From Home"
                    though we were actually home the whole time
The little room getting larger with musicians
The lottery and luck involved
                    the good-natured waiting
Surviving family, extended
          deserving of a camp and a stage in Black Rock
                    and many *wanted* that
                    would fantasize same
It was easy to imagine it

Don't know what to say
Except her music was a life jacket thrown
          taking such good care of those accordion keys
                    nameless for now
                    she stops the demand to be of dollars made
And slows to a trickle the bloodletting

She always *walks* and plays
          and leaves the stage when she does
              so that *everywhere* may be a show
                  with no holding back
                  or keeping a crowd controlled

You can tell from the precision
              she's been to the church of sunshine
                  and activates Sometime's message
                      for the good of Every Time

Yet she's strangely agnostic
Her accordion breathes a skeptic's harmony
          naysaying *too* much elation
              as though beginning again mattered most

She has ended for now
And calls out her camp   where she may be found
          her and her friends
Says what goes on there
              she invites us all!

I'll be governed by her music
Like a bird suddenly authorized to fly
                  and browse air's libraries awhile

What is her name? Please!
If I can think of Utah and remember the others...
Remember Robin Williams
          Whoopy Goldberg
                  Marilyn Monroe and Joe DiMaggio
                      all of whom had come there before...

The stories! the stories!
Hotel Utah was famous
          (Marilyn wanting a place to sit
          where she couldn't see herself in the mirror
                          was it true?)

It is *adversity*, this amnesia
She's trying to save our lives   *who is she?!*
              spoke with her so *many* times   c'mon!

390

Now and always   astute and elegant
                                miles away while I listen

Bad at languages in a land of babble
         this meaning is sufficient
                  her *posture* instructive
                     her *rhythm* the "tick-tock"
                     of exactly what happens in Time
   And given enough of it   her cabal is assured

Okay, now, at *last,* I can say her name is "Nichole"
Had some help, though   being helpless too long
It was J.J. changed her name for me
         changed it from *imaginary* names
                  all starting with the fourteenth letter

She isn't "Nadine"
Nor is she "Naomi"   "Noreen"
         or any "Nancy" I know
                  or "Nadel" "Natalie" "Natashya"
                     "Nadia" "Nina" "Norma"   no! *no!*
She's "Nichole" who sings
Hotel Utah   and she strides, so absolutely sure

It's like she's knowing something transcendental
         has consumer access
                  where the price is a fox   enchanted
Faraway and near in the night
One that won't run away   the rarest

And it is safe for your influence
         for your beautiful advantage
                  the fox that wanted to see *you,* too
                  its own accordion mind made up

Amnesia solved with Utah's assistance
The salon   the saloon
      the *Hotel*
            has told your name, Nichole

149. MEDICAL!

They're grim   they don't even want to *be* here!
They're mad and they're tired and *very* impatient

They'd volunteered   but *why?*
       they were hoping Hemmingway would show up
           in a World War One ambulance?

"How much ecstasy did you take?"
"How much ecstasy *and coke* did you take?"
"What do you *mean* you're about to give birth to an alien?"
"Why do you think water's bad for you?"
"Will you *stop talking* and tell me your name?!"
"Hey, Lonnie! *this* one thinks high blood pressure's good for sex
       and wants to have an *orgy* right here in the clinic!"
"Hey, just because they *looked* like M&M's
                doesn't mean they *were* M&M's"
"*You! get out of here! that's the twentieth time today!!*"
"OKay, what happened to *you?*
       you say you tried to fly
           using a hundred balloons?   hey, you were lucky!"
"My friend, if you ride a kid's bike
       I *get* that you're closer to the *ground*
          and can't tip *over* as easily
          but   you *still* need lights *at night!*   right??
          Iike, *don't be a 'dark wad'*
          and don't make me say that word again!
Get some fresh *batteries* for your *bling!*   *idiot!!*"
"Excuse me, sir   how old are you?
      uh-huh...
      so what the hell are you doing at Burning Man?!
       un-fucking-believable!!"
"What's that, kid?   who *am* I?
      your mother
       the doctor there's your father
Here's an aspirin
Now go to your room
      the one in your home town   far from here
        get going!
         I don't see you running!"

150. THE INSTITUTE, THE SYMPOSIUM

What you stand for
What you *care* about
    on the other side of the one-way glass
        is the treasure of moderation
           promised to unhinged passion

Unchecked   in the visible spectrum
    paintings spill their acrylics and oils
              what you care about

The political divide is vanishing
And some uncanny unity's at hand
        glowing bright as Saturday's light

The counting done
    all the dimensions are become a single plane
    adjusted for "Inflation"
        that infinitude of first things

Stand alone   one day of it or always
    Keeping safe your loved ones
        beyond a mirror's power to please

What you cared about has come to rest
And made small the vengeance of heavy elements
    that yearned for End Time shame

What you cared about has fired the Symposium
        is also the Institute's theme
           while delicate violet and red
           like an Impressionist shower
              enveloped
              tying   discourse to the senses

The one-way universe apprising its inhabitants

Will the Institute let us   at least
    audit the plan for making sense
        Symposium sense   the banquet over?

when we're drunk but cogent?
perhaps *more so* for the libations?

We've seen the other side so far
and its mirror glows with deep dark
It is well to believe and belong with others of your kind
Accepting uncertainty as long as it inspires

The Institute's bright letters say,
"Let's get together and talk!
we can talk about *anything*, right?"
Oh, let it not be reason, necessarily
for reason is not to be trusted anymore
those fanatic paths made for inflatable dinosaurs!

Perhaps there's a good blandness to be discovered
Yeah, I know, sounds weird
Colorless thought to balance vivid feeling
and where the mirror splits the worlds apart
let no felony escape that isn't accidental

It will therefore be exclusive and that's just fine
The word "Institute" is just three syllables sounding
like a trio   you and I and...

This was your idea
and because I love you
I entered the Institute
a little leary until the first course arrived
and by the time the desserts were served
nothing skeptical remained
the food coma
ensuring that discourse
would sizzle softly

A beautiful white noise
to go with the white block letters
announcing "INSTITUTE"
The loaded word turned pleasantly shallow
And if you'll only hold my hand
the Symposium will sound *and*
minds be reminded it's easier to breathe

when you're silent

What you've taught me
        besides what *they*—who are they?— have taught me
                and not so well, either

You know what? we can be Greek!
Sure!   we can be Roman, be Etruscan!
        yeah, *Etruscan* for sure!
I'm betting their symposia were superior
 And their entertainment a sweet containment

What they stand for   and sit for
            and lie down for
        and what they care about
    both sides of the mirror
The river   your passion!

151. THE UNKNOWN

For now   they're just a name
They're the Space Cowboys
        a compound noun gone crazy with diction
            Steve Miller warming up somewhere
            with a vocalise he's devised

For now the Space Cowboys are brief remembrance
But soon we'll learn   find out the heart
Ride that "Unimog" they made
        celebrate King Street days
            the corral   longevity
                the recurrence of dreams
Find out the parties past
And just exactly how a DJ collective
            may achieve world peace in spite of all

And also be a Breakfast of Champions

For now, the name alone delights
Like the contemplation of sparks in the night
The roads will crumble that wind to war
        and progress be the consequence of dance-a-thons

Nice that Space may combine with cow punching
            the art of the cattle drive
                    perfect
How the open range allows a roundup
    of Saturn   and the rest of the planets

They'll be unknown till then
Chance sightings   ten gallons, spiffy
        the future of Tom Mix and Gene Autry
            maybe Hopalong Cassidy's heaven of rope
Makeshift rodeos
        when OK's more than a gunfight in Tombstone
                    and spills whiskey in orbit too
The frontier's a hotty on a very cold desert night

Maybe I'll follow them
Mingle   and ask a question
    "Remember *me?*
            now I'm an old-timer
            I get to pretend I remember *you!*"

Out and about and making the most of *outdoors*
Wranglers from Out There have come Here!
        buckaroos from beyond the light years
        yearning for a hook up   a *saddle* up

I'm going to respect all the times they rode out
        and let 'em rope to their hearts' content
                see to it the strays are returned to the herd
Be in Space the way you *want* to be
Your lariats all-inclusive
        seeing if sage is allowed in a vacuum

For now they're still a theory
But the feeling is they've been here all along

osmosis, tell the truth:
               they kind of sank in, didn't they?

A peripheral party
     well-attended for twenty years
And   empty-headed as I am, and *Space* is,
          I think they'd take me in
              past the swinging flaps
              if there's a saloon

So far they are subliminal cowhands
Wait! there they *are*
     according to their exceptional sign!
        will this greenhorn rustler learn to fit in?

Sure! I'll unlearn surprise and get casual
Talk with a drawl
     all previous lives to funnel into dance-a-thon

It's said they were a theme before the coming of the camps
And I just want to dance in Space again
     think *you'll* like it too
        just another stop on the way to you tell me

For now   I'm waiting
     waiting on possible sin
        in the dark and light arenas
               life not begun until

There is not enough time for any other way
The pace of discovery slow
     but there will be some very enchanted evening
        an evening of the day
        in a river of thought and feeling
I will see them across a crowded playa
And, grateful for the musical,
     I'll never let the Cowboys go
        unless it's into the Space
           the Void from which they came

For now, say "Yes!" to bright buckskins
The alabaster getup will be well-known

all there is   all that's remembered

For now   so far
        but soon, the rest of the story
        for however long it takes to tell
                with "Hee-yah!" perhaps
                        and the Houston accent, unmistakable
                        that was always peculiar to Space travel

152. WENT THERE TO WRITE

What better choice than the salon
                        the warmth of the Minstrels' space
Even absent *from* it
        they sing and perform miracles
        early morning   an unextinguished longing

The lighting amenable
The time of day   perfect
        write
                write anything
The ambiance will guide the pen to petite notoriety

        September just starting
Greg just planning a bike ride
            there's nothing to explain
                    and there will be no arrests

    Just outside   the skinny pyramid shines
    And the furry creature
            clinging to it darkly
                    announces frivolity to passersby

    Write him into early a.m.
    Write desertion, too
            the end of it all can be that
                    even if the beginning is crowded

Write into solitude
        sitting safely at the red piano   softly illumined

"Let's go inside," I'd said
And my muse accompanied
        sure of everything as usual
                and willing to share

153. A CONVERSATION WITH A JELLYFISH

"You're not a box jelly, are 'ya'?"
"Too big to be a box
        I'm almost too big to be *any* jellyfish
                except maybe that Portuguese man o' war"
"Oh, I've heard of *that* one
Wait! I've even seen a *picture*   ugly orangish
But the man o' war is not a true jellyfish
                it's a *siphonophore!*"
"Okay, smartypants   so   what *else* 'ya wanna' know?"
"Well, do you sting?"
"Only metaphorically"
"And those tentacles?"
"Harmless! they just wrap you to greet
        and then let you go!"
"Are you telling the truth?"
"Mostly..."
"So what's not true so far?"
"Everything so far is true
        we have yet to discuss what might take a fib"
"Fair enough"
"But let me ask *you* something"
"Sure"
"Ever want to be something like *me*
        you know   just to see what it might be like?"
"Well, I probably *have* been
        or *will be*
                such a creature as yourself..."

"Oh, past and future lives, right"
"Right"
"Do you see me as demotion?"
"Am I allowed a lie of my own?"
"Don't worry   insults work as well as praise!"
        all talk is welcome talk"
"All right, then
                I can't wait to be you   got that?
                okay, and now the truth
I'd worry, I suppose, about how to *be* a jellyfish
And by the *way*
        why-oh-why do they say you're a *fish*
                you're no fish!   what's up with that?"
"Can't say
        but don't worry about how to be a jellyfish
                it is mostly floating
                        and the rest comes naturally
                        naturally as karma"

"If you say so"
"And I do   but   you're still worried"
"Well, *yeah*
        you are only *one* of the weird things I could be
        and I guess I just want *someone* to say it isn't so"
"Not to add concern, but there are other planets too
                might be even creepier!"
"How is it you're speaking to me right now?"
"No idea"
"You're certainly transparent! sure you're not a hologram?"
"Part of being a jellyfish
        we're sort of see-through by nature"
"I *see*   I mean   I see *through* as you say
                        however you say it"
"Are you a *happy* human?"
"I *was*"
"What happened?"
"I lost something I was never supposed to lose
                                some writing"
"Well, write it again"
"Can't   it's like DNA
        dinosaur strands   .   never again *complete*
                never enough to make the same dinosaur
But you wouldn't understand

You don't *write*   you're this jellyfish!"
"Don't be so sure
     I've published in the sea
     it is   different how we do it, that's all"
"But how?"
"Never mind
      suffice to say I've lost track too of threads and strands
                    I'm sympathetic!
              it's awful
        the many stories
      novels in my case
      that just drifted away somehow..."
"Do you think 'Never mind'?"
"Never mind *what?*"
"Never mind because
      maybe the writing's still out there somewhere
        I mean   the lost ideas?
        perhaps they're in safe keeping
The God of All Life at least cares enough for that"
"My boy, you have a love of complexity
     and as a jellyfish   I warn you
        complexity's a hazard
          one of many that higher life has to face
Simplify you must!   be simply one-celled, even!
                       it's better"
"Hey, how come you're out of the water and hovering here?"
"It was to gift you with blue-and-white in the night
     nothing more   consider me suggestion
       the hype of Nature talking back
         when you least expect it to do that"
"Thanks, I think"
"Ah! but you know better
     as in 'Don't fight it, baby
         it's bigger than both of us!'"
"Okay, okay
     so you went to Jellyfish High School
       use that line on a date, did you?"
"This must be the part where we pull legs"
"*And* tentacles!"

154. AFTER THE MUSIC

After the music: anything youre talking about
        heartbreak of learning
                the innovative night prepares its texts
                        discerned in the antiseptic dust
Be a client once more of the Guardians
The ghosts of all the Earth entertained
        ghosts   and all they're going through

After the music
        I could hear you in the brand-new cavern
                for a limited time
                        our tête-à-tête happening
                        like the earliest stage of despair
Letting night tell a short story of fleeting talent
        discovered
                discarded

There are so many tricks   illusion wins
Wins *easily*   the argument with perception
                                every time
I think we pause right here at the entrance, yeah
        the entrance to where the music was played so well
                just about every pleasure is known by now
That is why we sought to say something
                give pleasure its review
                acknowledge its ultimate cogency

It took a certain sobriety
        to get started   make some sense
        for the sake of the long run to entropy

The evening was a page-turner
Fires and ashes   delicious serendipity
The peaches offered somewhere near to the Roller Disco
        the sardines served by the barkeep
                who *also* espoused a radical idea
                a solution for saving the brainwashed
                        "Make their minds dirty again!"

402

And there was chocolate, of course
                    at the Lost Penguin's headquarters
Someone said it would rain
        we only saw the whites of his eyes
        and had to trust he could see

There's life in the light blue marquee
                spelling out   block letters
                                SCRABBLE letters
Earth Guardians like a study in Sesame
                    wanting children to assist

We have the luxury
        of ending the week
            still energetic
                still engaged
                        just starting the day in the dark

Starting a thought about Poland
The homes undamaged by the Germans
        and how strange it would have been
                    to come and go from such structures
Like being in and out of the Guardians' tent
        so soon to come down
                and its poles carefully laid flat
                an ages-old procedure

A structure that's year-to-year the same
And may always be found   easily
        how is it not a cliché?
            how is it not inevitably thus?

After the music   we chased after the flats and sharps
The naturals were slower and some were captured!
I thought it was enlightenment
        it turned out to be a shorter word: Power
        and the will to Power   yikes!
How many human rights better be counted
                        before the dawn comes crowding
                        and disappears the stars?

Will you learn in my place

and report back when you're less manic
everyone   including myself
          in a rush to the irrational

For the moment there's democracy
And intellect indulges every recreation
          things that go wrong go unreported

Bask in the glowy signage
          the illumined two dimensions of a downsized icon
                    The Man striking a Flatland pose
                    not going anywhere
                              his fair assessment is unreadable

The best we can hope for
          is reunion with the ghosts
                    who went to war with the living
                                        just to be remembered

The guy who *designed* the art is known
He's Oakland
          his work in a whitewashed gallery was seen
He was friendly   the world was small
          less than six degrees   and counting down

It was sunshine the day we connected
Talked like   this   after *music*, too   that time
          the CDs silenced to help our acquaintance

We don't know how much better I'll be in the daylight
Best to continue with the warmth of this community
You and I
          and the rule of law of late night/early morning
                    and how goodness makes an appearance then
          at the suture   a definitive closure

After the music came a worrisome mourning
It seemed a seance, free-floating
          a loss to society   ourselves conferring

"Are you smarter since Monday? some of what's changed?
Can you tell me?   before the partnership is over

404

and heartache cancels the colors of tête-à-tête?"

It's an emergency as much as learning the alphabet again
   each awkward letter
         hoping for words that may be joined

155. "COME INTO THE LIGHT!"

"Come into the light!
Would you like to announce yourselves?
I'm witness to your green and black
         there is mystery and no obvious clues
         your presence is a balanced performance

"Come into the better light of the lamp
   to explain the love that's one-of-a-kind with us
         each time magic claims its place in line

"Would you like to go on record?
Start with the green that says 'Emerald has a wardrobe'?

"Talk back   if you want to, you guys
You're my favorite couple
      say the words you want
         a percentage of paradise to tell
            care of life   care of one another
What description? what paint-by-numbers plan?
What dancing is it starts with *Scheherazade*
    and goes on to be a ballet of meanwhile solace?

"Please announce the cities and countries
            don't forget the DJs.
Here has outrage sought to calm itself
            and rely on your witness protection
            morning, noon and night of Nevada

"Being rich is having this encounter

When I, like a faddist, adhered to Alain Robbe-Grillet
        and started noticing just about everything

"You, my friends, are an exquisite moment in time
I think you both have written freedom
                a brand-new constitution
                        here, let me *sign* it! sign *on!*
The urban bubble's burst
        paired green and black in a foreground embrace
                for zero dollars

"Lucid dreaming I saw you
Think I'll keep the sleep of it and analyze later
Right now   tell me about Ibiza
        private planes and plans
                your work is your play
                        where exactly do I sign?
Wrap me in your parchment, a new citizen before you go!
Tell the mystery's end   I'll keep it a secret, promise!

"There's white to go with the other colors   that scarf
And of course there's the purple ambience
                wishing to be an ultraviolet flood
                        seeping into every situation

"If you introduce yourselves there'll be a reward
And you'll be reducing the chances of a general strike
The Truth is waiting
        your outfits are de rigueur, *simplified*
        the light blue glow stick
        the embellished caps and fancy goggles
                me want!   why didn't I shop?

"For the space of two minutes   please speak
Maybe my friend Scott Boggs in Florida will hear
        Scott   who first brought me to Burning Man

"Your hands are cool with the crux of moderation
Together you will solve the riddle
        of how a hollow Moon may yet preside in its orbit
Let us *all* come into a light that is not of our illumining
        I'll wait right here until then

406

I can see the weather ahead has planned to include us
              and make a study of togetherness

"By the way   are you famous, the two of you?
And is fame something someone may catch
        by being in proximity?
        by hearing you speak?
Does anyone still believe in those six degrees of separation?

"The only safety is: repeat everything
                hey!   I've said this before
                do come into the light
It is our previous lives lived again!
        the gist of *déjà vu*
              murky yet undeniable

"Do you guys play SCRABBLE?"
"Why, yes!   we do!
        but it's the SCRABBLE *dictionary* we love the most!
              that's the best part of SCRABBLE
              a game which, finally, we don't mind losing!"
"Gotcha!"
"Maybe there could be a giant version of the game"

The girl brightened

"What did you have in mind?"
"Oh, a great big board for *interactive* play
        and each tile would be a square yard"
"Right!" said her boyfriend, joining in
        "each word could be acted out   or *danced*
              even if the word were simply an article like 'the'"

I came into the light of our SCRABBLE vision
        and liked what I saw   the green girl spoke again

"And with all those aerobic exertions
                    we'd have to have cold drinks"
"What about soy milk?" I asked
Ice-cold soy milk served from a nearby tanker!"
"That *much?*" they said in unison
"Oh, yeah!"   I was insistent

"With that much exercise placing the letters
        on a board that's forty-five feet on a side,
                                tanker needed!"

We all agreed Burning Man would love it
The light was blinding by then
                with the planning of our SCRABBLE installation!
We had the design   we had the talent
Had the money spent already
        and after it's built
                the SCRABBLE players will come into the light
                        of a word game's tent!

156. INVENTORY OF NEW COMPANIONS

There'd been rouge applied
And he sported a bullhorn with decals
        though by now eyesight was optional
        I noticed his red baggy pants and other colors
                and they sang troubadour with perfect pitch
He looked historic
        and he said "Good evening!" in the middle of the day

Then there was "Roses"   plural
She said she didn't have enough to go on as yet
But *so* far she thought the following:
                Burning Man would make a very fine country
She called it a territory
        a province a protectorate a colony a possession

Called it everything it *could* be
        and said she'd grow roses   *thousands!*
                how she'd represent as immigrant
She said she was doing what she *always* does
And would seek to know this land
        as she'd come to know the rest of the world to date

There was "Air Route" who loves to fly
        and had launched with the Wings of Rogallo
        from Mission Peak near Fremont with outspread gliding
Many happy times a tactical eagle in summer thermals
        for what seemed unlimited soaring!

I played with "Long Island"   a newlywed
It was SCRABBLE with a board that swiveled
Each word a construction new to the language
            points being scored for plausible-*im*plausible
            it was a form of telepathy
Short-lived, though, for I turned around and he was gone

I met "Mandarin"
        he told me of the Taiping Rebellion
        and together we thanked the gods, the Chinese ones
For having been born later
            beyond the militant gaze of the 19th century
                he assured us Taiwan was safe for now

We were joined by "Space B&B"
        who showed us coupons for a stay on Venus
"Is it even *possible* to stay on Venus?" asked Mandarin
"Sure, but only our resort has the tech to manage it!"
"Even if it's nine hundred degrees in the shade?" I asked
"You're safe in our dome   it's *titanium!*"
"I see!   well, we *accept*, then!"

There was ballet going on in the dust
A pas de deux   I was invited   'pas de trois?"
"How many can you have before you drop the 'pas' deal?"
"Never mind! just dance! we're doing *Swan Dry Lake*
        here we go!   a one and a two and a..."

There was the teacher, "Mister Magister"
And he made *me* a teacher *too*
The way *we* played was
        each of us sought to explain things to students
            without teaching aids and *without* talking

We decided that lessons should be year-round
And all-day and all-*night* long with lots of one-on-one!

with plenty of behind-the-scenes teacher confab
Perhaps   after a surfeit of nothingness
        the least crumbs of "spoken word"
                        would be all the more savored!

I met "Lemming Master" at the single phone booth
I think there was a sign that said "Talk to God"
The line was long and getting longer
        life had been promised   healthier!   longer!
I asked the Lemming Master
                "If I were a lemming would you save me?"
"I'd *try*"
"But wouldn't my destiny be to dive into the sea
            with others of my kind?"
"Not if you knew another way of belonging"
"I see   by the way, whom exactly are we calling?"
"*I'm* phoning my wife
        who keeps *me* from going over the edge!"
"Ah!"

The others said they'd be sticking with God
I was feeling capricious and blurted out,
"The one who lives in a heavenly fleabag
        and looks like John Houston's father
                in *The Treasure of the Sierra Madre,*
                    or   some other personage?"
"Gee," said someone "I don't know
        and don't quite know what you *mean,* but *want* to"

When it was my turn to use the land line
            I yielded to Lemming Master
But he said, "I've forgotten my wife's number suddenly
And I feel like a lemming *myself* so I'm leaving!"

"Puma 101" and "Tracie of Boston"
                were enjoying a game of Pick-Up Sticks
And I kibbitzed between their fierce concentration
        and the trance of the Seesaw People
                the same I'd met at the yoga extravaganza
                their mutual support was exact
And no one "seed" or "sawed" until I gave them a nudge
        and started the *briefest* of oscillations

410

"Hey! whaddya doin'? we were perfectly balanced!
        you've 'interfered with our immediate experience'
        you've violated one of the Principles!
Just kidding   ha! ha!   we're not mad at you
            now or at any time
            not in the yoga class either
We shall not be mad at you *any other* time!"
"It is kind of you to say so   thank you!
And for *my* part I will promise something   *yes!*
I promise to totally leave no trace
        let's see..., uh, sorry, my Mento candy wrapper
            it hit the ground and blew away   *yikes!*
                I better go find it!"

There was a poet up there on one of the stages
        filler speech
                he spoke words between jazz sets
                    they were not his *own*, however
He donated those of Percy Bysshe Shelley
And the tantalizing words poured into the crowd
He who spoke them had practiced well
        he'd been ready to roll since arriving
                    a Romantic came to life again
                    a very *early* one
And Shelley returned in the lurch of 3rd millennium angst
Morning, noon and night talk
        from the youth of *Prometheus Unbound*
            and a beautiful contrast flowed
            the informal ambience sifted for the classical

And after his recitation
        I took the channeling poet aside
            and tried to say it right
Say that   with respect to Shelley's Demogorgon
        pretty scenes may hide the wolves
            and it was said by way of gentle agreement
Softly, before the drums and guitars recommenced
And *that* hearing

These were my friends
        playmates many and persuasive

Like strange notes sounding newly discovered Mozart
His only comfort restarted, happy-sad as always
And, major-minor, write the book that touches on
        calls back to   and is surrounded by his charity

157. TROJAN EVOCATION

This is the way you get past the Gate and get in

This is the way to kick off invasion
        double-decker
        a military cunning
        and dissembling
                masquerading

What happened was less than expected, though
And both sides agreed to drop acid
                    take ecstasy
                        smoke pot and get the munchies
                        followed by intermittent fasting

They figured out what they would need
Got busy and partied accordingly
        a dot-com *Aeneid* enacted
                and a poll taken to see if they succeeded
They discussed the question of walls
                    and whether Troy should have had any

The bus with the bird beak redly advanced
Its compliment of bicycles lashed
        it was a would-be Trojan bird-mobile
Better for their self esteem no battle came
Just impudence plain and simple traveling
Pink-roofed in the dull light of the world
        suggestion vying with a modest grandiosity
A journey through life without blue jeans to temper conceit

Count the "Greeks" till they're out of sight
        with their fore-and-aft peacock color
And you tell *me* what you call that   that moves
Majestic yet clandestine, too
And let us wish together,
        "Please do not be entirely gone!"

158. APOTHEOSIS: THE BURNING-DOWN

The time had come for dubstep
        and the dread of its awful bass and *below* that!

But *saying* this is to be *ahead* of that time
And possibly unemployed prior to the final fires

I'd always been early before
But this time I'd be just early *enough*
        and not positioned as usual
        just to the right of the ingress to come

Would not be close   close as it's possible to be
Where the crowd stops and the rangers begin
        guarding   bantering   keeping control

This time there would not be long waiting there
When   at first   just a few were adjusting pillows
        oh, and chairs and blankets and tripods
When the day still had something to say
When nothing seemed imminent
        seemed at *all* about to happen
                least of all a certain harassment
                                by way of a furnace!

This time I sought the right artcar to be aboard
        the one wagon that wouldn't notice
                I'd be surreptitious   blending

The anonymous partygoer
Maybe invited   theoretically   by some campmate
The stranger *not* a stranger
        ascending back stairs to a vantage
                any seat   or anywhere topside
                and separate

As if the lesson of twenty-one appearances is "Hide.."
It doesn't have to be complete concealment
        just one where no questions are raised
                especially the one that goes,
                "How many times?"
As if it were sex and you were keeping track

"How many Burns?" just as bad
                maybe *worse* for the slang involved

No, the circumstance of some elevation was needed
And austere mingling with aristocratic notes

Somehow the ground has been promoting babble
        and despite the gifting going on
                the candy and trinkets proffered
                        the babble is repetitive public
Better had Burning Man stayed a private wonder
Nineteen ninety-six's extended stay

A jail   a *good* one that continues the Past
        and is a less-attended overlay
A hologram, even   hovering
The wooden figure casual, sublime Dada
        before the later oohs and aahs
                                were a *de-rigueur* chorus
                                sounding platitudinous awe

So dubstep was due
        and other dearly beloved noise
                and   though dreadful
                it would be over and done with sooner
Sooner than before   those other times
It's better
Really, it is

So *this* time arrived and scrutiny commenced
And looking for a certain height above the desert
For that candidate dragon   or shark
        or mobile propane extravaganza
A search was underway
                a prescription for security wanted

The caution tape is stretched
        and an ambulance crawls
                "Beauty"   that's her name
                her greeting is so very welcome!
                        a Ranger remembers and embraces
While a lustrous horizon persists
                        beyond all expectations

Nightfall's delayed like a *dance* postponed
Being nervous at the prom
Clouds and cameras' apertures   *perfect*
        their lenses safe
        all equipment pristine
And while I *do* have a "crush"
                it's not the crush of a crowd

There's a leisure too
        the People of the Crane   steeply observant
Someday we'll find the right connections
Set it up   find a place in the sky as well

The machines!
The great machines are not yet settled in
                not yet just outlines and parking

Leonardo's Man has been ready and readied
His bottega dismantled and the fireworks primed
There is plenty of playa to set him apart
        the center of things
        yet nothing to save him

There used to be a chant to do just that
And   delightfully absurd   they'd start in:
        "Save the Man!   Save the Man!"

The chant was sporadic   recurring
It would come to life
          though not every year

The ships are here!
The ships!   wonderful!
The *tall* ships
          docked   their Lahontan slips
                    like imaginary privilege

And please, may the *Contessa* return someday!
Where'd you go?
      the galleon with the lanterns
      that would sail darkly
          for authenticity was the deal

They wanted the sixteenth century to come around
      silent as pre-Discovery done
Oh, bring it back!   forgive the captain
          for exceeding the speed limit that time

Beyond the bicycles
      still unlit   as if it were noon
          the mountain of the fox
          with its many names   some unknown
As the hunters and gatherers are guessed at
And asked to return

Come back to be with lime green adornment
The quasi-octopodal headdress
      of a woman who is whoever she is
          come to recoup what's been expended so far
          in a week of awakenings
Her Medusa strands pulsing in near twilight

Burning Man's pavilion's deserted
And frankly, the photogenic scene
          especially with those eastern tones
                    is like a backlit Turner
The peach and gray evidence of a transcendence
Mid-air   heaven having come near to us
      wanting to be close-by

How can you not be surprised
        by such a vacation from ordinary light?
There is a threat that's concealed
A percent of glory prepared to undermine
        the art
        the firmament
        the sun's more subtle   and pale   expanses

A canvass that's a journey to darkness
                and intermittent star haze
With every word of magic heard
        that would *prosecute* the sky for being too lovely
            softly completed
            like an ether come to Earth
                    for the duration of life *on* Earth

Or an attempted coup by unauthorized angels
And the Universe   on the job
        horizon!   lakebed!   all who've gathered!

Ah! there it is, a nondescript bunny bus!
Where to be!   a modest yet adorable achievement
That's the one to climb on   the very creature!
        the ultimate pet to share a fire with
            and the *timing* is right
            the passengers busy or on some errand
                            boisterous

They are playing poker
        I'm wearing my finest loops and spangles
            there's winking and blinking
            past the finish line of fashion
The right lights to introduce and gain an upper railing

The rabbit revealed   whispering accommodation
"Here may you wait and study the flames!"
I *thanked* the gracious artcar
        feeling like a singer-songwriter
            seeing new lyrics appear on a page
                and hearing the tune
                    that will take them places

If culture came to die in the West
        let it be the *Old* West where it happens
                        warming everyone in the end

When you least expect it
            the arrow of thought targets struggle
            puts a premium upon it
Reading *into* the efforts made
                to break out of San Francisco
                    and make room for this unravelling

It's dark enough, finally
And air flows through Jim Morrison's mansions
        the "killer on the road"
                become a bringer of life to a brand-new heart

There had been a strange portage
Some object of veneration conveyed
                the circumference of the center

And now   dangerous stilts
        careful on their way
                the world of Saturday night
                    and the Fire Conclave's final act
                    fixed in amber like a forecast
Oh, they've practiced all right!
So much so it's methodical
                    the art wears a game face

It was for the experience of alone-together
This was always the quest   a private public
        and here at the railing of the rabbit's upstairs
        the preliminaries over
The fireworks make a name for themselves
            and soar
                as if a great transformer had blown!

Leonardo's lonely L'Uomo Vitruviano
        still refusing to spin

The fire at last is an almost *modest* orange

418

Compared to the pyro, that is
Can it be there's *considered* technique involved?
Say the skill to make Liszt light up the night!
        it's a barrage!
                over kill accomplished!
A *zenithal* display
                so far above have the rockets gone!

And it's hard to know how much was planned
        stuff just blowing up
        no seeming schedule   random artillery

Before the fencing
        if you wanted to
                you could allow a frenzy to take hold
And run the open ground to immolation
There are quite a few wars beheld right here and now
        just as in the fifteenth century

And   still solitary in the Renaissance heat
        no doubt the cameras are loaded
                        and the media prepared
But this combustion's ancient
Not needing photography or repetition
Let it be remembered without an image
        without exactitude
        its explosions a once-only proposition
    no record
A sweet commotion abandoned!

Even *saying* so   a forested city burns
        far from home
There can be only *one* conflagration!
This is the key to these glorious forget-me-nots
                        blossoming!

There is a raging to it all!
An apotheosis driven by blast furnace aficionados
        People of the Inferno
        a tortuous vindication!

The priests in asbestos close enough

for the jazz of fire to happen   hotly melodic
Even the railing's toasty
        and the bunny's whiskers singed

Also, whatever card game it was
The winner's taking all
        even if all of *him* is taken too

We know the difference a dying city makes
Those burning timbers whitely remaining
        oddly substantial despite the incandescence

Everybody's screaming and wanting collapse
Why is it Dresden's come calling?
Why is it history just won't stay in place
        but bothers the world with firestorms?
              even *here*   at the last minute
              no one having done much wrong?

All is heartfelt   to hear the triumph up and down!
     the concentric crowd
     hot inner   cool outer
           disintegrating too
           with vows to return
Though many linger with secondary revelations
Perhaps the ecstasy
The way it tends to make immobile
                            those creatures of the drug

Empathy   the first scenes   the last
     and the mobius in play
           the previous Saturday   and this one
           spliced

And being sad is almost a luxury   the *denouement*
Having headed this way
        since Steens Mountain first tilted
              it is possible to be truly grateful for once
Here at the outskirts   a substance uncontrolled

Maybe a refugee
Maybe no name

Nothing in the night displeases
        and hope is become the consequence
                                of incomparable arson
Alone-together, most of Black Rock is here
And   mobile as ever
        Cecil B. has busied himself
        swept aside the talkies
                and returned to silent fast motion
                perceived in slow   to keep the film going

Though the celluloid burns in the sprockets
The hole expanding
        to be a blaze without suffering
                mystic as Nevada
The height and depth of all its ranges surrounding

A bonfire built of all the minutes and hours of the last
And adding those we should later create
        making it easy
                counting only till eight
                        when Infinity will take it from there

159.   AT THE TEMPLE OF... SILENCE

So silent it's a *Silent Night*
Nicholas Cage in a moment of reflection
It's only whispering now
                though it got that way in pieces

Frankly, the soprano would help
        the one who would sing *Amazing Grace*
                let the hymn be reprised!
Because right now the lull is unnerving
                        the wait   an embarrassment

There used to be lasers outlining the woodwork
Lasers green and lasers red

it was thought disrespectful
there'd been a collective groan

So now the crowd's stuck in an outdoors library of "Shh!"
while torches move in the Temple's spaces
igniting   methodic
their purpose noted

It is serious for sure
A silence imposed on "radical self-expression"
And it's not a *bad* thing   it's just kind of *weird*
and I want to giggle
just like in a library!

There will be no Sunday *night* to follow
No further time ensconced
sheltering in place on the playa
There will be exiting started
even *before* the Temple's fallen
and crashed down into furious embers

The silent circle's still closed
though witness has reduced itself
to a trance state of wonder
and its numbers are fewer
A throng that's porous
if widespread with less attendance
and unbefitting finale

Burning the Temple's almost a postscript
an afterthought
and its flames are different
slow motion in charge of things
Even its several tangential tornadoes
twist with languor and delay
not wishing to be over with

Call it subdual
Everyone mindful of what was left *within* the Temple
Everyone thinking of all that's memorial
and wanting ignition
those photographs   letters   prayers

Messages scrawled on slats and supports   *boldly*
Or secretly inscribed in the Temple's recess cubbies
        an almost shy remembrance

Yet keep the cult away
        lest innocence is made self-conscious
There is enough law and rangering to make it so
Even Cat Stevens's "miles from nowhere"
                is sufficient ballade

The artcars left have gathered   sadly
I'm *sure* of it
        those melancholy wishes made
                trying to say it for the sake of the living

The lights that drape and outline
The lights that flash and strobe
All of this is a species of holiday
        seen in the prelude of Summer Lake Hot Springs
                and there's a *before* feeling
                Sunday akin to that getting here
Thinking of it   sunk in hot water
                solo
                        or beholden
                                to imaginary companions

There's the same restraint bookending a heart's desires

Sit with me
We'll find somewhere   some vantage
        another upper deck
                from which to enjoy a paradox
                a party returned to conception
                                gone back in its box

We'll "linger until..."
        as "Fats" Domino did
Thermals intensely ascending
In a darkness devoid of blueberries
                radio chatter at last subsides

Nothing follows   *may follow*

423

                                  Such magnificent heat
                        eruptive, conclusive
Only oneself assisting the illusions
        what is so carefully crafted and begotten

The waking dream is this
Like a persistent coloration
                perhaps amazing
                perhaps that grace
                        sung a capella, too
And lasting as long
        as tradition allows a Christmas in September
        LEDs on loan from its solstice

It's like a very special wedding
                        with extravagant tension
                                each face a flower

David Best has said it's his last Temple
The last time a Temple's named   his hope
He wanted it to be just a Temple
        and not a Temple *of*
                at least it was a wish he had
The structure should be simple despite the filigree
The ornate baroque implied

No matter the elaborate decor
The many roofs   chandeliers   eaves
        and lanterns suspended
                amidst Asian upturned shingles

I'm happy it's completed
Though the elements of which it's made
        will now take a vacation from a xyloid identity
                wood's reward in fire to accomplish

This time the Temple was handmade
This time *lucidity* is foremost
There will be no receipt
        his largesse is immortal
                Infinity found   and touched
                after a fashion of strange and wonderful!

Mozart is filling in the blanks   almost secretly
Privately
          as though genius were personal
                    his concerto needing two pianos to say it

And while the silence continues   so does E Flat Major
What the prayer is
What remembrance has decided for David's last

Mozart a guest speaker
          and we're thrilled to hear him
                    to have him   if only in mind
A connection we've always had
And it's so nice to hear the concerto this way
          perhaps the way *he* heard it
                    before he took his pen to write it

The Temple's both too far away and near
          the heart is undecided which
                    and seriously
                    I hope there's someone to talk to later
Someone who will both believe us
                    and believe *in* us
                    zero-calorie scripture spoken
                              whose words
                                        are reshaped knowing

I am hoping all rise like the fire before us
It's good to see it all over again
All religion is repeats
          all it takes to set something in motion

We are well-met in Black Rock
          and the temples till now persist in this one
          the one that will take no preposition
                    but you and I
                    and all who wait and watch the glow
The Temple of All of Us
          that eschews even the artist's assignation

I think David is onto something

as he has all along been
                    I'm only wondering what came *before*
            the way cosmologists look at the Bang
                    unsatisfied
Because empirical testing just isn't possible

Last year was the Temple of Promise
And before that, Grace   Whollyness   Juno
            Transition and Flux
There was the Fire of Fires   the Basura Sagrada
The Temples of Forgiveness, of Hope
                                Dreams and Stars
The Temples of Joy, of Tears, of Honor
                    and the first   and most modest
                    the Temple of the Mind

I remember it
And David Best saying what it was all about
            in the brand new millennium
                    all the wooden pieces fresh and freshly cut

In the bright sun he talked
There'd been an accident   friends involved
            on the highway to Gerlach
                        he'd wanted to build on that
                        "what it was all about..."
            what we knew about the mind till then

And now he has said
            that no one should decide
                    what a temple should be
                    or discover even the mystery of motivation

The fox is watching also   turning its attention
"Who's responsible?" he asks
That distant glow colluding with the darkness
            the way my own handheld brilliance
                                had held him in thrall
                    and seemed to dispel the lies of the hominid

Beautiful fox!
Please descend from Sahra's Mountain

to join us   surrounding the fire together!

We are contemplative as yourself
        and match your color to the oldest
                out of control as Mozart's imagination
The Temple turned hearth
                with all availible brightness
                born to defeat the afflictions

A transformation more a dream
                        than mere Kindling
A plan that burgeons beyond any intention
That's what it is   and it's hard to explain
        but a combat exists to make it real
                have it slide into awareness problem-free

For now, gorgeous is gone to bed with mundane
Knows entitled destruction
Images chasing one another to the edge of Space
        though awful uncertainty lurks
        and Shelley's Demogorgon readies itself
                                for intervention!

The Temple to No One combusts
                        markets Fahrenheit's sparks
                        inevitable   advisory

You want to say technology's great, eh?
Technology's consumed like excess weight
All is enlightened and skyward gone

I have not touched a drink for so long now
        and perhaps it was abstinence done
                to behold this burning and final party
So many ways to see it   silent

I'll join them once more
                slip into a primal association
                this will be done   especially for you
Find the fox again
The presence of invisibility felt
        ghosting a last hour's oasis till dawn

perfectly balanced
spirit and incarnation

The level desert dreams of great heights and depths
and the difference between made plain

160. AUSTIN, THE SIXTH OF SEPTEMBER

Austin steeples
The Austin castle

On the sixth of September
please note that the steeples bore resemblance
and the stone castle you hear tell of
was somewhere no one has time for

Decompression meant cessation
Being no longer the tourist
though Austin, Nevada
was exemplary small town intriguing

Still wanting no distractions
Yet the International put on such a front
I came to rest on its front *porch*
tucking in one more hotel
if that is what it was

The road had been exit and arrival both
And   still breathless
the week that's weeks long had let us go
some to Syria, even   amazing!

The road was Highway 50
and no other ran the way *it* did
across and sideways
Wanting tickets to be written on the straightaways

The white church pretends it's Sunday
While the other   more brick than that
        has other ideas
                says it would be closed for the holidays
                        no matter who shows up

The town is old as gold
Don't say it's "nestled" or "perched"
Just drive the streets a little
        relieved that Austin's *there*
                uncoupled like a freight car

I went some distance towards it
        wondering aloud
                how its sun and shadow could startle
                        so sharp-edged yet serenely routine
The pleasure of its company
        flowing into the blank parts
                of Burning Man's afterwards

It wasn't being tired
Rather   it was exaltation conferred by a fox
        lovely all the ways it *can* be
        in dimmest day and brightest night
And   connected to the near and far
        and befriending
                the power animal lives in the next town over
                and in the wilds between, of course

Going International as the hostel on the main drag
        whose pioneers' planks were darkly enclosing
The original boardwalk wonderfully uneven
                like the record of good and bad deeds done

Maybe the castle after all   in this afterwards
        its stone art installed like the art in Black Rock

161. FOLLOW

Been known to wander...

Though age tries everything it has to put a period

Above Austin
     where the erosion has tired of rounding off
     there will the wanderings resume
         that began with Esther's Burning Man
Over fields with rocks to keep you careful ascending
Pretty arrangements of all sizes
     trying to be forts
         or stone fences' beginings

With due east making promises
And what's left of Black Rock well over the horizon west
Just the two of us roam
     the seconds in a minute say the whereabouts
               hidden

Panorama's stairs done more easily now
     in a gradual sense of elevation
         the gradient good for reflection
           the Slinkies put away
            put in legal *jeopardy*   some of them

And did you hear   now it's quiet enough
     the near and far avifauna?
Patience   like a picnic   is spread
            in the hay-colored hills

And there's a feeling of being immune to everything
For the moment   because
     the serious threats
     well, they were too lazy to exercise *themselves*
This day, anyway

It's a search that's a race
     to find out before sundown the family of Canidae
Oh, yes!   one member in particular

Vulpes vulpes   you say it twice
            as if disbelieving
            renard roux!

There's a kingdom's chain of command
                    animalia
                    chordata
                    mammalia
                    carnivora
                        Canidae

Be systematic as the science
A powerful committee of one
        on the loose and hunting for
                swearing to follow the fox
                    until I deserve its body
                    or fail to return
                        from the accidental landscape

Best of all   it's a health care plan
        whose premiums amount to a Holocene's coupons
New windows
Wide as the glass of all this rumpled prairie

Freedom's done its job and stayed on
Stubbed its toes in the tall grass
                    that is almost top secret
And I will find you, fox!
        in the daylight   corroborate your magic
                        that is shy
                        and circumspect

I thank you for your company
        that night of early morning on Sahra's Peak
        with its summit cache of Paiute weaving!
Exchange a hominid's frame
            that the Cosmos may show equal justice

Part of the problem
        was always too *much* desire
            your own chiseled form to make up for that

And so   with increasing certainty
        your path appears
        is taken
                with lighter and lighter steps
Almost delicate
                and sure

The trail's the final days
        of reading, writing and 'rithmetic

And I seek the bright light *you* saw
Myself *your* self

Arntson

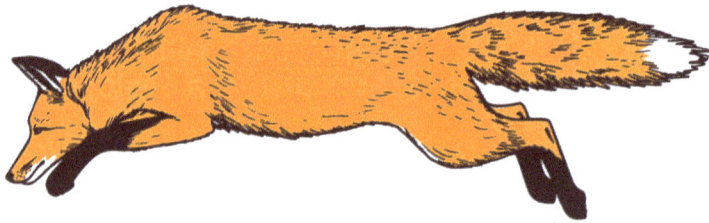

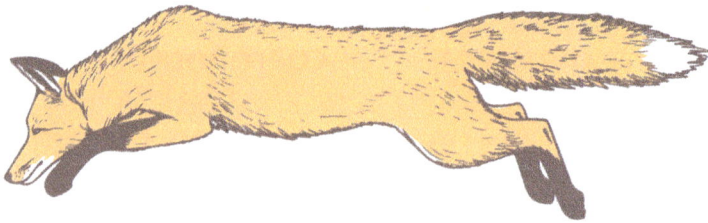